ECONOMIC ISSUES, PROBLEMS AND PERSPECTIVES

ECONOMIC POLICIES IN A TIME OF FINANCIAL CRISIS

Economic Issues, Problems and Perspectives

Additional books in this series can be found on Nova's website under the Series tab.

Additional E-books in this series can be found on Nova's website under the E-books tab.

ECONOMIC ISSUES, PROBLEMS AND PERSPECTIVES

ECONOMIC POLICIES IN A TIME OF FINANCIAL CRISIS

HEATHER D. PERKINS

EDITOR

Nova Science Publishers, Inc.
New York

For permission to use material from this book please contact us:
Telephone 631-231-7269; Fax 631-231-8175
Web Site: http://www.novapublishers.com

LIBRARY OF CONGRESS CATALOGING-IN-PUBLICATION DATA
Economic policies in a time of financial crisis / editor, Heather D. Perkins.
p. cm.
Includes index.
ISBN 978-1-61122-686-7 (hbk.)
1. United States--Economic policy--2009- 2. Financial crises--United States. 3. Recessions--United States. 4. Global Financial Crisis, 2008-2009. I. Perkins, Heather D.
HC106.84.E355 2011
330.973--dc22
2011002383

Published by Nova Science Publishers, Inc. † New York

CONTENTS

PREFACE

The financial crisis that began in 2007 spread and gathered intensity in 2008, despite the efforts of central banks and regulators to restore calm. By early 2009, the financial system and the global economy appeared to be locked in a descending spiral, and the primary focus of policy became the prevention of a prolonged downturn on the order of the Great Depression. The volume and variety of negative financial news, and the seeming impotence of policy responses, has raised new questions about the origins of financial crises and the market mechanisms by which they are contained or propagated. This book presents and discusses the economic policies which have been put into place by the United States government in order to address these problems.

Chapter 1- The following list of authoritative resources is designed to assist in responding to a broad range of questions and concerns about the American Recovery and Reinvestment Act (ARRA), P.L. 111-5. Links to the full text of the act, Congressional Budget Office (CBO) estimates, White House fact sheets, and federal, state, and municipal government websites are included, along with other useful information. This list reflects information that is currently available on the Internet.

The following list of authoritative resources has been compiled to assist in responding to a broad range of questions and concerns about the American Recovery and Reinvestment TAct of 2009 (ARRA), P.L. 111-5. Links to the full text of the act, Congressional Budget Office (CBO) estimates, White House fact sheets, and federal, state, and municipal government websites are included, along with other useful information. This list reflects information that is currently available on the Internet.

Chapter 2- The current financial crisis began in August 2007, when financial stability replaced inflation as the Federal Reserve's chief concern. The roots of the crisis go back much further, and there are various views on the fundamental causes.

It is generally accepted that credit standards in U.S. mortgage lending were relaxed in the early 2000s, and that rising rates of delinquency and foreclosures delivered a sharp shock to a range of U.S. financial institutions. Beyond that point of agreement, however, there are many questions that will be debated by policymakers and academics for decades.

Why did the financial shock from the housing market downturn prove so difficult to contain? Why did the tools the Fed used successfully to limit damage to the financial system from previous shocks (the Asian crises of 1997-1998, the stock market crashes of 1987 and 2000-2001, the junk bond debacle in 1989, the savings and loan crisis, 9/11, and so on) fail to work this time? If we accept that the origins are in the United States, why were so many financial systems around the world swept up in the panic?

Chapter 3- The budget deficit in FY2009 equaled $1.4 trillion, or 9.9% of gross domestic product (GDP). Combined with a shrinking economy, this increased the publicly held federal debt by 12.8 percentage points of GDP last year. Deficits of this size are not sustainable in the long run because the federal debt cannot indefinitely grow faster than output. If it did, a greater and greater share of national income would be devoted to servicing the debt, until eventually the government would be forced to monetize the debt (finance it through money creation) or default on it.

Although the debt cannot persistently rise relative to GDP, it can rise for a time, so it is hard to predict at what point investors would deem it to be unsustainable. A few other advanced economies have debt-to-GDP ratios higher than the United States. While some of those countries have seen their relative financing costs rise during the financial crisis, Japan has continued to be able to finance its debt at extremely low costs.

Chapter 4- This chapter presents current data on estimated ownership of U.S. Treasury securities and major holders of federal debt by country. Federal debt represents the accumulated balance of borrowing by the federal government. To finance federal borrowing, U.S. Treasury securities are sold to investors. Treasury securities may be purchased directly from the Treasury or on the secondary market by individual private investors, financial institutions in the United States or overseas, and foreign, state, or local governments. Foreign investment in federal debt has grown in recent years, prompting questions on the location of the foreign holders and how much debt they hold.

Chapter 5- Governments run deficits for several reasons. By running short-run deficits, governments can avoid raising taxes during economic downturns, which helps households smooth consumption over time. Running deficits can stimulate aggregate demand in the economy, thus giving policymakers a valuable fiscal policy tool to help support macroeconomic stability. In particular, short-run deficits may help boost economic activity when monetary policy loses its potency. When interest rates fall to low levels during an economic downturn, banks can become reluctant to lend when they perceive the risks of lending outweigh the gains, while fewer firms and consumers demand new loans. In such a situation, known as a liquidity trap, a monetary authority such as the Federal Reserve can do little to expand the money supply. Thus, while the monetary authority can cut short-term interest rates to nearly zero—or even to zero—lower interest rates or other monetary policy initiatives may do little to encourage new consumer spending or business investment. During a liquidity trap situation, fiscal policy tools such as increased government spending or tax cuts, which increase deficits, may be an important complement to monetary policy. So-called "fresh-water" economists have questioned the logic of these fiscal policies. So-called "salt-water" economists, who have sought to put Keynesian fiscal theories on a more modern foundation, contend that government interventions can mitigate economic downturns. Most professional economic forecasters find that deficits and fiscal policy measures can stimulate economic activity when the economy operates well below its potential.

Chapter 6- This chapter provides an overview of the role foreign investment plays in the U.S. economy and an assessment of possible actions a foreign investor or a group of foreign investors might choose to take to liquidate their investments in the United States. Concerns over the potential impact of disinvestment have grown as national governments have become more active investors in the U.S. economy and as innovation in creating financial instruments has increased volatility in financial markets. Such concerns seem out of step with the experience of the 2008-2009 financial crisis, during which the dollar became the preferred safe haven investment for foreign investors. If some foreign investors were to liquidate their holdings, these actions could affect the U.S. economy in a number of ways due to the role foreign investment plays in the United States and due to the current mix of economic policies the United States has chosen. The impact of any such action on the economy would also depend on the overall condition and performance of the economy and the financial markets. If the economy were experiencing a strong rate of economic growth, the impact of a foreign withdrawal likely would be minimal, especially given the dynamic nature of credit markets. If a withdrawal occurred when the economy were not experiencing a robust rate of growth or if credit financial markets were under duress, the withdrawal could have a stronger effect on the economy.

Chapter 7- Since the end of World War II, the United States has experienced almost continuous inflation—the general rise in the price of goods and services. It would be difficult to find a similar period in American history before that war. Indeed, prior to World War II, the United States often experienced long periods of deflation. It is worth noting that the Consumer Price Index (CPI) in 1941 was virtually at the same level as in 1807.

During the last two economic expansions, March 1991-March 2001 and November 2001-December 2007, the inflation rate remained low by the standards of previous decades, and has remained low since this recession began. This is true regardless of which index is used to calculate the rate at which the price of goods and services rose. A low inflation rate is especially significant since the U.S. economy was fully employed, if not over fully employed, according to many estimates for the last three years of the 1991-2001 expansion and during 2006-2007. Yet, contrary to expectations, the inflation rate accelerated only modestly. Keeping an economy moving along a full employment path without igniting a burst of inflation is a difficult policy task.

Chapter 8- The Federal Reserve (Fed) defines monetary policy as the actions it undertakes to influence the availability and cost of money and credit to help promote its congressionally mandated goals, achieving a stable price level and maximum sustainable economic growth. Since the expectations of market participants play an important role in determining prices and growth, monetary policy can also be defined to include the directives, policies, statements, and actions of the Fed that influence how the future is perceived. In addition, the Fed acts as a "lender of last resort" to the nation's financial system, meaning that it ensures its sustainability, solvency, and integrity. This role has become of great importance with the onset of the financial crisis in the summer of 2007.

Chapter 9- In the beginning of 2008, American International Group (AIG) was one of the world's largest insurers, generally considered to be financially sound with an AA credit rating. By the end of the year, it had undergone a near bankruptcy and had been forced to seek up to $173.4 billion in financial assistance from the U.S. government. The CEO had been replaced at the government's behest, executive compensation was under limits, and shareholders in AIG had been nearly wiped out as their equity was diluted by a new 79.9% stake held by the government. The government assistance to AIG has been largely ad hoc. The overarching AIG holding company was regulated by the Office of Thrift Supervision (OTS), but because the company was primarily an insurer, it was largely outside of the normal Federal Reserve (Fed) facilities that lend to thrifts facing liquidity difficulties. AIG was also outside of the normal receivership provisions that apply to banking institutions. Had

AIG not been effectively deemed "too big to fail" and given assistance by the government, bankruptcy seemed a near certainty in September 2008.

Chapter 10- In 2008, 39.8 million people were counted as poor in the United States—an increase of 2.6 million persons from 2007, and nearly the largest number of persons counted as poor since 1960. The *poverty rate*, or percent of the population considered poor under the official definition, was reported at 13.2%; this is up from 12.5% in 2007, and is the highest rate since 1997. The recent increase in poverty reflects the worsening of economic conditions since the onset of the economic recession in December 2007. Many expect poverty to rise further next year, and it will likely remain comparatively high even after the economy begins to recover. The incidence of poverty varies widely across the population according to age, education, labor force attachment, family living arrangements, and area of residence, among other factors. Under the official poverty definition, an average family of four was considered poor in 2008 if its pre-tax cash income for the year was below $22,025.

Chapter 11- The United States has been free of a national debt for only two years, 1834 and 1835. In its first year, 1790, the country faced a debt of $75 million. From FY1998 to FY2001, the federal government ran budget surpluses. Since then, the budget has returned to deficit, and the debt had risen to $7.5 trillion by 2009. It rose to a high of 108.6% of gross domestic product (GDP) at the end of World War II; declined to a post-World War II low of 23.8% of GDP in 1974; and, then, rose to another high of 49.5% of GDP in 1993.

The national debt results from borrowing to finance budget deficits. Historically, the major cause of debt accumulation has been war. The United States has financed the extraordinary expenditures associated with war by borrowing rather than by raising taxes or printing money. This pattern was broken by the large budget deficits of the 1980s, the first half of the 1990s, and the period subsequent to 2001, which caused the national debt to rise substantially as a fraction of GDP.

Chapter 12- Of the three broad categories of federal spending, the only category that cannot be reduced by legislative action is net interest payments. Net interest payments accounted for about 7% of federal spending between 1962 and the late 1970s. With the high interest rates in the late 1970s and the large budget deficits in the 1980s, net interest payments eventually rose to 15% of federal spending. The low interest rates combined with budget discipline in the 1990s reduced net interest payments back down to 7% of federal outlays by 2003. Low interest rates kept net interest payments low to 2009. However, net interest payments are projected to increase dramatically over the next 10 years.

Chapter 13- America's current account (CA) deficit (the trade deficit plus net income payments and net unilateral transfers) rose as a share of gross domestic product (GDP) from 1991 to a record high of about 6% of GDP in 2006. It began falling in 2007, and reached 3% of GDP in 2009. The CA deficit is financed by foreign capital inflows. Many observers have questioned whether such large inflows are sustainable. Even at 3% of GDP, the deficit is probably still too large to be permanently sustained, and many economists fear that the decline is temporary and caused by the recession. Further, a large share of the capital inflows have come from foreign central banks in recent years, and some are concerned about the economic and political implications of this reliance. Some fear that a rapid decline in capital inflows would trigger a sharp drop in the value of the dollar and an increase in interest rates that could lower asset values and disrupt economic activity. However, economic theory and empirical evidence suggest that the most plausible scenario is a slow decline in the CA deficit, which would not greatly disrupt economic activity because production in the traded goods sector would be stimulated.

Chapter 14- Petroleum prices rose sharply in the first half of 2008, at one time reaching more than $140 per barrel of crude oil. After July 2008, however, petroleum prices and import volumes fell at a historically rapid pace; in January 2009, prices of crude oil fell below $40 per barrel. Since then, crude oil prices have nearly doubled, while the average monthly volume of imports of energy-related petroleum products has fallen nearly 10% year over year. Despite the drop in the volume of crude oil imports, the rise in the cost of energy imports through 2009 and early 2010 could add more than $100 billion to the nation's trade deficit in 2010 over that experienced in 2009. The strength of the U.S. economic recovery in the second half of 2010 could increase both the volume of energy imports and the price of those imports. This chapter provides an estimate of the initial impact of the changing oil prices on the nation's merchandise trade deficit.

Chapter 15- Discretionary spending is provided and controlled through appropriations acts, which fund many of the activities commonly associated with such federal government functions as running executive branch agencies, congressional offices and agencies, and international operations of the government. Essentially all spending on federal wages and salaries is discretionary.

Federal spending in 2009 accounted for just under a quarter (24.7%) of the U.S. economy, as measured by gross domestic product (GDP). Federal spending since 1962 has averaged about a fifth of GDP. (Years denote federal fiscal years unless noted otherwise.) Discretionary spending accounted for 35.2% of total outlays in 2009, as extraordinary federal responses to financial turmoil sharply increased mandatory spending (59.5% of outlays in 2009), reducing discretionary spending's share of total spending.

Chapter 16- Foreign direct investment is sparking a national debate. Local communities compete for investment projects, while many of the residents of those communities fear losing their jobs to foreign outsourcing. Some opponents argue that such job losses have a disproportionately negative impact on local communities. Economists generally argue that free and unimpeded international capital flows have a positive impact on both domestic and foreign economies. This issue is complicated by the fact that broad, comprehensive data on U.S. multinational companies was not developed to address the issue of jobs outsourcing. This chapter provides an overview of CRS Report RL32461, *Outsourcing and Insourcing Jobs in the U.S. Economy: Evidence Based on Foreign Investment Data*, that analyzes the extent of direct investment into and out of the economy and the relationship between direct investment and the broader economic changes that are occurring in the U.S. economy.

Chapter 17- After the long economic expansion that characterized much of the current decade, the nation entered its 11th postwar recession in December 2007. The subsequent decrease in jobs and comparison of the latest recession to the Great Depression intensified congressional interest in passing legislation early in 2009 aimed at encouraging creation of new jobs and warding off further loss of jobs.

To mitigate all but one recession since the 1960s, Congress chose to increase federal spending on public works (infrastructure). (See CRS Report 92-93 9, *Countercyclical Job Creation Programs*.) Public works expenditures traditionally have gone to certain types of construction activities (e.g., building highways and bridges, dams and flood control structures) which indirectly increase demand in industries that supply their products to construction firms (e.g., manufacturing). Today, the definition of infrastructure has been expanded to include green economic activities (commonly referred to as green jobs), which include industries that utilize renewable resources (e.g., electricity generated by wind), produce energy-efficient goods and services (e.g., mass transit), and install energy-conserving products (e.g., retrofitting buildings with thermal-pane windows).

In: Economic Policies in a Time of Financial Crisis
Editor: Heather D. Perkins
ISBN: 978-1-61122-686-7

Chapter 1

AUTHORITATIVE RESOURCES ON THE AMERICAN RECOVERY AND REINVESTMENT ACT OF 2009 (ARRA)

Kim Walker Klaman and Julie Jennings

SUMMARY

The following list of authoritative resources is designed to assist in responding to a broad range of questions and concerns about the American Recovery and Reinvestment Act (ARRA), P.L. 111-5. Links to the full text of the act, Congressional Budget Office (CBO) estimates, White House fact sheets, and federal, state, and municipal government websites are included, along with other useful information. This list reflects information that is currently available on the Internet.

The following list of authoritative resources has been compiled to assist in responding to a broad range of questions and concerns about the American Recovery and Reinvestment TAct of 2009 (ARRA), P.L. 111-5. Links to the full text of the act, Congressional Budget Office (CBO) estimates, White House fact sheets, and federal, state, and municipal government websites are included, along with other useful information. This list reflects information that is currently available on the Internet.

FULL TEXT OF THE LAW

P.L. 111-5 (H.R. 1) was signed by the President on February 17, 2009.

Conference Report (H.Rept. 111-16) was passed by the House and Senate on February 13, 2009. This includes the Joint Explanatory Statement.

Congressional Budget Office Cost Estimates

Estimates of ARRA's impact on the budget and a detailed analysis of the budgetary effects by title. http://www.cbo.gov/ftpdocs/99xx/doc9989/hr1conference.pdf

White House Information

Fact Sheets

Provides general fact sheets on broad policy areas within the stimulus (e.g., education, energy, health, infrastructure) and estimates by state the number of jobs that will be created or saved.

http://www.whitehouse.gov/the_press_office/state_by_state_employment_impact/

Recovery.gov

This Administration's website is intended to be a repository for information related to implementation and oversight of the stimulus. It currently includes overview information about the legislation, accountability reports and actions, frequently asked questions, and funding data, including distribution of funds and major recipients.

http://www.recovery.gov

Each federal agency receiving funds from the act will submit reports on their recovery activities. Updated reports are submitted each week, as well as detailed major actions taken by each agency and how much money has been spent.

Agency Reported Data

http://www.recovery.gov/Transparency/agency/Pages/AgencyLanding.aspx

Recipient Reported Data

http://www.recovery.gov/Transparency/RecipientReportedData/Pages/RecipientLanding.aspx

Office of Management and Budget Guidance

The Office of Management and Budget (OMB) issued a detailed guidance document on February 18, 2009, directing executive branch agencies to develop a dedicated portion of their websites for information related to the recovery. This document was updated and expanded based on input from the various stakeholders on subsequent dates (April 3, 2009 and June 22, 2009). All three guidance documents are available on the recovery.gov website:

Initial Implementing Guidance (February 18, 2009)

http://www.recovery.gov/About/Documents/InitialRecoveryActImplementingGuidance_Feb18.pdf

Update Implementing Guidance (April 3, 2009)
http://www.recovery.gov/About/Documents/m09-15_April3.pdf

OMB also issued guidance on recipient reporting:

Memorandum on the Reports on Use of Recovery Act Funds (June 22, 2009)
http://www.whitehouse.gov/omb/assets/memoranda_fy2009/m09-21.pdf

Memorandum on Improving Recovery Act Recipient Reporting (September 11, 2009)
http://www.whitehouse.gov/omb/assets/agencyinformation_memoranda_2009_pdf/m09-30.pdf

Improving Compliance in Recovery Act Recipient Reporting (November 30, 2009)
http://www.recovery.gov/FAQ/recipient/Documents/m10-05%5B1%5D.pdf

Updated Guidance on the American Recovery and Reinvestment Act (December 18, 2009)
http://www.recovery.gov/FAQ/recipient/Documents/m10-08%20Updated%20Guidance%2012182009.pdf

Updated Guidance on the American Recovery and Reinvestment Act (March 22, 2010)
http://www.recovery.gov/FAQ/recipient/Documents/OMB212Sharp_omb_eop_gov_20100322_170428.pdf

OMB has created a nationwide data collection system for recipients of ARRA funds to use for submitting their required data. Only registered users may use this system. Data collected will be available to the public on the recovery.gov site beginning October 11, 2009.
http://www.federalreporting.gov/

CONGRESSIONAL SOURCES

The House Committee on Ways and Means provides instructions for requesting various benefits from the funding provided by the act. It also contains fact sheets on some of the tax provisions of the act.
http://waysandmeans.house.gov/press/PRArticle.aspx?NewsID=10421

GOVERNMENT ACCOUNTABILITY OFFICE REPORTS

The Government Accountability Office (GAO) is required to conduct bimonthly reviews of selected funding recipients and to report on the use of funds. These GAO reviews currently include 16 states and the District of Columbia and are available on the GAO website:

GAO-09-580, Recovery Act: As Initial Implementation Unfolds in States and Localities, Continued Attention to Accountability Issues is Essential (April 23, 2009) http://www.gao.gov/new.items/d09580.pdf

GAO-09-829, States' and Localities' Current and Planned Uses of Funds While Facing Fiscal Stresses (July 8, 2009) http://www.gao.gov/new.items/d09829.pdf

GAO-09-830SP, States' and Localities' Current and Planned Uses of Funds While Facing Fiscal Stresses (Appendixes) (July 8, 2009) http://www.gao.gov /new.items/d09830sp.pdf

GAO-09-1016, Funds Continue to Provide Fiscal Relief to State and Localities, While Accountability and Reporting Challenges Need to Be Fully Addressed (September 23, 2009) http://www.gao.gov/new.items/d091016.pdf

GAO-09-1017SP, Funds Continue to Provide Fiscal Relief to States and Localities, While Accountability and Reporting Challenges Need to Be Fully Addressed (Appendixes) (September 23, 2009) http://www.gao.gov/new.items/d091017sp.pdf

GAO-10-231, Status of States' and Localities' Use of Funds and Efforts to Ensure Accountability (December 10, 2009) http://www.gao.gov/new.items/d10231.pdf

GAO-10-232SP, Status of States' and Localities' Use of Funds and Efforts to Ensure Accountability (Appendixes) (December 10, 2009) http://www.gao.gov/new.items/d10232sp.pdf

GAO-10-437, Recovery Act: One Year Later, States' and Localities' Uses of Funds and Opportunities to Strengthen Accountability (March 3, 2010) http://www.gao.gov/new.items/d10437.pdf

GAO has developed a website covering not only the above-mentioned fund recipient reviews, but also links to other GAO products and instructions for reporting fraud or misuse of ARRA funds. Following the Money: GAO's Oversight of the Recovery Act is available at http://www.gao.gov/ recovery/.

Other available GAO products include the following:

GAO-09-453T, American Recovery and Reinvestment Act: GAO's Role in Helping to Ensure Accountability and Transparency http://www.gao.gov/new.items/d09453t.pdf

GAO-09-515T: American Recovery and Reinvestment Act: GAO's Role in Helping to Ensure Accountability and Transparency for Science Funding http://www.gao.gov/new.items/d09515t.pdf

FEDERAL AGENCY WEBSITES

Corporation for National and Community Service:
http://www.nationalservice.gov/about/recovery/index.asp

Department of Agriculture:
http://www.usda.gov/wps/portal/arra?navid=USDARECOVERY

Department of Agriculture – Plans:
http://www.usda.gov/documents/FY09_Stimulus_Enacted.pdf

Department of Commerce:
http://www.commerce.gov/Recovery/index.htm

Department of Commerce – National Institute of Standards and Technology:
http://www.nist.gov/ recovery/

Department of Defense:
http://www.defenselink.mil/recovery

Department of Education:
http://www.ed.gov/policy/gen/leg/recovery/index.html

Department of Energy:
http://www.energy.gov/recovery/index.htm

Department of Energy – Energy Efficiency and Renewable Energy:
http://apps1.eere.energy.gov/ news/daily.cfm/hp_news_id=156

Department of Energy – Western Area Power Administration:
http://www.wapa.gov/newsroom/ sec402.htm

Department of Health and Human Services:
http://www.hhs.gov/recovery/

Department of Health and Human Services – state Medicaid funding:
http://www.hhs.gov/ recovery/statefundsmap.html

Department of Housing and Urban Development:
http://www.hud.gov/recovery/index.cfm
Department of the Interior:
http://recovery.doi.gov

Department of Justice:
http://www.usdoj.gov/recovery/

Department of Labor:
http://www.dol.gov/recovery/

Department of Labor – Employee Benefits Security Administration (COBRA information):
http://www.dol.gov/ebsa/COBRA.html

Department of State:
http://www.state.gov/recovery/

Department of Transportation – Federal Transit Administration:
http://www.fta.dot.gov/ index_9118.html

Department of Transportation:
http://www.dot.gov/recovery/

Department of Treasury:
http://www.ustreas.gov/recovery/

Department of Veteran Affairs:
http://www.va.gov/recovery/Implementing_the_Recovery_Act.asp

Environmental Protection Agency:
http://www.epa.gov/recovery/

General Services Administration: http://www.gsa.gov/Portal/gsa/ep/contentView.do?contentType=GSA_OVERVIEW&contentId=25761&noc=T

Internal Revenue Service:
http://www.irs.gov/newsroom/article/0,,id=204335,00.html? portlet=6

National Aeronautics and Space Administration (NASA):
http://www.nasa.gov/recovery/

National Endowment for the Arts:
http://www.nea.gov/recovery/index.html

National Institutes of Health:
http://recovery.nih.gov/

National Institutes of Health (NIH), Director's statement:
http://www.nih.gov/about/director/ 02252009statement_arra.htm

National Science Foundation:
http://www.nsf.gov/recovery/

National Science Foundation, Director's statement:
http://www.nsf.gov/news/ news_summ.jsp?cntn_id=114277&org=OLPA&from=news

Small Business Administration:
http://www.sba.gov/recovery/

Small Business Administration – press release:
http://www.sba.gov/idc/groups/public/documents/sba_homepage/news_release_09-10.pdf

Social Security Administration:
http://www.ssa.gov/recovery/

State Government Websites

(The list below reflects states that currently post ARRA information on the Web. CRS will update the list regularly as more information becomes available.)

Alabama: http://www.stimulus.alabama.gov/
Alaska: http://omb.alaska.gov/10_omb/budget/IndexEconomicStimulus.htm
Arizona: http://az.gov/recovery
Arkansas: http://recovery.arkansas.gov
California: http://www.recovery.ca.gov
Colorado: http://www.colorado.gov/recovery
Connecticut: http://www.recovery.ct.gov Delaware:
http://recovery.delaware.gov/default.shtml
Florida: http://www.flarecovery.com/ Florida-transportation:
http://www.dot.state.fl.us/planning/economicstimulus/
Georgia: http://stimulusaccountability.ga.gov
Georgia-transportation: http://www.dot.state.ga.us/informationcenter/gastimulus/Pages/default.aspx
Hawaii: http://hawaii.gov/recovery
Idaho: http://accountability.idaho.gov
Illinois: http://recovery.illinois.gov/default.htm
Indiana: http://in.gov/gov/INvest.htm Iowa: http://www.iowa.gov/recovery/
Kansas: http://governor.ks.gov/issues-a-initiatives/american-recovery-act
Kentucky: http://kentuckyatwork.ky.gov/ Louisiana: http://www.stimulus.la.gov/
Louisiana-energy: http://dnr.louisiana.gov/sec/execdiv/techasmt/programs/ARRA_2009/
Maine: http://www.maine.gov/recovery/
Maryland: http://statestat.maryland.gov/recovery.asp
Massachusetts: http://www.mass.gov/recovery
Michigan: http://www.michigan.gov/recovery/
Minnesota: http://www.mmb.state.mn.us/stimulus
Mississippi: http://stimulus

Missouri: http://transform.mo.gov/
Montana: http://recovery.mt.gov/
Nebraska: http://www.recovery.nebraska.gov/
Nevada: http://nevada.gov/recovery/
New Hampshire: http://www.nh.gov/recovery
New Jersey: http://www.state.nj.us/recovery
New Mexico: http://www.recovery.state.nm.us/
New York: http://www.recovery.ny.gov/
North Carolina: http://www.ncrecovery.gov/
North Dakota: http://www.nd.gov/recovery
Ohio: http://recovery.ohio.gov/
Oklahoma: http://www.ok.gov/recovery/
Oregon: http://www.oregon.gov/recovery
Pennsylvania: http://www.recovery.pa.gov/
Rhode Island: http://www.recovery.ri.gov/
South Carolina: http://stimulus
South Dakota: http://recovery.sd.gov/
Tennessee: http://www.tnrecovery.gov
Texas: http://txstimulusfund.com/
Utah: http://www.recovery.utah.gov/
Vermont: http://recovery.vermont.gov/
Virginia: http://stimulus.virginia.gov/
Washington: http://recovery.wa.gov/
West Virginia: http://www.recovery.wv.gov/
Wisconsin: http://www.recovery.wisconsin.gov/
Wyoming: http://wyoming.gov/recovery/

State Funding Allocations

Department of Education:
http://www.ed.gov/about/overview/budget/statetables/recovery.html

Department of Health and Human Services-Community Health Center Grants:
http://www.hhs.gov/recovery/hrsa/napawards.html

Department of Heath and Human Services-Medicaid:
http://www.hhs.gov/recovery/ statefunds.html

Department of Health and Human Services-State Funding:
http://transparency.cit.nih.gov/RecoveryGrants/

Department of Housing and Urban Development:
http://portal.hud.gov/portal/page/portal/HUD/ recovery

Department of Justice-Justice Assistance Grant Program:
http://www.ojp.usdoj.gov/BJA/ recoveryJAG/recoveryallocations.html

Department of Justice-Crime Victims Fund Compensation and Assistance Programs:
http://www.ovc.gov/fund/recoverycvfa2009.html

Department of Justice-Stop Violence Against Women Formula Grant Awards:
http://www.ovw.usdoj.gov/recovery-grants-awards.htm

Department of Labor-Workforce Investment Act Youth Activities:
http://www.dol.gov/opa/media/ press/eta/eta20090249-chart.pdf

Department of Transportation-Funds for Highway Infrastructure Investment:
http://www.fhwa.dot.gov/legsregs/directives/notices/n4510705t2.htm

Department of Transportation-Public Transportation Programs:
http://www.dot.gov/recovery/ docs/E9-4745.pdf

Environmental Protection Agency-Clean Water and Drinking Water Revolving Fund:
http://www.epa.gov/water/eparecovery/docs/Final_SRF_eco_recovery_allotments.pdf

State and Municipal Sources

The Council of State Governments has compiled information on executive orders and state legislation related to ARRA, as well as key deadlines and grants information: http://www.staterecovery.org/ and http://www.staterecovery.org/state-responses

The US Conference of Mayors has prepared a summary of the act, highlighting those provisions they consider to be important for cities: http://www.usmayors.org/recovery/

State-by-State Breakdown of ARRA Dollars: http://www.usmayors.org/recovery/documents/report-stateprog.pdf

Key Program Summaries: http://www.usmayors.org/recovery/documents/program-summaries.xlsx

The National Conference of State Legislatures has prepared overview summaries of selected sections of the package (e.g., Medicaid, transportation, labor and economic development, energy and water, broadband): http://www.ncsl.org/?tabid=16779

NON-GOVERNMENT SOURCES

ProPublica, an independent, nonprofit investigative journalism organization, tracks the stimulus and its projects: http://www.propublica.org/ion/stimulus

In: Economic Policies in a Time of Financial Crisis
Editor: Heather D. Perkins
ISBN: 978-1-61122-686-7

Chapter 2

CAUSES OF A FINANCIAL CRISIS

Mark Jickling

SUMMARY

The current financial crisis began in August 2007, when financial stability replaced inflation as the Federal Reserve's chief concern. The roots of the crisis go back much further, and there are various views on the fundamental causes.

It is generally accepted that credit standards in U.S. mortgage lending were relaxed in the early 2000s, and that rising rates of delinquency and foreclosures delivered a sharp shock to a range of U.S. financial institutions. Beyond that point of agreement, however, there are many questions that will be debated by policymakers and academics for decades.

Why did the financial shock from the housing market downturn prove so difficult to contain? Why did the tools the Fed used successfully to limit damage to the financial system from previous shocks (the Asian crises of 1997-1998, the stock market crashes of 1987 and 2000-2001, the junk bond debacle in 1989, the savings and loan crisis, 9/11, and so on) fail to work this time? If we accept that the origins are in the United States, why were so many financial systems around the world swept up in the panic?

To what extent were long-term developments in financial markets to blame for the instability? Derivatives markets, for example, were long described as a way to spread financial risk more efficiently, so that market participants could bear only those risks they understood. Did derivatives, and other risk management techniques, actually increase risk and instability under crisis conditions? Was there too much reliance on computer models of market performance? Did those models reflect only the post-WWII period, which may now come to be viewed not as a typical 60-year period, suitable for use as a baseline for financial forecasts, but rather as an unusually favorable period that may not recur?

Did government actions inadvertently create the conditions for crisis? Did regulators fail to use their authority to prevent excessive risk-taking, or was their jurisdiction too limited and/or compartmentalized?

The multiple roots of the crisis are mirrored in the policy response. Two bills in the 111th Congress—H.R. 4173, passed by the House on December 11, 2009, and Senator Dodd's

Restoring American Financial Stability Act, as ordered reported by the Senate Banking Committee on March 22, 2010—address many of the purported causal factors across the entire financial system. The bills address systemic risk, too-big-to-fail, prudential supervision, hedge funds, derivatives, payments systems, credit rating agencies, securitization, and consumer financial protection. (For a summary of major provisions, see CRS Report R40975, *Financial Regulatory Reform and the 111th Congress*, coordinated by Baird Webel.)

This chapter consists of a table that presents very briefly some of the arguments for particular causes, presents equally brief rejoinders, and includes a reference or two for further reading.

INTRODUCTION

The financial crisis that began in 2007 spread and gathered intensity in 2008, despite the efforts of central banks and regulators to restore calm. By early 2009, the financial system and the global economy appeared to be locked in a descending spiral, and the primary focus of policy became the prevention of a prolonged downturn on the order of the Great Depression.

The volume and variety of negative financial news, and the seeming impotence of policy responses, has raised new questions about the origins of financial crises and the market mechanisms by which they are contained or propagated. Just as the economic impact of financial market failures in the 1930s remains an active academic subject, it is likely that the causes of the current crisis will be debated for decades to come.

This chapter sets out in tabular form a number of the factors that have been identified as causes of the crisis. The left column of **Table 1** below summarizes the causal role of each such factor. The next column presents a brief rejoinder to that argument. The right-hand column contains a reference for further reading. Where text is given in quotation marks, the reference in the right column is the source, unless otherwise specified.

Table 1. Causes of the Financial Crisis

Cause	Argument	Rejoinder	Additional Reading
Imprudent Mortgage Lending	Against a backdrop of abundant credit, low interest rates, and rising house prices, lending standards were relaxed to the point that many people were able to buy houses they couldn't afford. When prices began to fall and loans started going bad, there was a severe shock to the financial system.	Imprudent lending certainly played a role, but subprime loans (about $1- 1.5 trillion at the peak) were a relatively small part of the overall U.S. mortgage market (about $11 trillion) and of total credit market debt outstanding (about $50 trillion).	CRS Report RL3 3775, *Alternative Mortgages: Causes and Policy Implications of Troubled Mortgage Resets in the Subprime and Alt-A Markets*, by Edward V. Murphy.
Housing Bubble	With its easy money policies, the Federal Reserve allowed housing prices to rise to unsustainable levels. The crisis was triggered by the bubble bursting, as it was bound to do.	It is difficult to identify a bubble until it bursts, and Fed actions to suppress the bubble may do more damage to the economy than waiting and responding to the effects of the bubble bursting.	CRS Report RL33666, *Asset Bubbles: Economic Effects and Policy Options for the Federal Reserve*, by Marc Labonte.
Global Imbalances	Global financial flows have been characterized in recent years by an unsustainable pattern: some countries (China, Japan, and Germany) run large surpluses every year, while others (like the U.S and UK) run deficits. The U.S. external deficits have been mirrored by internal deficits in the household and government sectors. U.S. borrowing cannot continue indefinitely; the resulting stress underlies current financial disruptions.	None of the adjustments that would reverse the fundamental imbalances has yet occurred. That is, there has not been a sharp fall in the dollar's exchange value, and U.S. deficits persist.	Lorenzo Bini Smaghi, "The financial crisis and global imbalances – two sides of the same coin," Speech at the Asia Europe Economic Forum, Beijing, Dec. 9, 2008. http://www.bis.org/review/ r081212d.pdf
Securitization	Securitization fostered the "originate-to-distribute" model, which reduced lenders' incentives to be prudent, especially in the face of vast investor demand for subprime loans packaged as AAA bonds. Ownership of mortgage-backed securities was widely dispersed, causing repercussions throughout the global system when subprime loans went bad in 2007.	Mortgage loans that were not securitized, but kept on the originating lender's books, have also done poorly.	Statement of Alan Gree-nspan before the House Committee on Overs-ight and Government Reform, October 23, 2008. ("The brea-kdown has been most apparent in the securitization of home mortgages.")

Table 1. (Continued)

Cause	Argument	Rejoinder	Additional Reading
Lack of Transparency and Accountability in Mortgage Finance	"Throughout the housing finance value chain, many participants contributed to the creation of bad mortgages and the selling of bad securities, apparently feeling secure that they would not be held accountable for their actions. A lender could sell exotic mortgages to homeowners, apparently without fear of repercussions if those mortgages failed. Similarly, a trader could sell toxic securities to investors, apparently without fear of personal responsibility if those contracts failed. And so it was for brokers, realtors, individuals in rating agencies, and other market participants, each maximizing his or her own gain and passing problems on down the line until the system itself collapsed. Because of the lack of participant accountability, the originate-to-distribute model of mortgage finance, with its once great promise of managing risk, became itself a massive generator of risk."	Many contractual arrangements did provide recourse against sellers or issuers of bad mortgages or related securities. Many non-bank mortgage lenders failed because they were forced to take back loans that defaulted, and many lawsuits have been filed against MBS issuers and others.	Statement of the Honorable John W. Snow before the House Committee on Oversight and Government Reform, October 23, 2008.
Rating Agencies	The credit rating agencies gave AAA ratings to numerous issues of subprime mortgage-backed securities, many of which were subsequently downgraded to junk status. Critics cite poor economic models, conflicts of interest, and lack of effective regulation as reasons for the rating agencies' failure. Another factor is the market's excessive reliance on ratings, which has been reinforced by numerous laws and regulations that use ratings as a criterion for permissible investments or as a factor in required capital levels.	All market participants underestimated risk, not just the rating agencies. Purchasers of MBS were mainly sophisticated institutional investors, who should have done their own due diligence investigations into the quality of the instruments.	Securities and Exchange Commission, "SEC Approves Measures to Strengthen Oversight of Credit Rating Agencies," press release 2008-284, Dec. 3, 2008.

Table 1. (Continued)

Cause	Argument	Rejoinder	Additional Reading
Mark-to-market Accounting	FASB standards require institutions to report the fair (or current market) value of securities they hold. Critics of the rule argue that this forces banks to recognize losses based on "fire sale" prices that prevail in distressed markets, prices believed to be below long-term fundamental values. Those losses undermine market confidence and exacerbate banking system problems. Some propose suspending mark-to-market; EESA requires a study of its impact.	Many view uncertainty regarding financial insti-tutions' true condition as key to the crisis. If acco-unting standards—however imperfect—are relaxed, fears that published balance sheets are unreliable will grow.	"Understanding the Mark-tomarket Meltdown," *Euromoney*, Mar. 2008.
Deregulatory Legislation	Laws such as the Gramm-Leach-Bliley Act (GLBA) and the Commodity Futures Modernization Act (CFMA) permitted financial institutions to engage in unregulated risky transactions on a vast scale. The laws were driven by an excessive faith in the robustness of market discipline, or self-regulation.	GLBA and CFMA did not permit the creation of unregulated markets and activities; they simply codified existing markets and practices. ("There is this idea afloat that if you had more regulation you would have fewer mis-takes," [Gramm] said. "I don't see any evidence in our history or anybody else's to substantiate it." Eric Lipton and Stephen Labaton, "The Reckoning: Deregulator Looks Back, Unswayed," *New York Times*, Nov. 16, 2008.)	Anthony Faiola, Ellen Nakashima, and Jill Drew, "What Went Wrong?" *Washington Post*, Oct. 15, 2008, p. A1.
Shadow Banking System	Risky financial active-ties once confined to regulated banks (use of leverage, borrowing short-term to lend long, etc.) migrated outside the explicit government safety net provided by deposit insurance and safety and soundness regulation. Mortgage lending, in particular, moved out of banks into unregulated institutions. This unsupervised risk-taking amounted to a financial house of cards.	Regulated banks—the recipients of most of the $700 billion Treasury TARP program—have not really fared much better than investment banks, hedge funds, OTC derivatives dealers, private equity firms, et al.	Nouriel Roubini, "The Shadow Banking System is Unravelling," *Financial Times*, Sep. 22, 2008, p. 9.

Table 1. (Continued)

Cause	Argument	Rejoinder	Additional Reading
Non-Bank Runs	As institutions outside the banking system built up financial positions built on borrowing short and lending long, they became vulnerable to liquidity risk in the form of non-bank runs. That is, they could fail if markets lost confidence and refused to extend or roll over short-term credit, as happened to Bear Stearns and others.	Liquidity risk was always present, and recognized, but its appearance at the extreme levels of the current crisis was not foreseeable.	Krishna Guha, "Bundesbank Chief Says Credit Crisis Has Hallmarks of Classic Bank Run," *Financial Times*, Sep. 3, 2007, p. 1.
Off-Balance Sheet Finance	Many banks established off-the-books special purpose entities (including structured investment vehicles, or SIVs) to engage in risky speculative investments. This allowed banks to make more loans during the expansion, but also created contingent liabilities that, with the onset of the crisis, reduced market confidence in the banks' creditworthiness. At the same time, they had allowed banks to hold less capital against potential losses. Investors had little abil-ity to understand banks' true financial positions.	Beginning in the 1 990s, bank supervisors actually encouraged off-balance sheet finance as a legiti-mate way to manage risk.	Adrian Blundell-Wignall, "Structured Products: Implications for Financial Markets," *Financial Market Trends*, Nov. 2007, p. 27.
Government-Mandated Subprime Lending	Federal mandates to help low-income borrowers (e.g., the Community Reinvestment Act (CRA) and Fannie Mae and Freddie Mac's affordable housing goals) forced banks to engage in imprudent mortgage lending.	The subprime mortgage boom was led by non-bank lenders (not subject to CRA) and securitized by private investment banks rather than the GSEs.	Lawrence H. White, "How Did We Get into This Financial Mess?" Cato Institute Briefing Paper no. 110, Nov. 18, 2008.
Failure of Risk Management Systems	Some firms separated analysis of market risk and credit risk. This division did not work for complex structured products, where those risks were indistingui-shable. "Collective common sense suffered as a result."	Senior management's responsibility has always been to bridge this kind of gap in risk assessment.	"Confessions of a Risk Manager; A Personal View of the Crisis," *The Economist*, Aug. 9, 2008.

Table 1. (Continued)

Cause	Argument	Rejoinder	Additional Reading
Financial Innovation	New instruments in structured finance develo-ped so rapidly that market infra-structure and systems were not prepared when those instruments came under stress. Some propose that markets in new instru-ments should be given time to mature before they are permitted to attain a systemically significant size. This means giving accountants, regulators, ratings agencies, and settlement systems time to catch up.	In a global marketplace, innovation will continue and national regulators' attempts to restrain it will only put their countries' markets at a competitive disadvantage. Moreover, it is hard to tell in advance whether innovations will stabilize the system or the reverse.	Joseph R. Mason, "The Summer of '07 and the Shortcomings of Financial Innovation," *Journal of Applied Finance*, vol. 18, Spring 2008, p. 8.
Complexity	The complexity of certain financial instruments at the heart of the crisis had three effects: (1) investors were unable to make independent judgments on the merits of investments, (2) risks of market transactions were obscured, and (3) regulators were baffled.	Standard economic theory assumes that investors act rationally in their own self-interest, which implies that they should only take risks they	Lee Buchheit, "We Made It Too Complicated," *International Financial Law Review*, Mar. 2008.
Human Frailty	Behavioral finance posits that investors do not always make optimal choices: they suffer from "bounded rationality" and limited self-control. Regulators ought to help people manage complexity through better disclosure and by reinforcing financial prudence.	Since regulators are just as human as investors, how can they consistently recognize that behavior has become suboptimal and that markets are headed for a crash?	Cass Sunstein and Richard Thaler, "Human Frailty Caused This Crisis," *Financial Times*, Nov. 12, 2008.
Bad Computer Models	Expectations of the performance of complex structured products linked to mortgages were based on only a few decades worth of data. In the case of subprime loans, only a few years of data were available. "[C]omplex systems are not confined to historical experience. Events of any size are possible, and limited only by the scale of the system itself."	Blaming models and the "quants" who designed them mistakes a symptom for a cause—"garbage in, garbage out."	James G. Rickards, "A Mountain, Overlooked: How Risk Models Failed Wall St. and Washington," *Washington Post*, Oct. 2, 2008, p. A23.

Table 1. (Continued)

Cause	Argument	Rejoinder	Additional Reading
Excessive Leverage	In the post-2000 period of low interest rates and abundant capital, fixed income yields were low. To compensate, many investors used borrowed funds to boost the return on their capital. Excessive leverage magnified the impact of the housing downturn, and deleveraging caused the interbank credit market to tighten.	Leverage is only a symptom of the underlying problem: mispricing of risk and a credit bubble.	Timothy F. Geithner, "Systemic Risk and Financial Markets," Testimony before the House Committee on Financial Services, July 24, 2008.
Relaxed Regulation of Leverage	The SEC liberalized its net capital rule in 2004, allowing investment bank holding companies to attain very high leverage ratios. Its Consolidated Supervised Entities program, which applied to the largest investment banks, was voluntary and ineffective.	The net capital rule applied only to the regulated broker/dealer unit; the SEC never had statutory authority to limit leverage at the holding company level.	Stephen Labaton, "Agency's '04 Rule Let Banks Pile Up New Debt, and Risk," *New York Times*, Oct. 3, 2008, p. A1, and Testi-mony of SEC Chairman Christopher Cox, House Oversight and Government Reform Committee, Oct. 23, 2008. (Response to question from Rep. Christopher Shays.)
Credit Default Swaps (CDS)	"An interesting paradox arose, however, as credit derivatives instruments, developed initially for risk management, continued to grow and become more sophisticated with the help of financial engineering, the tail began wagging the dog. In becoming a me-dium for speculative transactions, credit derivatives increased, rather than alleviated, risk."	Speculation in derivatives generally makes prices of the underlying commodities more stable. We do not know why this relation-ship sometimes breaks down. Even in CDS, the feared "explosion" of defaults has not happened, albeit the expensive taxpayer rescue of AIG may have prevented such an event.	Jongho Kim, "From Vanilla Swaps to Exotic Credit Derivatives," *Fordham Journal of Corporate & Financial Law*, Vol. 13, No. 5 (2008), p. 705.
Over-the-Counter Derivatives	Because OTC derivatives (including credit swaps) are largely unregulated, limited info-rmation about risk exposures is available to regulators and market participants. This helps explain the Bear Stearns and AIG interventions: in addition to substantial loss-es to counterparties, a dealer default could trigger panic because of uncertainty about the extent and distribution of those losses.	The largest OTC markets—interest rate and currency swaps—appear to have held up fairly well.	Walter Lukken, "How to Solve the Derivatives Problem," *Wall Street Journal*, Oct. 10, 2008, p. A1 5.

Table 1. (Continued)

Cause	Argument	Rejoinder	Additional Reading
Fragmented Regulation	U.S. financial regulation is dispersed among many agencies, each with responsibility for a particular class of financial institution. As a result, no agency is well positioned to monitor emerging system- wide problems.	Countries with unified regulatory structures, such as Japan and the UK, have not avoided the crisis.	U.S. Treasury, *Blueprint for a Modernized Financial Regulatory Structure*, Apr. 2008.
No Systemic Risk Regulator	No regulator had comprehensive jurisdiction over all systemically important financial institutions. (The Fed had the role of systemic risk regulator by default, but lacked authority to oversee investment banks, hedge funds, nonbank derivatives dealers, etc.)	Some question whether the problem was lack of authority or failure to use existing regulatory powers effectively.	Henry Kaufman, "Finance's Upper Tier Needs Closer Scrutiny," *Financial Times*, Apr. 21, 2008, p. 1 3.
Short-term Incentives	Since traders and managers at many financial institutions receive a large part of their compensation in the form of an annual bonus, they lack incentives to avoid risky strategies liable to fail spectacularly every 5 or 10 years. Some propose to link pay to a rolling average of firm profits or to put bonuses into escrow for a certain period, or to impose higher capital charges on banks that maintain current annual bonus practices.	Shareholders already have incentives and authority to monitor corporate compensation structures and levels.	Andrew Ross Sorkin, "Rein in Chief's Pay? It's Doable," *New York Times*, Nov. 3, 2008.
Tail Risk	Many investors and risk managers sought to boost their returns by providing insurance or writing options against low-probability financial events. (Credit default swaps are a good example, but by no means the only one.) These strategies gener-ate a stream of small gains under normal market conditions, but cause large losses during crises. When market participants know that many such potential losses are distributed throughout	Dispersal of systematic risk via financial innovation was believed to make the financial system more resilient to shocks.	Raghuram Rajan, "A Tale of Two Liquidi-ties," Remarks at the University of Chicago Graduate School of Business, Dec. 5, 2007, online at http://www.chicagogsb.edu/news/12-5-07_Rajan.pdf.

Table 1. (Continued)

Cause	Argument	Rejoinder	Additional Reading
	the system (but do not know exactly where, or how large), uncertainty and fear are exacerbated when markets come under stress.		
Black Swan Theory	This crisis is a once-in-a-century event, caused by a confluence of factors so rare that it is impractical to think of erecting regulatory barriers against recurences. According to Alan Greenspan, such regulation would be "so onerous as to basically suppress the growth rate of the economy and ... [U.S.] standards of living." Testimony before the House Oversight and Government Reform Committee, Oct. 23, 2008.	"Some might be tempted to see recent events in the financial markets as just such black swans. But this would be quite wrong, in our view. Many of the flaws that have led to current turbulent conditions have not ridden on the back of a black swan. Instead, they are the result of weaknesses and failings in the interpretation of risk analysis and the process of oversight." (Booth and Mazzawi)	Geoff Booth and Elias Mazzawi, "Black Swan or Fat Turkey?" *Business Strategy Review*, vol. 19, Autumn 2008, p. 34. Also: Michael J. Boskin, "Our Next President and the Perfect Economic Storm," *Wall Street Journal*, Oct. 23, 2008, p. A17.

Source: Table Compiled by CRS.

Note: Passages in quotation marks are from the source cited in the right-hand column, unless otherwise noted.

In: Economic Policies in a Time of Financial Crisis
Editor: Heather D. Perkins
ISBN: 978-1-61122-686-7

Chapter 3

ECONOMIC EFFECTS OF A BUDGET DEFICIT EXCEEDING $1 TRILLION

Marc Labonte

SUMMARY

The budget deficit in FY2009 equaled $1.4 trillion, or 9.9% of gross domestic product (GDP). Combined with a shrinking economy, this increased the publicly held federal debt by 12.8 percentage points of GDP last year. Deficits of this size are not sustainable in the long run because the federal debt cannot indefinitely grow faster than output. If it did, a greater and greater share of national income would be devoted to servicing the debt, until eventually the government would be forced to monetize the debt (finance it through money creation) or default on it.

Although the debt cannot persistently rise relative to GDP, it can rise for a time, so it is hard to predict at what point investors would deem it to be unsustainable. A few other advanced economies have debt-to-GDP ratios higher than the United States. While some of those countries have seen their relative financing costs rise during the financial crisis, Japan has continued to be able to finance its debt at extremely low costs.

If investors as a whole currently deemed the debt to be unsustainable, the yields and the cost of credit default swaps on Treasury securities would be expected to rise. Instead, the former have been low by historical standards and the latter have risen only slightly. This may seem surprising, given that the debt is currently growing more rapidly than output, and it is projected to continue to do so under current policy. Over the next few years, the deficit is projected to fall somewhat, but if tax provisions scheduled by law to expire are extended and discretionary spending stays at recent levels, the deficit would not fall enough under current policy to stabilize the debt. Further, the debt is projected to begin rising much more rapidly in the long term under current policy because of the rising costs of Social Security, Medicare, and Medicaid. The willingness of investors to finance the federal debt at low interest rates in light of these projections suggests that investors believe that policy changes will eventually be made that will place the federal debt on a sustainable path.

Standard macroeconomics predicts that the increase in the deficit will temporarily boost overall spending at a time when there is significant slack in the economy. Were the deficit to be harmful to the economy, it would likely occur in two ways. First, it could raise interest rates and "crowd out" private investment. Because private investment has fallen so much as a result of the recession and interest rates are currently low, there is little evidence that crowding out is a significant factor at the moment. Second, the deficit could fail to boost GDP if it led to more borrowing from abroad. This factor also does not seem significant at present, as borrowing from abroad has fallen significantly during the recession.

Once the economy stabilizes, private investment demand can be expected to rebound. When it does, a large deficit would be expected to place a major strain on resources that are available to finance investment. By accounting identity, domestic investment spending must equal national saving plus net borrowing from abroad. The budget deficit is currently more than half the size of private saving. Even before this year's increase in the deficit, national saving was insufficient to finance domestic investment spending, and the United States was borrowing from abroad at unprecedented rates. Unless the deficit is reduced, the economy will require some combination of higher private saving, lower investment, and higher borrowing from abroad. Some economists have argued that borrowing much more from abroad is unrealistic, and the already heavy U.S. reliance on borrowing from abroad makes the maintenance of a large deficit even less sustainable.

Introduction

The federal budget deficit for FY2009 totaled $1.4 trillion, the first time it has ever topped $1 trillion. The government's ability to finance a budget deficit depends on the size of the economy. For this reason, and to compare the deficit to historical or foreign deficits, it is more meaningful to measure the deficit relative to gross domestic product (GDP). By this measure, the 2009 deficit is unusual but not unprecedented. The Congressional Budget Office (CBO) recorded an actual 2009 deficit equaling 9.9% of GDP. Seven times in U.S. history the federal budget deficit has exceeded 10% of GDP, which were during or following the Civil War (1865), World War I (1918, 1919), and World War II (1942-1945).

Federal budget deficits cause the publicly held federal debt to increase.[1] The FY2009 deficit of 9.9% of GDP, in a year when GDP fell, caused the debt-to-GDP ratio to rise by 12.8 percentage points.

Some Members of Congress have questioned whether a deficit of this magnitude is manageable and what effects it will have on the economy. This chapter will evaluate those questions.

At What Point Does the Public Debt Become Unsustainable?

Some economists worry that if the debt keeps rising, it will become unsustainable. By definition, the debt becomes unsustainable when private investors are no longer willing to hold it, at least at normal interest rates. Private investors become unwilling to hold a nation's debt when they become convinced that the government will either default on (in other words, renege on promises to repay) or monetize the debt (in other words, finance it through money creation). If the government chose the latter, it would result in rapidly increasing price inflation that reduces the existing debt's relative value.

Although it is not possible to predict the level when a country's debt becomes unsustainable, the trend that causes unsustainability is well known: a country cannot continually increase its debt at a rate that exceeds the growth rate of the economy. When it does, it causes debt service to absorb more and more of national income. As private investors observe the debt burden increasing, they will decide to flee the country's debt before the point where the government is forced to default or monetize. The decision by some investors to flee the debt will make it more onerous for the government to finance the debt, because it will now have to offer higher yields to attract new buyers. Thus, unsustainability tends to be triggered rapidly, as no investor wants to be the one still holding the debt when default or hyperinflation occurs. The exact point when investors choose to flee depends on psychological factors that cannot be predicted with accuracy and are likely to vary with circumstances.

Because it is the upward trend in debt that leads to unsustainability, investors may accept very large deficits for a year or a few years as long as they are convinced that in the future the government will reduce the deficit to a sustainable level before it is too late. For example, governments are often able to finance large deficits in wartime—the largest deficits in U.S. history occurred as a result of the Civil War, World War I, and World War II—because investors expect a rapid decline in the deficit once peacetime leads to a rapid decline in military spending.

Investors' willingness to accept large deficits for a time will depend in part on the current level of debt relative to GDP. In that regard, the 16 percentage point reduction in debt to GDP between 1993 and 2001 leaves the United States in a relatively good starting point, even after the 20.5 percentage point increase in debt that has already occurred since 2001. Although the increase in debt in 2009 brings the federal debt as a share of GDP to its highest level since 1955, it will remain at about half of its World War II peak.[2]

Are Financial Markets Treating the Debt as Unsustainable?

Standard financial market measures currently show no evidence to suggest that the fear of default is a large one. Although investors' views on the sustainability of the deficit cannot be observed directly, they are implicit in Treasury yields. If investors believed that the government would default on its debt or erode its value through inflation, they would demand higher yields to compensate against these risks. Yet Treasury yields have gone down, instead of up, as the deficit has increased. By December 2008, the yield on 10-year Treasury securities had fallen to 2.4%, its lowest level since 1954. (Yields have risen since then, but remain lower than they have been in decades.) Besides Treasury yields, another indicator of market fears of default are prices for credit default swaps, which can be thought of as a type of insurance against default.[3] Although the cost of credit default swaps for U.S. Treasuries rose during the recent financial crisis to atypical levels, they still implied a very low probability of default. Since February 2009, they have fallen, although they remain above levels that prevailed before September 2008.[4] These data strongly indicate that investors do believe that future deficits will be reduced to sustainable levels.

The ease of financing this year's historically large deficit is partly attributable to unique economic conditions. The United States entered its longest post-war recession in December 2007, featuring the most severe disruption to financial markets since the Great Depression.[5] September 2008 saw a "flight to quality" by investors who shunned risky assets and sought to hold only the safest assets. Investors perceived Treasury securities to be the safest assets.

Of course, although investors have not shown concern about the sustainability of government borrowing so far, this does not prove that borrowing is on a sustainable path. Investor behavior is compatible with a belief that policy steps will be taken to reduce the deficit to a level that stabilizes debt compared to GDP, but there is no guarantee that those steps will be taken. There is nothing preventing investors from re-evaluating their views at any time, however. As long as federal deficits remain at unsustainable levels, there is the risk—however small—that interest rates could rise quickly as a result of a perceived rise in default risk. Waiting until investor confidence has fallen would require larger policy changes because higher interest rates would cause debt service costs to rise.

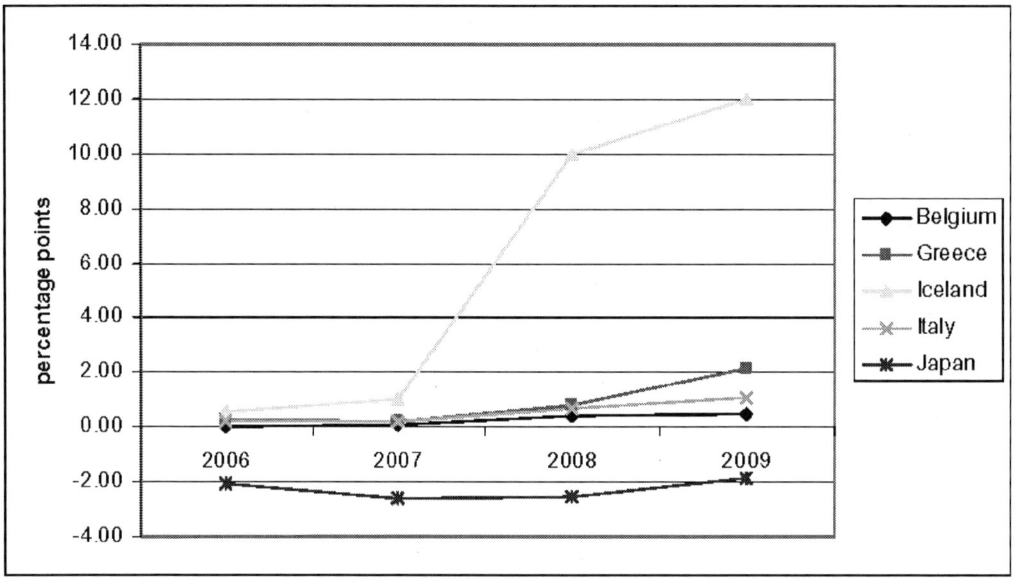

Source: Economist Intelligence Unit.

Notes: 2009 data for France, Germany, and Japan reflect actual yields on long-term bonds, where as the 2009 figures for Belgium, Greece, Iceland and Italy are projected.

Figure 1. Spread Between Interest Rates in Germany and Selected Countries Long-term Government Securities

Evidence from Abroad

One way to determine how high a debt level investors will be willing to finance is to look at how high the public debt has reached in other countries. Different countries have different reputations, so an acceptable debt level is likely to vary from country to country. Because more developing countries have defaulted on their debt in recent decades, advanced economies are generally seen as more able to sustain higher debt levels than developing ones. Thus, in gauging how much higher the U.S. public debt could get before it faces sustainability concerns, it is more useful to compare the United States to other advanced economies. There were seven Organization for Economic Cooperation and Development (OECD) members in 2009 that were projected to have higher government debt levels as a share of GDP than the United States: Belgium, France, Greece, Hungary Iceland, Italy, and Japan. U.S. debt was a projected 84% of GDP by the OECD's measure, while debt exceeded 100% of GDP for all these countries excluding France and Hungary, and it has been high in all but Iceland for many years.[6]

As seen in **Figure 1**, the five countries with debt exceeding 100% of GDP have had divergent experiences with financing debt at these levels. Using Germany as a comparison of a country that is generally viewed as a low default risk, **Figure 1** compares the spread between interest rates on government debt in Germany and the high debt advanced economies. At one extreme, the spread between Iceland's and Germany's debt was projected to be 12 percentage points in 2009. This large spread emerged when Iceland experienced a financial crisis in 2008 and its currency became non-convertible on international markets. But in fact, it was the crisis that caused the high debt level, rather than the high debt level causing the crisis—Iceland's debt was reported in 2008 to be only 25% of GDP. At the other extreme, Japan is able to finance its debt at a lower interest rate than Germany despite having a debt that surpassed 100% of GDP in 1997 and was projected to rise to 189% of GDP in 2009. The ability to finance debt at this level at low interest rates may be possible because Japan has a high rate of national saving overall, despite its large budget deficits, and because it has had lower inflation rates than Germany (which reduces the spread after adjusting for inflation).

The divergent experiences of Iceland and Japan point to another important factor in determining interest rate differentials—the size of a country's net foreign debt, including public and private debt. Of the five countries in **Figure 1**, only Iceland and Greece have significant net foreign debts—as does the United States. Before the crisis, neither Belgium, Greece, nor Italy paid significantly more than Germany to finance its debt. Belgium, Greece, and Italy have all joined the euro area, and their interest rate differentials with Germany fell significantly after joining.

Recent fiscal challenges experienced by Greece illustrate that investor willingness to finance large budget deficits can shift quickly. The country's current financial crisis began in October 2009, when newly elected Prime Minister George Papandreou announced that Greece's annual budget deficit reached 12.7% of GDP, significantly higher than previously announced.[7] On December 9, 2009, the Greek government bond market received a major setback when Fitch Ratings downgraded the nation's debt from A- to BBB+, marking the first time in a decade that a major credit rating agency had assessed Greece credit below an A grade.[8] Following additional bond rating cuts in December by Standard & Poor's and Moody's, the Greek government released a revised fiscal stability plan on January 14, 2010, that projected to reduce the country's deficit further to 2.8% of GDP by 2012.[9] But despite these renewed pledges of fiscal austerity, growing market concerns increased the spread between yields on Greek and German long-term bonds to approximately 3.9 percentage points on January 28, 2010, the highest level in 11 years.

In response to uncertainty about investor willingness to finance Greece's deficit, euro zone nations are faced with the dilemma of having to pledge financial assistance to Greece or face the potential credit default of a member nation. EU heads of state issued a joint statement on February 11, 2010, committing to coordinated action if necessary to safeguard euro zone economies.[10] Although this announcement offered few specifics regarding specific financial support that might be provided, some analysts now expect EU governments to disburse funds if Greece proves unable to raise the funds needed to cover outstanding government bond redemptions and coupons due in April and May of this year. Without investor perception of support from neighbors, current pressure on Greece's finances could be more acute.

Will Future Budget Deficits Remain at Unsustainable Levels under Current Policy?

If the budget deficit remained at its FY2009 level, it would be unsustainable because it would cause the national debt to continually rise relative to GDP. But will deficits remain at elevated levels in future years, or return to more normal levels under current policy?

In the medium term, there are reasons to believe that the deficit will fall somewhat from FY2009 levels without any policy changes. The recession causes certain outlays (such as unemployment insurance) to automatically rise and revenues to automatically fall. CBO projected that the business cycle increased the deficit by 2.1 percentage points of GDP in 2009. In addition, CBO recorded a subsidy cost of $152 billion in FY2009 for Treasury Department activities initiated under the Troubled Asset Relief Program (TARP), and net cash infusions to Fannie Mae and Freddie Mac totaled another $91 billion.[11] CBO projects that the effect of these programs on the debt and deficit will be small in future years under current policy. Finally, a stimulus package was enacted in February 2009 (P.L. 111-5) that increased the deficit by $200 billion in 2009, and a projected $404 billion in 2010, $135 billion in 2011, and $123 billion over 2012 to 2019. It seems most reasonable to assume that all three of these sources of pressure on the deficit are of a temporary nature. (There may be political support to extend some temporary TARP or stimulus provisions, but that would require legislative action.) Once the programs' costs have largely dissipated by 2012, the deficit would be significantly smaller, all else equal.

CBO's projections of current law under the baseline show deficits falling to less than 3% of GDP after 2014. The projections would seem to indicate that the budget deficit is already on a sustainable path under current law. These projections assume three important differences from current policy, however. First, CBO assumes that all tax provisions, including the tax cuts enacted in 2001 and 2003, will be allowed to expire as scheduled. Second, CBO projections of the deficit are based on assumptions that discretionary spending, which is determined annually, will grow at a rate that is significantly below the historical average. Third, CBO assumes that the routine one-year "patches" to adjust the alternative minimum tax (AMT) for inflation will not be extended, and as a result millions more taxpayers will fall under the AMT each year. If any of these three assumptions were altered, deficits would be much higher. Modifying the baseline to assume that tax provisions will not expire and discretionary spending (excluding the stimulus) will stay relatively steady as a share of GDP would cause deficits to exceed 7% of GDP from 2012 to 2017 and 9% of GDP in 2019.[12]

These projections do not take into account the possible enactment of new policy proposals currently being considered, which could further increase the deficit. Because deficits of this size would cause a persistent increase in the debt as a share of GDP, policy changes are required to put the budget deficit on a sustainable path.[13]

Moreover, long-term projections of current policy estimate that a large increase in Social Security, Medicare, and Medicaid spending will cause the budget deficit to grow continuously following the retirement of the Baby Boomers. Although deficit projections show some improvement in the short run, the long-term projection estimates even larger deficits under current policy, assuming health care costs continue to rise more rapidly than output. In the long term, reducing the growth rate of health care costs below the growth rate of the economy would have the largest impact on the budget deficit; however, the effects of health care cost growth on the deficit are very gradual, and play little role in the sustainability of the deficit in the near term.[14]

Because interest rates are currently so low, CBO recorded debt service payments of $187.3 billion for FY2009, the lowest level in dollar terms since 2005, even though the debt has risen by more than $1.7 trillion in the last year. As discussed below, financing the deficit may become more costly once economic conditions normalize. Even if interest rates return only to average levels in recent years, the cost of debt service will rise significantly. CBO's projections assume a relatively low interest rate paid on government debt over the next 10 years, largely because the starting point for its projections is today's very low rates. Some commentators have questioned whether this assumption is reasonable given the size of current and projected budget deficits. If investors respond to large deficits by demanding above-average interest rates, the cost of debt service would become large.[15]

SUSTAINABILITY AND FOREIGN HOLDERS OF THE DEBT

Some economists believe the government's reliance on foreign investors to finance the federal debt makes the United States more vulnerable to sudden shifts in investors' willingness to hold federal debt.[16] Foreigners currently hold $3.50 trillion (or a little more than half) of the total privately held federal debt.[17] Foreigners are perceived as less willing to passively buy and hold federal debt, in part because they bear exchange-rate risk when holding federal debt. If so, their demand for federal debt could be more sensitive to perceptions of sustainability, since default or monetization typically leads to currency devaluation that would reduce the debt's value in foreign currencies. If foreigners were to become less willing to hold federal debt, presumably, significantly higher interest rates would be required for Americans to absorb such large sums. Furthermore, if debt service costs were to rise suddenly, higher debt payments to foreigners would result in a fall in U.S. income, while higher debt payments to Americans would transfer income with no net effect on overall U.S. income.

Is foreign unwillingness to hold U.S. debt in the future a serious concern? Perhaps the strongest argument against it is the behavior of investors during the recent crisis. During a financial crisis that first emerged in U.S. subprime mortgage markets and potential financial writedowns from U.S. assets estimated by the International Monetary Fund (IMF) to be twice as large as losses from the Euro area, United Kingdom, and Japan combined,[18] foreigners increased their net purchase of Treasury securities from $216 billion in 2007 to $750 billion in 2008—a trend that continued even after financial conditions deteriorated in September 2008. If Treasury securities maintained their "safe haven" status amidst rapidly rising budget deficits and rapidly deteriorating financial conditions, it is arguably difficult to imagine a plausible scenario today in which investors would shun Treasury securities.

Nevertheless, in the long run, the sustainability of foreign borrowing falls under the same mathematical rules as the sustainability of government borrowing—the net debt owed to foreigners cannot indefinitely rise faster than GDP, or else an ever-increasing share of national income will be needed to service it. Since 2000, the current account deficit (a measure equal to net borrowing from abroad) has exceeded the growth in the economy. The current account deficit has fallen significantly since 2007, but it remains to be seen whether this change is cyclical or longer lasting. Thus, independent of concerns about the size of the federal debt, the upward trend in the net debt owed to foreigners raises concerns about the long-term sustainability of large scale borrowing from abroad.[19]

The willingness of foreign investors to hold U.S. Treasury securities is further complicated by the role of foreign governments. From 2003 to 2008, foreign governments (mostly through their central banks) have purchased on net an average of $213 billion of Treasury securities each year, or about two-thirds of the average purchased on net by all foreigners each year.[20] While it can be reasonably assumed that private investors are purchasing Treasury securities because they are seen as good investments (and would sell them if they no longer were), foreign governments may have other motivations. It is not clear if these other motivations would make them more or less likely to hold Treasury securities in the future because of sustainability concerns. Regardless of the motivation for initially purchasing Treasury securities, now that some foreign governments hold large portfolios of federal debt, they have an incentive to maximize their return. Collectively, this would call for governments to cooperate to avoid taking actions, such as large sales of holdings, that destabilize Treasury prices. But individually, any particular government has the incentive to sell its holdings before everyone else if it believes that the debt has become unsustainable; this incentive could hamper collective action.

IS A LARGE DEFICIT HARMFUL TO THE ECONOMY?

When the economy is at full employment (meaning practically all labor and capital resources are in use), government budget deficits "crowd out" private investment spending in the standard macroeconomic model. Setting aside foreign capital flows for the moment, borrowing can only be financed through saving, and government borrowing competes with business borrowing for the same pool of national saving. By increasing the demands on that pool of national saving, government borrowing pushes up the cost of all borrowing through higher interest rates, causing businesses to finance less capital spending than they otherwise would.[21] Business borrowing finances capital spending on plant and equipment, and lower capital spending results in lower potential gross domestic product, and hence lower future national income, than would otherwise occur.

In the current context, the economy is not at or near full employment. In this context, government deficits are unlikely to crowd out private business borrowing. On the contrary, business investment was contracting until the fourth quarter of 2009, either because investment demand declined or businesses are credit constrained. This greatly reduced the potential for large government deficits to crowd out private investment spending. As discussed above, low interest rates support the view that the deficit is currently causing little crowding out to occur. (Of course, this could change if investor concern about sustainability pushed up interest rates.) In this case, the decline in aggregate spending caused by falling investment spending can be offset, at least in part, by the rise in (deficit-financed) government spending, which directly increases GDP. Most economic forecasters predict that the rise in the budget deficit will, on balance, raise GDP over the next couple of years, despite a possible crowding out effect. Indeed, it is the increase in the deficit that is the primary reason that the stimulus package was projected to stimulate the economy in standard macroeconomic models.[22]

With international capital mobility, borrowing can also be financed by foreign saving. In the standard macroeconomic model with perfect capital mobility, the boost in aggregate spending from the stimulus would cause the trade deficit to rise as foreign capital is attracted to higher domestic interest rates. The availability of foreign credit would avoid the crowding out of domestic capital investment. But the boost to aggregate spending from the budget deficit would be negated (or "crowded out") by the higher trade deficit. The United States relies heavily on foreign borrowing, and this is another reason that large budget deficits could be less effective at stimulating the economy. The lack of perfect capital mobility and large output gap in the United States at present means that a larger trade deficit is unlikely to completely negate the stimulus as theory would suggest, but it is likely to make it less effective at boosting aggregate spending. Since the recession began, the trade deficit has fallen substantially, so the problem of crowding out from the trade deficit does not seem significant at this time. It should also be noted that if capital spending is financed by foreigners, the income generated by that capital will accrue to foreigners instead of Americans.

As the economy returns to full employment, large budget deficits will no longer provide any stimulus to aggregate spending.[23] At this point, crowding out will become a more serious concern if the budget deficit is not reduced. By accounting identity, domestic investment must equal national saving plus net borrowing from abroad. From 2000 to 2007, domestic investment averaged about 20% of GDP, as seen in **Table 1**. Because national saving averaged about 15% of GDP, three-quarters of this investment was financed by national saving and one-quarter was financed by borrowing from abroad. In 2000 and 2001, the federal government ran a budget surplus that increased national saving. From 2002 to 2007, the government ran a deficit that reduced national saving. The deficit was more than 2% of GDP from 2003 to 2005, and less than 2% of GDP in the other years. In 2008, national saving fell to 12.6% of GDP, in part because the budget deficit rose to 3.2% of GDP. Despite the fall in national saving that year, net borrowing from abroad remained relatively steady because investment spending fell to 17.5% of GDP.

The budget deficit was 9.9% of GDP in FY2009, more than half the size of total private saving, which is the sum of household and business saving. Although investment was low in 2009 because of the deepening of the recession, it can be expected to rebound when the economy recovers.

Table 1. Saving and Investment, 2000-2008 (Percentage of GDP)

	2000-2007	2008
Gross Domestic Investment	20.3	17.5
Gross National Saving	15.4	12.6
Net Borrowing from Abroad	4.9	4.9
Federal Budget Deficit[a]	-1.3	-3.2

Source: CRS Report RS21480, *Saving Rates in the United States: Calculation and Comparison*, by Brian W. Cashell, Congressional Budget Office

Notes: Gross domestic investment is the sum of private and government investment. Gross national saving is the sum of business, household, and government saving.

a. Fiscal Year, as measured by federal budget conventions.

At that point, even if the deficit were to fall by half as a share of GDP, either private saving would need to rise significantly above its average over the past ten years or net borrowing from abroad would have to be significantly higher than the 2000 to 2007 average, which was already at a historical high. Private saving has been fairly steady over the past 10 years, between 13.8% to 16.0% of GDP. Some of the rise in saving during the recession may prove lasting, but it is doubtful it would continue to rise enough to offset the rise in the budget deficit. In other words, even before the rise in the budget deficit, the combination of low rates of national saving and high rates of borrowing from abroad to finance domestic investment spending was unsustainable in the long run. If the budget deficit remains at elevated rates, national saving will be even lower, requiring either lower rates of domestic investment (that would reduce GDP from what it otherwise would have been) or higher rates of borrowing from abroad.

The willingness of foreigners to buy U.S. assets in the future will depend not only on the desirability of U.S. investment opportunities, but also on investment opportunities abroad. Here too, future trends may point to a shift away from U.S. assets. Even if foreign investors were unconcerned about the sustainability of U.S. debt, foreign countries may find more internal demand for their saving as the world economy recovers. U.S. public debt will also be competing to attract funds with a large increase in borrowing by foreign governments. The IMF estimates that public debt in the G-20 advanced economies will rise from 92% of GDP in 2009 to 105% of GDP in 2012 to 109% of GDP in 2014. [24]

Furthermore, foreign private demand for U.S. assets has been much smaller than total U.S. borrowing needs in recent years, and foreign governments have filled the gap. From 2002 to 2005, net foreign official capital inflows have exceeded $200 billion, and from 2006 to 2007, they exceeded $400 billion. These official inflows were motivated by factors that may prove to have been specific to the context of the previous economic expansion, and not sustainable over the long term going forward. Countries may have been accumulating official reserves in recent years (1) to prevent their currency from appreciating against the dollar or against a major trading partner's (or competitor's) currency; (2) because the price of a major export, such as oil, had suddenly risen and the country decided to invest some of its windfall in foreign assets; (3) to guard their currency against a sudden withdrawal of investment from their country during a future downturn; or (4) to rebuild their reserves after a prior defense of their currency drained them away. None of these explanations would imply a permanent desire to continuously accumulate official dollar-denominated assets.

Will Large Deficits Lead to High Inflation?

Another concern that has been raised is that large deficits will lead to high inflation. A significant increase in inflation is ultimately a result of changes in the money supply, and the Federal Reserve controls the money supply independently of the Treasury and its financing needs. Large deficits would lead to higher inflation if the Fed begins to finance unfunded government operations by increasing the money supply. Under current law, this is prevented by Section 14 of the Federal Reserve Act, which forbids the Federal Reserve from purchasing debt directly from the Treasury, and Section 2A, which mandates that the Fed keep inflation low, among other goals.[25] In a well-known article, economists Thomas Sargent and Neil Wallace pointed out some "unpleasant arithmetic," however.[26] They observed that in order to avoid default, a central bank might ultimately be forced to monetize the debt if private investors become unwilling to finance it and the government refuses to raise taxes or cut spending. Investors may perceive this future outcome and raise their inflationary expectations today. If investors anticipate that the debt will be monetized, they will require higher interest rates to finance it in the meantime, so inflation will ultimately be higher than if the deficit had been monetized from the outset. In that example, future inflation is a function of fiscal decisions as well as monetary decisions taken today. To date, there is no evidence that inflation expectations have risen significantly.

End Notes

[1] References in this chapter to the national debt refer to the publicly held federal debt unless otherwise noted because this is the debt that is financed in private capital markets and affects the economy. The gross federal debt is the sum of the publicly held debt and intra-governmental debt that arises from surpluses in government trust funds. Changes in intragovernmental debt are unrelated to the budget deficit.

[2] For more information, see CRS Report RL34712, *Ebbs and Flows of Federal Debt*, by Mindy R. Levit.

[3] For more information on credit default swaps, see CRS Report RS22932, *Credit Default Swaps: Frequently Asked Questions*, by Edward V. Murphy and Rena S. Miller.

[4] International Monetary Fund, *Fiscal Implications of the Global Economic and Financial Crisis*, Staff Position Note 2009/13, June 9, 2009.

[5] See CRS Report R40198, *U.S. Economy in Recession: Similarities To and Differences From the Past*, by Marc Labonte.

[6] Organization for Economic Cooperation and Development, *Economic Outlook*, vol. 86, December 2009, Annex Table 32. The OECD attempts to standardize the measurement of debt for cross-country comparison, and may not use the same measure as the federal government. To account for different systems of federalism, the OECD uses a measure that includes state and local and federal debt. This is the primary reason the OECD figure is higher for the United States than data from CBO.

[7] "Greece in EU Dock Over Dodgy Budget Data", *EU Business*, October 20, 2009.

[8] Ingrid Melander and Lefteris Papadimas, "Fitch Rating Cut Piles Pain on Troubled Greece," *Reuters*, December 8, 2009.

[9] Karen Hope and David Oakley, "Greece unveils 3-year plan to curb deficit," *Financial Times*, January 14, 2010.

[10] Simon Kennedy and James G. Neuger, "EU Leaders Deploy 'Bazooka' to Repel Attack on Greece," *Bloomberg*, February 12, 2010.

[11] In the case of TARP and transfers to the GSEs, the effect of the programs on the deficit do not closely match their effect on the national debt. Under the Credit Reform Act, CBO scores the deficit costs of the programs as the net present value of the subsidy implicit in the assistance, and counts that cost in the budget year it is outlayed, with no cost recorded for future years. The national debt is affected by the programs as securities are bought and sold. This means that the programs will increase the debt more than CBO's score of the deficit in the short term, but reduce the debt in future years (as securities are sold). In addition, the debt has increased this year by about $200 billion without any recorded effect on the deficit because of the Treasury Supplementary Financing

Program, a program under which Treasury issues extra debt in order to deposit funds at the Federal Reserve. It is expected that this program will not permanently increase the debt, although it is unclear how much longer it will continue. From a sustainability perspective, the effect of all these programs on the debt may be more relevant than CBO's score of their effect on the deficit.

[12] One category of spending that might not continue at current levels is overseas military spending. Assuming that this falls to zero would reduce the deficit by about 1% of GDP annually.

[13] Budget projections are subject to high margins of error, even over relatively short periods of time. Thus, the actual deficit in future years could turn out to be larger or smaller than CBO's projection, requiring larger or smaller policy changes, respectively, to place the debt on a sustainable path.

[14] See CRS Report RL32747, *The Economic Implications of the Long-Term Federal Budget Outlook*, by Marc Labonte.

[15] For example, assuming interest rates of 10.5% after 2014 would increase the 2019 deficit under the President's budget by $1.2 trillion. See Congressional Budget Office, *Letter to Honorable Paul Ryan*, June 30, 2009.

[16] See, for example, Kenneth Rogoff, "Foreign Holdings of U.S. Debt: Is Our Economy Vulnerable?", Testimony before the Committee on the Budget, U.S. House of Representatives, June 26, 2007; Brad Setser, *U.S. External Debt and Power*, Brookings Institute, working paper, 2008.

[17] U.S. Department of Treasury, Financial Management Service, *Treasury Bulletin*, December 2009. Privately held debt omits debt held by government trust funds and the Federal Reserve. It includes debt held by state and local governments.

[18] International Monetary Fund, *Global Financial Stability Report*, April 2009, Table 1.3.

[19] For more information, see CRS Report RL33186, *Is the U.S. Current Account Deficit Sustainable?*, by Marc Labonte.

[20] For more information, see CRS Report RS21951, *Financing the U.S. Trade Deficit: Role of Foreign Governments*, by Marc Labonte.

[21] In the case of current budget deficits, some government borrowing is being used to purchase assets from the financial sector, notably preferred stock. Borrowing to buy assets would not be expected to have the same crowding out effect as borrowing to buy goods and services. Asset purchases are not the primary cause of the current budget deficit, however.

[22] See, for example, Congressional Budget Office, *A Preliminary Analysis of the President's Budget*, March 2009.

[23] By definition, an economy near full employment does not have any slack that can be spurred into use by stimulus. Further, it is the increase in the deficit that stimulates spending—were the level of the deficit to be held steady, the economy would receive no further stimulus in future years.

[24] International Monetary Fund, *World Economic Outlook: Sustaining the Recovery*, data from Figure 1.7, October 2009.

[25] While the law forbids the Fed to directly finance the deficit, it can indirectly reduce the government's financing costs by purchasing Treasury securities on the secondary market. While the Treasury must pay the Fed interest on the Treasury securities it holds, the Fed remits its profits to the Treasury. The Fed has purchased Treasury securities on the secondary market in 2009 in order to provide liquidity to the economy, but the planned size of the purchases ($300 billion) is small relative to the projected deficit.

[26] Thomas Sargent and Neil Wallace, "Some Unpleasant Monetarist Arithmetic," Federal Reserve Bank of Minneapolis, *Quarterly Review*, Fall 1981.

In: Economic Policies in a Time of Financial Crisis
Editor: Heather D. Perkins
ISBN: 978-1-61122-686-7

Chapter 4

FOREIGN HOLDINGS OF FEDERAL DEBT

Justin Murray and Marc Labonte

SUMMARY

This chapter presents current data on estimated ownership of U.S. Treasury securities and major holders of federal debt by country. Federal debt represents the accumulated balance of borrowing by the federal government. To finance federal borrowing, U.S. Treasury securities are sold to investors. Treasury securities may be purchased directly from the Treasury or on the secondary market by individual private investors, financial institutions in the United States or overseas, and foreign, state, or local governments. Foreign investment in federal debt has grown in recent years, prompting questions on the location of the foreign holders and how much debt they hold.

SELECTED STATISTICS ON FOREIGN HOLDINGS OF FEDERAL DEBT

Federal debt represents, in large measure, the accumulated balance of federal borrowing of the U.S. government. The portion of gross federal debt held by the public consists primarily of investment in U.S. Treasury securities.[1] Investors in the United States and abroad include official institutions such as the U.S. Federal Reserve, financial institutions such as private banks, and private individual investors. **Table 1** provides December 2009 data, available as of March 2010, on estimated ownership of U.S. Treasury securities by type of investment and the percentage of that investment attributable to foreign investors.[2]

As the table shows, during the past five years, foreign holdings of debt increased by nearly $1.8 trillion to more than $3.6 trillion from December 2004 to December 2009. During the same period, total privately held debt increased by approximately $3.3 trillion to $7 trillion.

Table 1. Estimated Ownership of U.S. Treasury Securities (in Billions of Dollars)

End of Month	Total Public Debt Held by All Private Investors	Total Debt Held by Foreign Investors	Foreign Holdings as a Share of Total Privately Held Public Debt
Dec. 2009	$7,034.5	$3,614.0	51.4%
Dec. 2008	$5,893.4	$3,076.3	52.2%
Dec. 2007	$4,395.7	$2,352.9	53.5%
Dec. 2006	$4,122.1	$2,105.0	51.1%
Dec. 2005	$3,970.6	$2,036.0	51.3%
Dec. 2004	$3,690.6	$1,853.4	50.2%

Source: Table OFS-2: Estimated Ownership of U.S. Treasury Securities from the March 2009 *Treasury Bulletin.* See link for "Ownership of Federal Securities" tables at http://www.fms.treas.gov/bulletin/index.html.

Notes: Table data represent estimated figures current as of March 22, 2010. For the most current data, connect to the link listed above. Percentage shares calculated by CRS.

Although gross federal debt is the broadest measure of the debt, it may not be the most important one. The debt measure that is relevant in an economic sense is debt held by the public. This is the measure of debt that has actually been sold in credit markets and has influenced interest rates and private investment decisions. This table reflects that portion of public debt held by all private investors in federal securities and the portion of that debt held by foreign investors. See CRS Report RL31590, *The Federal Government Debt: Its Size and Economic Significance*, by Brian W. Cashell.

Table 2. The Top 10 Foreign Holders of Federal Debt, by Country (Data Current as of March 9, 2010)

Country	Amount Held ($ in billions; as of Dec. 2009)	Percentage of all foreign holdings in federal debt	Country	Amount Held ($ in billions; as of Dec. 2004)	Percentage of all foreign holdings in federal debt
Mainland China	$894.8	24.3%	Japan	$689.9	37.3%
Japan	$765.7	20.8%	Mainland China	$222.9	12.1%
Oil Exporters	$207.4	5.6%	United Kingdom	$95.8	5.2%
United Kingdom	$178.0	4.8%	Taiwan	$67.9	3.7%
Brazil	$169.3	4.6%	Oil Exporters	$62.1	3.4%
Hong Kong	$148.7	4.0%	Korea	$55.0	3.0%
Russia	$141.8	3.8%	Carribean Banking Centers	$51.1	2.8%
Carribean Banking Centers	$128.2	3.5%	Germany	$50.3	2.7%

Table 2. (Continued)

Country	Amount Held ($ in billions; as ofDec. 2009)	Percentage of all foreign holdings in federal debt	Country	Amount Held ($ in billions; as of Dec. 2004)	Percentage of all foreign holdings in federal debt
Taiwan	$116.5	3.2%	Hong Kong	$45.1	2.4%
Switzerland	$89.7	2.4%	Switzerland	$41.7	2.3%
Total Top 10 Countries of Foreign Investors in Federal Debt	$2,840.1	77.0%	Total Top 10 Countries of Foreign Investors in Federal Debt	$1,381.8	74.9%
Total All Foreign Investment in Federal Debt	$3689.0	100%	Total All Foreign Investment in Federal Debt	$1,849.3	100%

Source: Treasury Department International Capital System (TIC), at http://www.treas.gov/tic/mfhhis01.txt.

Notes: Data, including estimated foreign holders of federal debt historically by month, in these Treasury Department tables are periodically adjusted. Current monthly estimates are available at http://www.treas.gov/tic/ mfh.txt. Aggregate data totals in **Table 1** vary slightly from aggregate data totals in **Table 2** because of minor valuation differences of a few securities for a few of the countries in the complete list of International Financial Statistics data used by the TIC data. Percentage approximations calculated by CRS. Percentages may vary slightly due to rounding.

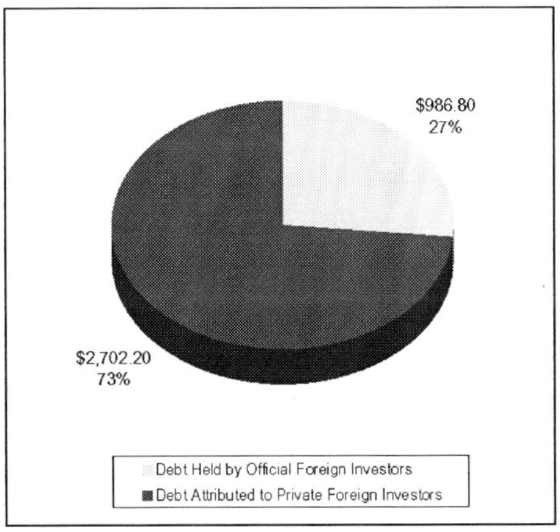

Source: Treasury Department International Capital System, http://www.treas.gov/tic/mfhhis01.txt. Notes: Data in the chart represent estimated figures current as of March 9, 2010. Figures are in billions of dollars. Data in the Treasury Department tables are periodically adjusted. For the most current estimates, click on the URL address listed above.

The estimated combined total of all foreign holdings for December 2009 was $3,689.0 billion. Data consist of reported December 2009 figures from the Treasury Department International Capital System http://www.treas.gov/tic/mfh.txt. The breakdown between estimated official and private holdings is not publically available on a country-by-country basis. Approximate percentages calculated by CRS.

Figure 1. Breakdown of Official vs. Private Foreign Holdings of U.S. Federal Debt

In December 2004, total foreign investment in U.S. federal debt was approximately $1.9 trillion (50.2%) of the total of approximately $3.7 trillion in privately held debt. By December 2009, total foreign investment in U.S. federal debt grew by 1.2 percentage points to $3.6 trillion (51.4%) of the total of approximately $7 trillion in debt held by private investors.[3]

Data on major foreign holders (investors) of federal debt by country are provided in **Table 2**. According to the data, the top three estimated foreign holders of federal debt by country, ranked in descending order as of December 2009, are China ($894.8 billion), Japan ($765.7 billion), and oil-exporting countries ($207.4 billion). Based on these estimates, China holds approximately 24.3% of all foreign investment in U.S. privately held federal debt; Japan holds approximately 20.8%; and the oil-exporting countries hold approximately 5.6%.[4]

Foreign holdings as estimated by the Treasury Department can be divided into official (governmental investment) and private sources. **Figure 1** provides data on the current breakdown of estimated foreign holdings in U.S. federal debt. As the figure shows, 73.3% of foreign holdings in U.S. federal debt are held by governmental sources. Private investors hold the other 26.7%.

FOREIGN INVESTMENT IN U.S. FEDERAL DEBT: WHY IS IT AN ISSUE OF CONCERN?

Foreign ownership of federal debt has become a growing concern among some Members of Congress because of the nation's large and rising trade deficit. During the past three decades, U.S. national saving has not been adequate to finance its capital investment needs, and borrowing from abroad has covered the gap. For foreigners to invest in the U.S. economy on net, the United States must import more than it exports (run a trade deficit). When the government runs a budget deficit, as it has done since 2002, it reduces the national saving rate. This implies that domestic investment must fall, unless private saving rises or borrowing from abroad increases.[5]

As seen in **Table 1**, as the national debt has increased, foreign ownership of U.S. Treasuries has followed closely, suggesting that the budget deficit has been financed, in part, through borrowing abroad. By June 2004, foreigners held more than 50% of the public debt held by private investors for the first time. Although this percentage has no particular economic significance, it may have other significance.

Since 2002, some observers have been concerned that the nature of foreign purchases of U.S. Treasuries has changed. Beginning in that year, a significant fraction of the trade deficit was financed through official purchases of U.S. assets, such as purchases by foreign central banks. Although no direct data on official purchases of Treasuries by country exist, it can be inferred that the Treasuries may have been purchased by certain Asian and oil-producing countries because they were the only countries that had large increases in their foreign reserves during that period. Although the effect on the U.S. economy of official purchases of Treasuries is the same as private purchases, the motivations behind the purchases are different. Whereas private purchases are typically motivated by the profit incentive, official purchases may be motivated by a country's desire to keep its exchange rate constant or mitigate its rise against the dollar.[6] Many observers are concerned that the large fraction of national debt held by foreigners has the potential to be harmful to the U.S. economy.

Specifically, they fear that if foreigners suddenly decided to stop holding U.S. Treasury securities or decided to diversify their holdings, the dollar could plummet in value and interest rates would rise. Others are concerned that China's accumulation of hard currency assets will allow it to undertake activities in the foreign affairs and military realms that are not in the U.S. interest. Some economists argue that foreign borrowing at current levels is unsustainable and could cause problems for the U.S. economy down the road.[7]

When foreigners purchase U.S. Treasuries, or any other U.S. asset, the interest rate is lower than when borrowing is financed domestically out of national saving. Thus, when overall interest rates are lower as a result of net capital inflows, more interest-sensitive spending is undertaken. Interest-sensitive spending includes capital investment (e.g., production plants and equipment), residential investment (e.g., new homes), and durable consumption goods (e.g., automobiles and appliances). On the other hand, U.S. foreign borrowing induces a trade deficit by reducing exports and import-competing production. The trade deficit occurs because foreigners must first purchase U.S. dollars before purchasing U.S. assets. When the demand for dollars increases, the dollar appreciates, making U.S. exports and import-competing goods relatively more expensive. Thus, foreign borrowing shifts production out of the trade sector and into the interest-sensitive sector.[8]

Since the financial turmoil began in August 2007, the supply of Treasury securities has risen sharply, as a result of the increase in federal borrowing to finance spending on economic and financial recovery.[9] At the same time, the demand for Treasury securities has risen as there has been a "flight to quality" caused by greater investor preference for Treasury securities compared with riskier private securities. Thus, although an increase in the supply of Treasury securities would be expected to cause Treasury yields to rise, they instead fell relative to pre-crisis levels. Likewise, although the financial turmoil originated in U.S. markets, after the turmoil deepened in September 2008, net capital inflows pushed up the value of the dollar.

SELECTED CRS REPORTS

CRS Report RS21409, *The Budget Deficit and the Trade Deficit: What Is Their Relationship?*, by Marc Labonte and Gail E. Makinen.

CRS Report RL34314, *China's Holdings of U.S. Securities: Implications for the U.S. Economy*, by Wayne M. Morrison and Marc Labonte.

CRS Report RL31590, *The Federal Government Debt: Its Size and Economic Significance*, by Brian W. Cashell.

CRS Report RL34319, *Foreign Ownership of U.S. Financial Assets: Implications of a Withdrawal*, by James K. Jackson.

CRS Report RL33186, *Is the U.S. Current Account Deficit Sustainable?*, by Marc Labonte.

CRS Report RL30520, *The National Debt: Who Bears Its Burden?*, by Marc Labonte.

CRS Report RL31032, *The U.S. Trade Deficit: Causes, Consequences, and Cures*, by Craig K. Elwell.

CRS Report RS21951, *Financing the U.S. Trade Deficit: Role of Foreign Governments*, by Marc Labonte.

End Notes

[1] Figures on federal debt held by the public are available on the Department of Treasury Bureau of Public Debt website, "The Debt to the Penny and Who Holds It," at http://www.treasurydirect.gov/NP/BPDLogin?application=np.

[2] This chapter discusses foreign holdings of U.S. federal debt. Foreign investors also hold U.S. private securities. For data on foreign holdings of U.S. private securities, see "Survey of Foreign Holdings of U.S. Securities," at http://www.ustreas.gov/tic/shlhistdat.html, produced by the Treasury Department International Capital System.

[3] Data are excerpted from Table OFS-2 in the March 2010 *Treasury Bulletin*. Table OFS-2 presents the estimated ownership of U.S. Treasury securities. Information is primarily obtained from the Federal Reserve Board of Governors Flow of Funds data, Table L209. State, local, and foreign holdings include special issues of nonmarketable securities to municipal entities and foreign official accounts. They also include municipal, foreign official, and private holdings of marketable Treasury securities.

[4] Foreign holdings are estimated by the Treasury Department based on the location of the holdings, not the nationality of the holder. For certain countries, such as the Carribean Banking Centers, many of the holdings are likely owned by third country citizens.

[5] CRS Report RS21409, *The Budget Deficit and the Trade Deficit: What Is Their Relationship?*, by Marc Labonte and Gail E. Makinen.

[6] See CRS Report RS21951, *Financing the U.S. Trade Deficit: Role of Foreign Governments*, by Marc Labonte.

[7] See CRS Report RL33186, *Is the U.S. Current Account Deficit Sustainable?*, by Marc Labonte.

[8] CRS Report RL31032, *The U.S. Trade Deficit: Causes, Consequences, and Cures*, by Craig K. Elwell.

[9] For details on the liquidity crisis in financial markets starting in August 2007, see CRS Report RL34182, *Financial Crisis? The Liquidity Crunch of August 2007*, by Darryl E. Getter et al.

In: Economic Policies in a Time of Financial Crisis
Editor: Heather D. Perkins
ISBN: 978-1-61122-686-7

Chapter 5

Running Deficits: Positives and Pitfalls

D. Andrew Austin

Summary

Governments run deficits for several reasons. By running short-run deficits, governments can avoid raising taxes during economic downturns, which helps households smooth consumption over time. Running deficits can stimulate aggregate demand in the economy, thus giving policymakers a valuable fiscal policy tool to help support macroeconomic stability. In particular, short-run deficits may help boost economic activity when monetary policy loses its potency. When interest rates fall to low levels during an economic downturn, banks can become reluctant to lend when they perceive the risks of lending outweigh the gains, while fewer firms and consumers demand new loans. In such a situation, known as a liquidity trap, a monetary authority such as the Federal Reserve can do little to expand the money supply. Thus, while the monetary authority can cut short-term interest rates to nearly zero—or even to zero—lower interest rates or other monetary policy initiatives may do little to encourage new consumer spending or business investment. During a liquidity trap situation, fiscal policy tools such as increased government spending or tax cuts, which increase deficits, may be an important complement to monetary policy. So-called "fresh-water" economists have questioned the logic of these fiscal policies. So-called "salt-water" economists, who have sought to put Keynesian fiscal theories on a more modern foundation, contend that government interventions can mitigate economic downturns. Most professional economic forecasters find that deficits and fiscal policy measures can stimulate economic activity when the economy operates well below its potential.

In better economic times, deficits may crowd out private investment or worsen trade deficits. But long-run deficits may transfer economic resources from younger to older generations, allowing older generations to enjoy anticipated benefits of future economic growth—long-run deficits may also impose large burdens on future generations. Some have argued this allows politicians to act opportunistically by providing benefits to current constituents while leaving future generations, an unrepresented constituency, with substantial fiscal burdens.

Between 2007 and 2009, federal tax revenues fell by 18.0% and corporate tax revenues fell 62.7%. Government outlays rose during the recession due to "automatic stabilizer" programs such as unemployment insurance and income support programs; federal support provided to Fannie Mae, Freddie Mac, AIG, and other companies; and economic stimulus legislation such as the American Recovery and Reinvestment Act of 2009 (ARRA; H.R. 1, P.L. 111-5).

Anticipation of changes in partisan control of government can motivate deficits, as current policy makers may wish to restrict their successors' options. Research on state and foreign governments suggests that balanced-budget rules force governments to adjust spending and taxes sharply during economic downturns. Budget enforcement legislation, such as the 1990 Budget Enforcement Act (P.L. 101-508), may have helped preserve budgetary compromises between parties, which may have contributed to a reduction in federal deficits.

Deficits can seriously harm national economies. In the short run, fiscal overstimulation leads to inflation. In the long term, deficits either reduce capital investment, which retards economic growth, or increase foreign borrowing, which swells the share of national income going abroad. Governments can spend more than they collect in revenues by printing money, which causes inflation, or by borrowing. In the long run, governments risk default and bankruptcy if they fail to repay borrowers, at least to the extent of stabilizing the ratio of government debt to gross domestic product.

WHY DO GOVERNMENTS RUN DEFICITS?

In the past half century, the federal government has run annual deficits in all but six years.[1] The FY2009 federal deficit swelled to $1.414 trillion, or nearly 10% of gross domestic product (GDP), as the economic recession depressed federal revenues and as financial interventions and "automatic stabilizer" income support programs increased federal spending. The size of recent deficits has added to longstanding concerns regarding the federal government's long-term fiscal condition. Nonetheless, deficit finance can serve as an important policy tool. This chapter discusses how deficit finance can help governments manage their economies and how large and persistent deficits can lead to severe economic problems.

Public finance theory suggests three reasons for deficit financing by government. First, governments can prevent sudden changes in taxes by borrowing. Second, debt finance gives governments a powerful macroeconomic policy tool. Third, debt finance can redistribute resources among generations.

Government borrowing can shift revenues and expenses into different time periods more easily or more cheaply than households, which allows governments to use deficits to make taxpayers better off by smoothing tax levels.[2] The federal government can spread the cost of major capital investments over many years by issuing debt in the form of bonds or Treasury bills. Deficit finance can spread an especially large cost such as a major war over several generations, or even centuries,[3] and enables governments to keep taxes steady during temporary economic downturns, thus smoothing consumption for households. Government debt that nears unsustainable levels, however, can inject turmoil into an economy, and governments may go bankrupt if they fail to repay what they borrow.[4]

Increased government spending financed by borrowing can stimulate economic activity, giving government a fiscal policy tool to counteract recessions. A countercyclical fiscal policy, in which taxes are cut or spending is increased, can dampen economic fluctuations and limit the depth of economic downturns. Pro-cyclical fiscal policy, in which taxes are raised or spending is cut during recessions, tends to amplify economic fluctuations. During economic downturns, government revenues fall and expenditures rise as more people become eligible for unemployment insurance and income support programs, causing deficits to increase or surpluses to shrink. These programs are known as "automatic stabilizers" because deficit spending then provides a countercyclical stimulus to economic activity in the short run without the need for new legislative action.[5]

Finally, deficit finance can transfer the benefits of future economic growth to current generations. Continuing real economic growth would allow future generations to experience higher standards of living than previous generations. Deficit finance provides a means of transferring some of those gains to current generations by shifting some costs onto future generations. If deficits are large or if future economic growth is slow, then deficit finance could lead to a deterioration of living standards over time.

RECENT FEDERAL POLICY RESPONSES

The federal government's response to the recent recession may reflect the aims discussed above. The government cut some taxes and increased spending to stimulate the economy, while issuing new debt at an accelerated pace. The American Recovery and Reinvestment Act of 2009 (ARRA; H.R. 1, P.L. 111-5) funded programs that are projected to provide $862 billion to stimulate the economy with financial assistance, loans provided to financial firms, and increased government spending including aid given to states.[6] In 2008, tax cuts and income tax refunds under President Bush also provided increased liquidity allowing for higher levels of consumption. The Emergency Economic Stabilization Act of 2008 (EESA; P.L. 110-343), injected capital into key financial markets as part of the Troubled Assets Relief Program (TARP).[7] The "Cash for Clunkers" program (P.L. 111-47) was created to generate auto sales and improve fuel efficiency. Some argue that the program helped the automobile manufacturers General Motors and Chrysler remain viable concerns, encouraged greater sales of cars made in the United States, and prevented larger increases in unemployment.[8] ARRA extended a first-time home-buyer tax credit that provides up to an $8,000 credit to first-time home buyers for sales occurring between January 1, 2009, and April 30, 2010.[9] While these programs stimulated home and auto sales, many suspect that they were more effective in shifting the timing of sales rather than affecting the overall volume of sales.[10]

Is the Deficit the Right Measure of Fiscal Policy?

The federal deficit is an imperfect measure of the federal government's fiscal stance. While the total deficit indicates the federal government's current interaction with the U.S. economy, it does not reflect other aspects of the government's fiscal condition.[11] First, because the federal government is essentially run on a cash basis, the deficit does not fully reflect changes in future fiscal conditions of the government.[12] Second, some federal programs may create additional fiscal exposures that federal budget concepts may not fully reflect. The budgetary cost estimates of federal loan and loan guarantee programs omit risk adjustments, with the exception of programs funded by the Emergency Economic Stabilization Act (EESA) such as the Troubled Assets Relief Program (TARP).[13] Some contend that risk adjustments provide a more accurate description of the economic costs of federal credit programs. Other federal responses to financial turmoil may have created fiscal exposures that are harder to quantify. Recent federal interventions, to the extent that they convince private firms that the government will shoulder some costs of future adverse events through further public interventions, may expose taxpayers and federal program beneficiaries to other contingent costs that are difficult to quantify.

Bringing a federal budget to balance, temporarily, can occur beyond the straightforward measures of raising taxes or decreasing spending. Governments can increase current revenues by borrowing against future income, allowing a smaller deficit today at the expense of higher taxes or lower public program benefits. For example, Greece met certain European Union deficit and debt rules by selling rights to future airport fees and lottery income.[14] The City of Chicago in February 2009 sold the rights to parking fee revenues for the next 75 years for a $1.15 billion lump-sum payment that mostly funded current municipal expenses.[15] Government asset sales and trades of future income streams for lump-sum payments can improve deficit figures reported on a cash-accounting basis, but may signal a deterioration of a government's overall fiscal condition.

Finally, deficits are residuals resulting from spending that exceeds revenues. While policymakers can control economic policy instruments such as taxes and spending, economic fluctuations affect the tax base.[16] For that reason, many economists rely on deficit measures that take business cycle effects into account.

Benefits and Costs of Using Deficits to Smooth Consumption

Helping households smooth income, according to standard public finance theory, may justify short-run deficits. If governments were required to balance their budgets in each fiscal year, so that current spending were constrained by available cash reserves and incoming revenues, then negative economic shocks would require spending cuts or tax increases. Public spending tends to rise during recessions due to the effect of automatic stabilizers, while revenues fall. Thus, such strict balanced-budget requirements would force governments to run a pro-cyclical fiscal policy, which could either strain household budgets via tax increases or force painful cuts in public programs. Governments can also smooth income by maintaining "rainy day" funds or sinking funds.

Economists have studied balanced-budget requirements in state governments, as well as budgetary restrictions used by other national governments.[17] All states except Vermont have balanced-budget requirements, though the strictness of those requirements varies. Many studies have found that the strictness of the balanced-budget requirement affects fiscal performance. Inman and Bohn found that tight balanced-budget rules cause states to reduce deficits by cutting spending, whereas softer constraints have little short-term effect.[18] Other researchers found that balanced-budget rules force governments to adjust spending and taxes sharply during economic downturns.[19] Fiscal crises may put strains on states and their citizens, but may also force policy makers to face tough fiscal decisions that would otherwise be avoided. Balanced-budget rules also appear to hold down taxes and spending, at least in the short run. Over the longer term, both spending and taxes adjust, although state and local governments with tight budget-balance measures appear to spend less per capita than those with less stringent requirements.

State budget-balance rules may also complicate broader macroeconomic stabilization efforts. One study found that reductions in state spending in 2008-2009 essentially offset federal stimulus spending.[20] Thus, according to that analysis, while federal spending prevented a steeper decline in economic activity, it did little to counteract a fall in private sector demand.

Does Economic Stimulus Generate New Spending or Just Shift Spending?

Deficit finance aimed at helping households smooth consumption will generate few gains if households can smooth consumption on their own. For example, economist Robert Barro argued that deficit spending caused by tax cuts has no fiscal effect because households save in anticipation of future tax increases, offsetting any short-term stimulative effects. This concept is known as Ricardian equivalence.[21] The theory of Ricardian equivalence implies that only the net present value of government expenditures and taxes needed to pay for them matter, but that the timing of taxes does not.[22]

Empirical research has failed to find evidence of Ricardian equivalence in its pure form, but some research has identified some Ricardian effects in savings behavior.[23] Even if a large proportion of households face liquidity constraints that limit their ability to smooth out income fluctuations by borrowing and saving, however, many high-net-worth households are well equipped to shift buying power across time in response to government policies.

The overwhelming evidence of economic research and macroeconomic experience, contrary to the predictions of Ricardian equivalence, suggests that deficit spending creates a short-term fiscal stimulus.[24] Despite the imprint that New Classical Macroeconomics, of which Ricardian equivalence is a central tenet, has left on macroeconomic modeling, most empirical economists believe deficits affect prices and output in the short run and recognize the usefulness of fiscal policy as a tool for macroeconomic management, at least in some circumstances. Even if Ricardian equivalence fails to hold in a pure form, it may help explain why economic stimulus measures may have limited effect when households can shift purchases backwards or forwards in time. The effects can also vary with the instrument used. For example, many contend that the Cash for Clunkers program (P.L. 111-47) and the First-Time Homebuyers' tax credit may have encouraged households planning to buy either cars or homes in the medium term to shift purchases forward in time, rather than stimulating new purchases by households that had no plans to buy.

New Dimensions of Federal Economic Policy?

Economists typically view fiscal policy and monetary policy as the basic tools of macroeconomic management. Congress, in conjunction with the President, controls fiscal policy by making taxing and spending decisions, while the Federal Reserve sets monetary policy, using tools such as reserve requirements, and open-market trading of Treasury securities to affect key short-term interest rates. Responses to the financial crisis in late 2007 and 2008, however, included policies that do not fit squarely into the normal framework of fiscal and monetary policy. Some economists have referred to these initiatives as "credit policy" tools.[25] Many have argued that credit policy has developed because monetary and fiscal policy tools are ill-suited to deal with severe liquidity problems that may emerge due to credit quality issues.[26] Other economists note that over the longer term, financial regulation and consumer credit protection policies may also have important macroeconomic implications.

To avert a wider panic, the Federal Reserve set up facilities that loan funds to a broad assortment of private companies using a wide range of assets as collateral for longer terms, leading to a dramatic expansion of the Federal Reserve's balance sheet. In addition, in 2008, the federal government took on risky assets as part of financial interventions involving the Treasury Department and the Federal Reserve. In March 2008, as part of the arranged sale of the collapsing investment bank Bear Stearns to JP Morgan Chase, the federal government agreed to absorb certain Bear Stearns assets into the Maiden Lane I special purpose vehicle.[27] The federal takeover of mortgage giants Fannie Mae and Freddie Mac in September 2008 also required substantial government resources. The federal bailout of the insurer AIG resulted in the creation of the Maiden Lane II and III vehicles. Treasury officials have contended that supporting AIG avoided the collapse of other major financial firms and helped stabilize credit markets. [28]

New Federal Reserve loan facilities that provide liquidity to financial markets could expose the federal government to more risk than traditional monetary policy mechanisms. Medium-term collateralized lending through Fed liquidity facilities can provide economic relief to cash-constrained, yet solvent, companies. Federal Reserve facilities generally impose a "haircut" on loans, which depends on the type of collateral. For example, an asset with a par value of $100 might be assessed a 15% haircut, so that a borrowing firm could obtain an $85 loan. While the Federal Reserve is mandated to avoid credit risks and has implemented conservative loan collateral requirements, a severe financial disruption could impose costs on the Federal Reserve. For instance, if assets posted as collateral dropped sharply in value, the Federal Reserve could suffer losses. While the Federal Reserve is not part of the federal budget, net earnings of the Federal Reserve are transferred to the U.S. Treasury Department; capital losses on the Federal Reserve's balance sheet might also be transmitted to the federal government. Federal Reserve system earnings transferred to the U.S. Treasury, according to OMB estimates, are expected to reach $77 billion in FY2010.

Macroeconomic Demand Management: Theory and Policy

Keynesian economic theories, which call for governments to engage in active demand management through fiscal policy, had enormous influence in post-World War II economic policy. Governments, according to Keynesian theories, can influence economic activity through policies that affect investment and savings (IS) and liquidity and the money supply (LM).[29] Fiscal policy can influence investment and savings through government consumption and taxation. Monetary policy can affect the money supply and short-term interest rates, which can encourage investment. The IS-LM model, which describes the effects of fiscal and monetary policies, remains a widely used applied macroeconomics policy tool, even as academic research has focused on more mathematically sophisticated modeling approaches.

When interest rates fall to low levels during an economic downturn, banks can become reluctant to lend because they perceive the risks of lending outweigh the gains, while fewer firms and consumers demand new loans. In such a situation, known as a liquidity trap, a monetary authority such as the Federal Reserve can do little to expand the money supply. Thus, while the monetary authority can cut short-term interest rates to nearly zero—or even to zero—lower interest rates or other monetary policy initiatives may do little to encourage new consumer spending or business investment. Some monetary policy rules of thumb might in a severe recession indicate that short-term nominal interest rates should be negative. But a monetary authority cannot induce negative nominal interest rates because firms and households guarantee themselves a zero nominal return by simply holding cash.[30] When a central bank faces a zero lower bound (ZLB) on interest rates, fiscal policy tools such as increased government spending or tax cuts, which increase deficits, may be a necessary complement to monetary policy.[31] Some recent research suggests that fiscal stimulus is more effective when the zero lower bound applies.[32]

In better economic times, government spending becomes a less effective means of stimulating economic activity and can elbow out private consumption and investment or worsen trade deficits. When the economy is not below its potential, fiscal policy expansions are likely to lead to higher inflation or a displacement of private consumption and investment. When fiscal policy becomes less effective, though, monetary policy can be more effective in either encouraging or restraining economic activity.

In the 1970s, Keynesian theories began to face intense intellectual challenges.[33] The modern debate over Keynesian demand management and fiscal policy eventually precipitated into a division between the so-called "salt-water" and "fresh-water" schools of thought. Salt-water macroeconomics is often associated with the coast-proximate departments of economics at Berkeley, Harvard, MIT, UCLA, and Yale, while fresh-water macroeconomics is often associated with the lake-proximate Universities of Chicago, Minnesota, and Rochester.[34] These differences in views about the proper role of macroeconomic policy have become more prominent during the recent economic recession.

"Fresh-Water" Macroeconomics

Fresh-water economists are typically skeptical of the government's ability to improve economic performance. Fresh-water economists, critical of Keynesian theories, view recessions not as reflections of market instability, but as the result of the emergence of new economic structures or the responses to external shocks. This school of thought, often called the New Classical Macroeconomics, argues that market forces naturally balance labor supply and demand and lead to economic efficiency. According to some economists, the actions by the private sector are more effective and efficient at changing market forces than the government's response, which allows for a faster rebound from downward-trending economic forces. During the 1970s some Keynesian economists had argued that demand management policies could exploit an observed inverse relationship between unemployment rates and inflation, known as the Phillips curve. Policymakers who tried to reduce unemployment by tolerating higher inflation rates saw the Phillips curve break down, as slow economic growth and persistent inflation rates—termed "stagflation"—led to wide unhappiness with macroeconomic conditions.

While the joint appearance of inflation and high unemployment confounded many Keynesian economists, research in New Classical Macroeconomics argued that firms and households simply learned to anticipate inflation and developed inflationary expectations. Thus, the microeconomic responses of families and companies would counteract efforts of macroeconomic policymakers to exploit the Phillips curve relationship, which then resulted in high inflation rates without any persistent gains in employment levels. Prominent New Classical Macroeconomists argued, therefore, that monetary policy authorities should stick to simple, predictable rules.[35]

New Classical Macroeconomists also argued that microeconomic decisions of households and firms could undermine the effectiveness of fiscal policy. Further they believe in the flexibility of prices and wages throughout the economy. The Ricardian Equivalence view, as noted above, assumes households respond to tax cuts by saving funds to finance subsequent tax increases. This view, which assumes households can easily borrow and lend to shift buying power across time periods, has had mixed empirical support.

New Classical Macroeconomics research typically assumes that individuals have strong forecasting abilities. Rational expectations, a central tenet of New Classical Macroeconomics, presumes that firms and families are not systematically wrong when they form their economic plans. In particular, the rational expectations assumption implies that households and businesses foresee the consequences of changes in government policies and act in their own best interests in response, although economic agents may make mistakes because of changing circumstances and uncertainty. In many economic models, the combination of rational expectations with other technical assumptions, such as no-bubble conditions, often results in strong efficiency properties—meaning that resources are not wasted, productive equipment is not idle, costs are minimized, and firms produce a mix of goods that match what consumers want.[36] The New Classical Macroeconomics critique of Keynesian demand management policies has relied on models that combine neoclassical micro-foundations for macroeconomics (meaning that households make consumption decisions to maximize their long-term well-being) and the assumption that economic agents are foresighted, even when faced with complex dynamic decisions.

"Salt-Water" Macroeconomics

Salt-water economists tend to see recessions as evidence of economic instability that governments can mitigate to allow steadier economic growth.[37] More recent "salt-water" research sets older Keynesian theories upon more modern foundations, while emphasizing that the structure of labor markets may create wage rigidities. For example, the price of soybeans may change by the millisecond, but the wages of employees do not. Wage rigidities may lead to involuntary unemployment or excess capacity during economic downturns, and thus provide a role for traditional Keynesian demand management.[38]

Salt-water economists contend that individuals and firms, for various reasons, may have trouble lifting the economy out of a recession.[39] Federal fiscal policy actions and the Federal Reserve monetary policies, in this view, can help stabilize the economy and mitigate recessions. The Great Depression of the 1930s, according to salt-water economists, demonstrates that the American economy could remain persistently below its potential despite individual efforts by households and firms. If households are unwilling to spend because they fear continuing economic weakness, then firms may cut investment in the face of weak demand, generating a self-enforcing recessionary cycle. Falling prices, rather than adjusting the balance between supply and demand, may give households further reason to delay consumption. Government fiscal stimulus, salt-water economists claim, can restore market balance by temporarily replacing private consumption and investment with government outlays, thus providing the demand to help push the economy back to its full potential. Deficit spending can be used to increase aggregate demand in the economy, causing output and prices to increase. When the economy is running below its potential level of output, expansionary fiscal policies such as deficits stimulate economic activity, bringing idle economic capacity back into use and pushing the economy back toward its full potential.

If the economy is running near its full potential, expansionary fiscal policies can lead to inflation, may displace private economic activity, and could cause large trade deficits. Running government surpluses reduces aggregate demand in the economy and helps restrain inflation.

Dynamic Statistical Agnosticism and Macroeconomics Engineering

While fresh- and salt-water research has increased the technical sophistication of academic macroeconomic models, some contend that more atheoretical approaches that focus on the statistical dynamics of large economies may be more useful for policy analysis.[40] Moreover, models used by central banks and commercial economic forecasters often have a more pragmatic foundation than leading academic macroeconomic models. Such models can predict effects of a policy change, such as inflation, when given an accurate assessment of current conditions. Some see such applied economic models as a form of engineering, in contrast to the more scientific concerns of academic researchers.[41] While applied models used by the Federal Reserve, CBO, private forecasters, and major central banks, which generally rest on Keynesian foundations, may work reasonably well in normal circumstances, they might function less well in unusual circumstances where microeconomic responses of households and firms diverge from Keynesian assumptions.[42] New Classical models, while highly influential in academic research, have not yet achieved wide use in forecasting and policy analysis.[43]

How Effective Has Economic Stimulus Been?

ARRA was passed in February 2009 with the aim of stimulating economic growth by increasing government spending on certain programs and by cutting some taxes. The effectiveness of economic stimulus is often measured using estimates of multipliers, which calculate the cumulative effect of an extra dollar of government spending on overall economic activity.[44] According to CBO estimates, some recent programs have increased GDP by as much as $2.50 per dollar of stimulus spending, while others may have increased growth by as little as 20 cents per stimulus dollar. When tax breaks or transfer payments are saved rather than spent, multipliers are smaller.[45] Some economists would argue that during times of a liquidity trap, when monetary policy loses potency, spending multipliers are higher. Households that are liquidity constrained are more likely to spend one-time cash payments, yielding a high spending multiplier. For households that are not liquidity constrained, one-time payments are more likely to be saved, rather than spent. The expenditure multiplier is higher when the economy is operating below full potential.[46] When the economy operates at its full potential government spending is more likely to crowd out private consumption.

Figure 1 shows CBO estimates of multipliers associated with government spending programs funded by ARRA. Direct purchases by the government or transfer payments to state and local governments and to individuals generated the highest multipliers, while one-time payments had a relatively low multiplier in comparison to other forms of government spending. The multiplier for payments to retirees is even weaker because members of older generations may not face financial constraints such as those facing younger generations who often have higher levels of debt.

Corporate tax provisions generated the lowest multiplier. The extension of the First-Time Homebuyer Credit also had a very weak multiplier effect. Some economists contend that these purchases came at the expense of future purchases, where consumers took advantage of tax credits by acting now instead of opting to delay consumption.[47]

Other Considerations

Using deficit finance to expand government spending and federal aid during economic downturns is only sustainable if governments run surpluses during economic expansions to repay debt or accumulate reserves, or stabilize the debt to GDP ratio. Running surpluses during normal economic conditions may strengthen a government's capacity to manage its economy, not only by reducing public debt levels, but also by enhancing its reputation for fiscal prudence, which may widen its policy options in the event of a subsequent downturn.[48] Critics of deficit finance and active fiscal policy, however, argue that policy makers are more willing to increase government spending when economic growth slows than to cut spending when growth accelerates.[49]

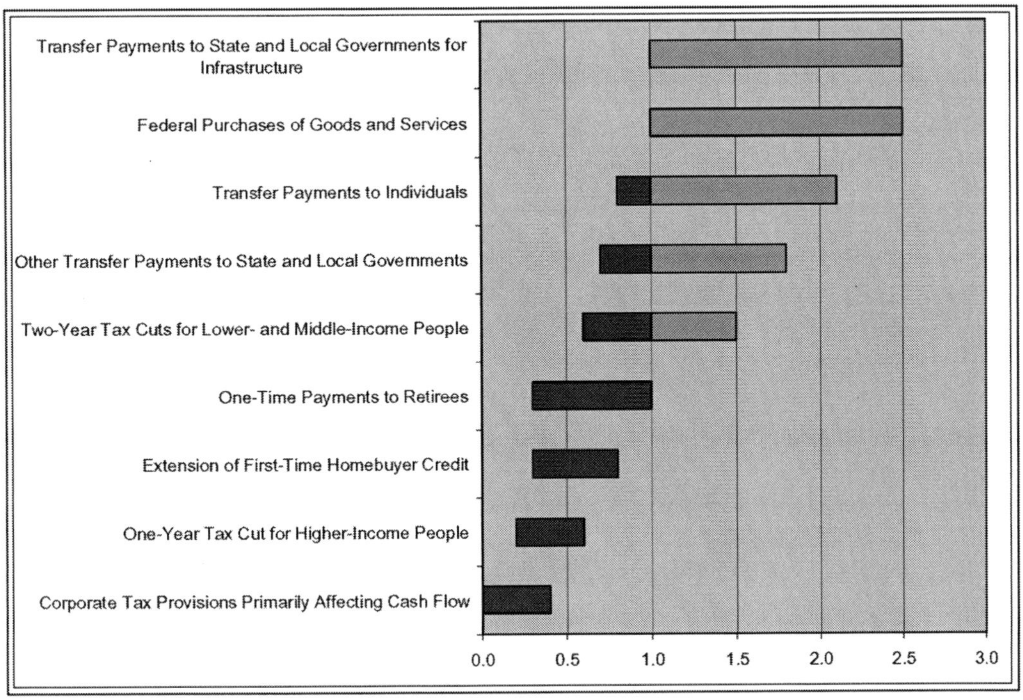

Source: Congressional Budget Office, Estimated Impact of the American Recovery and Reinvestment Act on Employment and Economic Output as of September 2009, available at http://www.cbo.gov/ftpdocs/106xx/ doc10682/11-30-ARRA.pdf.

Notes: Includes projections by CBO or JCT as having the total budget $5 billion or more over the 2009-2019 period. Certain provisions with lower total costs were included if the costs in the 2009-2011 period were large. Some elements have different multipliers, by CBO's estimates; in those cases the elements are listed with the multiplier used for the majority of the 2009-2019 budgetary cost. Major provisions as identified above are provided by the JCT, *Estimated Budget Effects of the Revenue Provisions Contained in the Conference Agreement for H.R. 1*, JCX-19-09 (February 12, 2009), available at http://www.jct.gov/x-19-09.pdf. The output multiplier is the cumulative impact on real gross domestic product over several quarters for each dollar of spending or reduction in tax revenues.

Figure 1. Estimated Multipliers of the American Recovery and Reinvestment Act Range of Estimated Government Multiplier Effects of Selected Programs

In addition, designing fiscal policy is a slow and deliberative process, whereas economic downturns can emerge suddenly and are difficult to predict. Because economic shocks affect spending patterns with substantial lags, economic conditions may have changed significantly before new federal spending actually reaches the public. Few economists believe that large changes in fiscal policy designed to counterbalance short-term economic downturns can be timed precisely, although many economists believe fiscal policy is an important tool during prolonged periods of slow or negative growth. Effects of severe economic downturns, however, often persist so that timing issues become less important. In particular, unemployment rates, widely considered a lagging economic indicator, may remain high well after other signs of economic growth appear.

While government spending can stimulate economic growth when private consumption is weak, excessive government spending can hinder growth. When the costs of financing government spending exceed its benefits, economic well-being is reduced. This can occur in one of two ways. First, it can raise interest rates and crowd out public consumption. Second, it can fail to improve GDP and generate higher levels of debt than before.[50]

While government spending can stimulate economic growth when private consumption is weak, excessive government spending can hinder growth. When the cost of financing government spending exceeds its benefits, economic well-being is reduced. While some government programs provide benefits that private markets cannot easily supply, taxes that fund government operations can distort economic incentives. Other government programs might fail to generate benefits that balance their costs to taxpayers. Thus, reducing some types of government spending might lead to higher levels of economic growth. One study using a panel of Organization for Economic Cooperation and Development (OECD) countries found government spending had sizeable negative effects on profits and business investments.[51] The size of the government sector in the United States is much smaller than most large OECD member states.

The effectiveness of aggressive fiscal policies, such as running deficits, also depends on the perception of investors that a government is solvent. If investors who might buy government bonds view a government's long-term fiscal situation as unsustainable and doubt that the government has the financial or political means to address its fiscal situation, then increased deficit spending may well lead to large interest rate increases that may overwhelm any positive stimulative effect.

POLITICAL EXPLANATIONS

The political business cycle literature provides a theory of economic fluctuations based on politicians' desire to maximize their chances of reelection. Early versions of political business cycle models presumed politicians could fool myopic voters by pumping up government spending before elections.[52] More sophisticated versions assume voters are rational and not myopic, but are unable to distinguish between sustainable prosperity based on policy and administrative competence from temporary prosperity based on deficit spending.[53] Drazen reviewed the literature and found strong evidence that voters react to economic conditions, but weak evidence that macroeconomic policy is manipulated to sway elections.[54]

The alternation of partisan control of government may explain a persistent tendency towards deficit spending. Several articles in the economics of politics literature, such as Alesina and Tabellini or Persson and Svensson, contend the government of the day can constrain its successors' choices by running budget deficits.[55] If a successor government has different spending priorities, the current government may be tempted to influence future fiscal policies by using debt to change the incentives and constraints facing future decision makers. Such policies are highly unlikely to be as economically efficient as a more consistent fiscal policy. Some argue that budget enforcement legislation, such as pay-as-you-go requirements and discretionary budget caps, may help provide political underpinnings to a more consistent fiscal policy. Some budget analysts contend that mechanisms created by the 1990 Budget Enforcement Act (P.L. 101-508) led to more sustainable fiscal policies. European Union fiscal rules on public deficits and debt-to-GDP ratios, however, may not have led to sustainable fiscal policies in some countries.[56]

Intergenerational Transfers

Political considerations may also affect how the benefits and costs of government programs are allocated among generations. Political leaders might seek to please their current constituents by increasing government spending; however, this shifts fiscal burdens onto unborn taxpayers and younger cohorts, whose lower voting participation rates may leave them with a weaker voice in policy discussions. This will hold true because individuals will favor fiscal policy that increases their lifetime wealth.[57] Leaving future taxpayers to pay for higher spending today simply transfers the burden to future generations as opposed to focusing on deficit reduction or actual solutions to higher costs.[58] Public debt then becomes a tool used to transfer wealth between generations.

One explanation of persistent deficits is that future generations do not vote, and young citizens usually vote less often than older citizens. Generations now alive face a temptation to pass on the costs of programs that benefit themselves to following generations that have no say. Some shifting of resources to older generations is seen by some as justified on the basis of equity. To the extent that technological change leads to greater prosperity over time, future generations will have access to higher standards of living. To the extent that population growth increases the size of the economy, the burden of financing pay-as-you-go retirement systems is reduced. If some of those gains are shifted from younger to older generations, then incomes and levels of well-being would be more equal among generations. Furthermore, in this view, a fiscal policy that shifts some resources from younger to older generations can raise living standards of all following generations by transferring a portion of the benefits of future economic growth into the present.

A simple example illustrates this possibility.[59] Consider an economy with a fixed population divided among age-specific cohorts. For the sake of simplicity, suppose individuals live 75 years. Also assume that income of each cohort is the same, arrives from a source outside the economy, and grows 3% per year. Consider a fiscal policy that causes each age-specific cohort (except the oldest) to transfer 2% of its income to the one-year-older cohort. All transfers, except for the oldest and youngest cohorts, cancel out. The youngest cohort gets 98% of its pre-transfer income, and the oldest gets 102% of its pre-transfer income. Although the loss to the youngest cohort and gain to the oldest cohort balance out for each year, each individual born after the start of the plan gains because of economic growth (so long as the economy's interest rate is below 3% per year). With a 3% growth rate over 74 years, income increases by 891%. Therefore, the gain in buying power per dollar of income in present value terms for a cohort born after the start of the policy is

$$1.02*\left(\frac{1.03}{1+r}\right)^{74} - (.98)$$

where r is the real interest rate. So long as the real interest rate is less than 3%, which is true for long-term historical real rates of return for U.S. Treasury bills, the policy of shifting resources to older generations makes all generations better off.[60] This highly simplified example shares the same basic structure as pay-as-you-go social insurance programs, in which young workers pay contributions that are more or less immediately used to pay benefits to older retirees.[61]

Raising current standards of living by shifting resources from younger to older generations has its limits. The example above relies on the assumption that the policy continues indefinitely into the future. With a finite ending point this policy would be unsustainable because some young cohorts near that end point would be made worse off and would be unwilling to give up resources.

The current fiscal policies' paths of entitlement spending of the United States imply that large transfers will be made to the baby-boom generation from younger generations.[62] Computations by Auerbach, Gokhale, and Kotlikoff indicate that future generations will pay much more in taxes than they will receive from the government.[63] In 2000, Gokhale and others estimated that a newborn male in 1998 would pay $142,500 more in taxes than what he would receive from the government; the corresponding estimate for a newborn female was $71,300.[64] Due to increased federal deficits, the introduction of Medicare Part D, and falling tax revenues due to the recent economic recession, those estimates would be higher for current newborns. Despite the projected magnitude of these intergenerational transfers, younger generations might not be worse off than their parents if the economy grew at a sufficiently swift pace.

These generational transfers are largely driven by the growth in the number of beneficiaries of entitlement programs relative to the work force, as well as by rapid increases in health care costs. The possibility that some future generation may eliminate fiscal policies that it perceives will lower its standard of living introduces political risk into social insurance programs funded by a pay-as-you-go mechanism.[65] If a generation anticipates that a younger generation will stop contributing to a pay-as-you-go social insurance program, then it may decide to end the program itself. A generation whose descendants are unwilling to finance its benefits would have little to gain, apart from altruistic impulses, by continuing its contributions.[66]

THE LONG-TERM BUDGET OUTLOOK

While the recent economic recession and past policy choices have led to large deficits in FY2008 and FY2009, the divergence between government revenues and expenditures is projected to grow. The "fiscal gap," the estimated magnitude of revenue increases or spending decreases necessary to stabilize the ratio of public debt to GDP over a given time horizon, is one measure of that divergence.[67] According to CBO extended baseline projections, the "fiscal gap" between government revenues and spending over the next 25 years may be as high as 2.1% of GDP or a total of an additional $7.1 trillion in debt over the next decade.[68] CBO's alternative fiscal scenario, which many analysts believe gives a more realistic approximation of future policy, puts the 25-year fiscal gap even higher at 5.4% of GDP.[69] Over longer horizons, the fiscal gap is projected to become wider still. The CBO extended baseline projects the 75-year fiscal gap at 3.2% of GDP, while the alternative scenario puts it at 8.1% of GDP.[70] The growing fiscal gap signals that younger and unborn generations may bear larger fiscal burdens, which could hinder their ability to achieve a higher standard of living than their parents. Without significant changes in fiscal policy, future generations will face the need to adjust tax rates, or government spending levels, or both, in major ways in order to avoid default.[71]

Costs of Financing Deficits

A government that runs deficits and is unwilling to raise taxes or cut spending faces three choices. First, domestic borrowing can be increased at the cost of crowding out domestic investment. Second, a government can borrow from foreign investors and governments. Borrowing from the rest of the world prevents deficits from crowding out investment. That is, foreign investors can provide financial resources now in exchange for future interest payments and profits. As foreign investors accumulate larger portfolios of stocks, bonds, and other assets, the flow of interest payments, dividends, and repatriated profits abroad increases as well. Third, a central government can print money to reduce the real value of debt denominated in domestic currency.

All three options have unpleasant consequences. While fiscal imbalances may gradually build over time, the consequences of unsustainable fiscal policies may arrive suddenly. Simple supply and demand theory implies that a smaller supply of savings for private investment will lead to higher interest rates and lower growth in private capital stocks. Lower stocks of private capital threaten economic growth, and slower economic growth translates into lower average living standards in the future. Borrowing from the rest of the world permits higher levels of investment and faster growth at the cost of sending a higher fraction of earnings abroad. If foreigners lend capital by purchasing stocks and bonds rather than by building auto plants, for example, they may decide suddenly someday to take their investments elsewhere. This could strain domestic and international financial systems, thus constricting firms' and households' access to capital.

Foreign investment in the United States plays an important role between balancing domestic supply and demand of capital. For instance, China held 22.8% of the United States' debt as of September 2009.[72] The financial crisis and economic downturn, however, have sharply reduced the demand by foreign investors.[73]As the share of the federal debt held by foreign entities has grown, so has concern about possible consequences. While the risk of a sudden or coordinated sale of U.S. Treasury securities is low, the large foreign holdings of U.S. debt may introduce new contingencies that could complicate financial and foreign policy.

Finally, inflation caused by printing money distorts the flow of information generated by the price system and disrupts financial markets. Investors, who wish to avoid capital losses in real terms, typically demand higher nominal interest rates when they see signs of inflation. During the 1970s, the real value of the federal debt fell sharply as inflation accelerated. While inflation in the past has helped ease the burden of federal debt, bringing inflation under control can be costly. Many economists believe that the restrictive monetary policies needed to squeeze rapid inflation out of an economy would require substantial economic disruption, at least in the short run. Moreover, in the current fiscal environment, inflation might not be an effective means of reducing the value of federal debt for two reasons. First, some Treasury securities are now indexed for inflation. Second, much of the fiscal imbalance facing the federal government is linked to the implicit cost of funding scheduled benefits for large entitlement programs such as Medicare and Social Security, rather than accumulated federal debt.

Reducing government deficits can improve economic performance in at least three ways. First, paying off government debt increases the supply of investment funds available for domestic investment. Second, paying off government debt held by foreign governments or investors reduces the amount of interest payments going abroad. Alternatively, paying off debt held by domestic investors gives them the opportunity to rebalance their portfolios by buying foreign assets, which offsets some of the flow of dividends and profits going abroad, or by buying domestic assets that otherwise would have been bought by foreign investors. Third, scaling down the federal debt decreases the temptation to reduce its real value by printing money, lessening the possibility of a major acceleration in inflation. Finally, most economists believe reducing government borrowing lowers interest rates, which in turn encourages investment and growth.

CONCLUSION

Some economists disagree on the effects of government's ability to smooth economic recessions. The ability of governments to run deficits can help avoid short-term fiscal crises caused by adverse economic shocks. Long-term deficits can be used to allow older generations to enjoy some of the anticipated fruits of future economic growth. A government can sustain a debt indefinitely, so long as the size of the debt relative to the size of the economy does not grow without bound. Maintaining a large debt requires large interest payments and can retard economic growth. Thus deficits can serve as a useful tool of economic management in the short run, but also can cause substantial economic damage to the economy over the long term.

End Notes

[1] The federal government ran surpluses in FY1960, FY1969, and FY1998-FY2001. Only in FY1960, FY1999, and FY2000 did the federal government run an on-budget surplus, which excludes off-budget surpluses that flow largely from Social Security payroll taxes net of beneficiary payments.

[2] So-called "rainy day" funds, used by many state governments, allow smoothing of tax levels without deficit finance.

[3] The British government still pays interest on consol bonds issued during the Napoleonic Wars.

[4] A more precise definition of fiscal sustainability is that the public debt does not grow without bound.

[5] The Congressional Budget Office (CBO) computes a measure of the deficit that adjusts for business cycle effects to allow a more meaningful comparison of short-term fiscal stance across different years.

[6] U.S. Congressional Budget Office, *The Budget and Economic Outlook: Fiscal Years 2010 to 2020*, January 2010, available at http://www.cbo.gov/ftpdocs/108xx/doc10871/01-26-Outlook.pdf, p. 98; and CRS Report RS21126, *Tax Cuts and Economic Stimulus: How Effective Are the Alternatives?*, by Jane G. Gravelle. ARRA (H.R. 1, P.L. 111-5) also raised the federal debt limit to $12.1 trillion. The initial CBO estimate of ARRA on federal deficits was $787 billion over the 2009-2019 period.

[7] CRS Report R41001, *Redirecting Troubled Asset Relief Program (TARP) Funds to Other Uses*, by Marc Labonte, Edward V. Murphy, and Baird Webel.

[8] A reorganized General Motors emerged from bankruptcy on April 30, 2009; Chrysler filed for bankruptcy and on July 10, 2009, was sold to the Italian car maker Fiat. For details, see Micheline Maynard, "A Primer on the New General Motors," *New York Times*, July 10, 2009. Michael J. De La Merced and Micheline Maynard, "Fiat Deal With Chrysler Seals Swift 42-Day Overhaul," *New York Times*, June 11, 2009, p. B4.

[9] A first-time home buyer tax credit was included in the 2009 Recovery Act (P.L. 110-289, Sec. 3011[a]). ARRA extended this credit and relaxed some requirements. The credit was again extended by the Worker, Homeownership, and Business Assistance Act of 2009 (P.L. 111-92) to homes bought before May 1, 2010. For details, see CRS Report R40955, *An Economic Analysis of the Homebuyer Tax Credit*, by Mark P. Keightley.

[10] Mark Trumbull, "Extending home-buyer credit: another clunker?" *Christian Science Monitor*, October 29, 2009. This issue is discussed in more detail below.

[11] The total deficit combines on-budget deficits with off-budget surpluses stemming from the difference between Social Security payroll taxes and benefit payments.

[12] *The Financial Statement of the United States* has for many years included accrual accounting measures that reflect some changes in future federal costs. Those measures, however, do not include scheduled benefits for programs such as Social Security and Medicare, which some contend leads to underestimation of the fiscal overhang facing the federal government. For details, see CRS Report RL33623, *Long-Term Measures of Fiscal Imbalance*, by D. Andrew Austin; "Accrual Budgeting and Fiscal Policy," *OECD Journal on Budgeting*, vol. 2009/1, pp. 1-29.

[13] Section 123 of EESA requires that TARP costs be estimated as specified by the Federal Credit Reform Act of 1990 (P.L. 101-508, amended by P.L. 105-33) and that estimates incorporate risk adjustments. Cost estimates for other federal loan and loan guarantee programs omit risk adjustments.

[14] Louise Story, Landon Thomas Jr., and Nelson D. Schwartz, "Wall St. Helped to Mask Debt Fueling Europe's Crisis," *New York Times*, February 14, 2010, p. A1.

[15] Dan Mihalopoulos, "Company Piles Up Profits From City's Parking Meter Deal," *New York Times*, November 20, 2009, p. A29A.

[16] Also see CRS Report RL31235, *The Economics of the Federal Budget Deficit*, by Brian W. Cashell.

[17] For a review of research using U.S. state data, see James M. Poterba, "Budget Institutions and Fiscal Policy in the U.S. States," *American Economic Review*, vol. 86, no. 2 (1986), pp. 395-400. For a review of European budgetary rules, see Giancarlo Corsetti and Nouriel Roubini, "European versus American Perspectives on Balanced-Budget Rules," *American Economic Review*, vol. 86, no. 2 (1986), pp. 408-413.

[18] Henning Bohn and Robert P. Inman, "Balanced Budget Rules and Public Deficits: Evidence From the U.S. States," NBER Working Paper No. 5533, April 1996.

[19] James M. Poterba, "State Responses to Fiscal Crises: The Effects of Budgetary Institutions and Politics," *Journal of Political Economy*, vol. 102, no. 4 (August 1994), pp. 799-821.

[20] Joshua Aizenman and Gurnain Kaur Pasricha, "On the Ease of Overstating the Fiscal Stimulus in the U.S., 2008-9" NBER Working Paper No. 15784, February 2010, available at http://www.nber.org/papers/w15784.pdf.

[21] This concept is named after David Ricardo (1772-1823), a London financier and economist engaged in debates about the management of debts accumulated during the Napoleonic Wars. Ricardo, while providing examples pointing out that the real burden of a stream of interest payments was essentially the same as the burden of immediate payment of borrowing associated with those payments, was concerned that the opportunity to carry public debt could encourage "profligacy" in government expenditure. David Ricardo, *The Principles of Political Economy and Taxation*, 3rd ed., (London: Murray, 1821), ch. 17.

[22] Robert J. Barro, "Are Government Bonds Net Wealth?" *Journal of Political Economy*, vol. 82, no. 6. (November-December, 1974), pp. 1095-1117. Robert Barro assumes that public spending is fixed and any decrease in taxes on consumers only induces households to save more to prepare for future tax increases.

[23] M. Gabriella Briotti, "Economic Reactions to Public Finance Consolidation: A Survey of the Literature," European Central Bank Occasional Paper no. 38, October 2005.

[24] Alan J. Auerbach and William G. Gale, "Activist Fiscal Policy to Stabilize Economic Activity," working paper, September 29, 2009, available at http://elsa.berkeley.edu/~auerbach/activistfiscal.pdf; Robert E. Hall, "By How Much Does GDP Rise If the Government Buys More Output?" *Brookings Papers on Economic Activity*, Fall 2009, pp. 183-249.

[25] Marvin Goodfriend, Carnegie Mellon University and National Bureau of Economic Research, "We Need an 'Accord' for Federal Reserve Credit Policy," *Shadow Open Market Committee Cato Institute*, April 28, 2008.

[26] Claudio Borio and Haibin Zhu, "Capital Regulation, Risk-Taking and Monetary Policy; A Missing Link In The Transmission Mechanism?" *BIS Working Papers*, December 2008.

[27] The New York Federal Reserve Bank's back door opens onto Maiden Lane in lower Manhattan.

[28] U.S. Department of Treasury, "Remarks by Secretary Henry M. Paulson, Jr. on Financial Rescue Package and Economic Update," press release, November 12, 2008, http://www.ustreas.gov/.

[29] The IS-LM interpretation of John Maynard Keynes's economic theories was developed by John Hicks. See John R. Hicks, "Mr. Keynes and the 'Classics': A Suggested Interpretation," *Econometrica* 5 (1937), pp. 147-59.

[30] The Taylor rule relates a short-term interest rate target to current inflation, a target inflation rate, and the level of economic slack in the economy, measured by the gap between actual and potential GDP. See John B. Taylor, "Discretion versus Policy Rules in Practice," *Carnegie-Rochester Conference Series on Public Policy*, vol. 39 (1993), pp. 195-215.

[31] Managing monetary policy can become more challenging when a central bank faces the ZLB. When economic activity becomes so weak that the price level falls, causing deflation, then those who hold cash enjoy a positive real rate of return, which the real value of debts increases. Consumers who expect deflation to continue may wish to delay purchases, further reducing aggregate demand. A central bank may seek to reverse those deflationary expectations by committing to policies that would help increase the price level. The credibility of a central bank may play an important role in the success of such policies.

[32] Lawrence Christiano, Martin Eichenbaum, and Sergio Rebelo, "When is the Government Spending Multiplier Large?" paper presented at the Allied Social Sciences Association meetings, January 4, 2010.

[33] Arjo Klamer, *Conversations with Economists* (Lanham, MD: Rowman & Littlefield , 1984).

[34] These departments of economics are not monolithically divided along fresh- versus-salt-water lines, and mostly comprise economists with diverse views.

[35] Finn E. Kydland and Edward C. Prescott, "Rules Rather than Discretion: The Inconsistency of Optimal Plans," *The Journal of Political Economy*, vol. 85, no. 3 (June 1977), pp. 473-492.

[36] These Ramsey-type models, in which infinitely lived households choose consumption paths over an infinite time horizon, incorporate other conditions and assumptions as well.

[37] Peter T. Kilborn, "'Fresh Water' Economists Gain," *The New York Times*, July 23, 1988.

[38] For a critique of fresh-water macroeconomics, see Robert J. Gordon, "Is Modern Macro or 1978-era Macro More Relevant to the Understanding of the Current Economic Crisis?" Northwestern University working paper, September 12, 2009, available at http://faculty-web.at.northwestern.edu/economics/gordon/GRU_Combined_090909.pdf.

[39] William White, "Modern Macroeconomics Is On The Wrong Track" *Finance & Development,* December 2009.

[40] Christopher A. Sims, "Policy Analysis with Econometric Models," *Brookings Papers on Economic Activity*, vol. 1 (1982), pp. 107-164. For a review of recent research that combines some limited assumptions about the structure of the economy with dynamic statistical approaches (structural autoregressive vector regressions), see Alan J. Auerbach and William G. Gale, "Activist Fiscal Policy to Stabilize Economic Activity," working paper, September 29, 2009; Robert E. Hall, "By How Much Does GDP Rise If the Government Buys More Output?" *Brookings Papers on Economic Activity*, Fall 2009, pp. 183-249.

[41] N. Gregory Mankiw, "The Macroeconomist as Scientist and Engineer," working paper, Harvard University, May 2006, available at http://www.economics.harvard.edu/files/faculty/40_Macroeconomist_as_Scientist.pdf. Mankiw was President George W. Bush's Chairman of the Council of Economic Advisors and is currently a professor of economics at Harvard University.

[42] Some applied revenue estimation models are Ramsey-type rather than Keynesian models.

[43] Mankiw, op. cit.

[44] Robert J. Barro and Charles J. Redlick, "Stimulus Spending Doesn't Work," *The Wall Street Journal*, October 1, 2009.

[45] U.S. Congressional Budget Office, *Estimated Impact of the American Recovery and Reinvestment Act on Employment and Economic Output as of September 2009*, November 2009.

[46] John F. Cogan, Tobias Cwik, John B. Taylor, and Volker Wieland, "New Keynesian versus Old Keynesian Government Spending Multipliers," February 2009.

[47] U.S. Congressional Budget Office, *Estimated Impact of the American Recovery and Reinvestment Act on Employment and Economic Output as of September 2009*, November 2009, available at http://www.cbo.gov/ftpdocs/ 106xx/doc10682/11-30-ARRA.pdf.

[48] This often referred to as creating "policy-space," or more colloquially as "reloading the fiscal cannon." See Olivier Blanchard, Giovanni Dell'Ariccia and Paolo Mauro, "Rethinking Macroeconomic Policy," *IMF Staff Position Note*, SPN/10/03, 12 February 2010.

[49] Milton Friedman, *Capitalism and Freedom* (Chicago: Univ. of Chicago Press, 1962), pp. 75-84.

[50] CRS Report R40770, *Economic Effects of a Budget Deficit Exceeding $1 Trillion*, by Marc Labonte.

[51] Alberto Alesina, Silvia Ardagna, Roberto Perotti, and Fabio Schiantarelli, "Fiscal Policy, Profits, and Investment," *American Economic Review*, vol. 92, no. 3 (June 2002), pp. 571-589.

[52] William D. Nordhaus, "The Political Business Cycle," *Review of Economic Studies*, vol. 42, no. 2 (April 1975), pp. 169-190.

[53] Kenneth Rogoff, "Equilibrium Political Business Cycles," *American Economic Review*, vol. 80, no.1 (1990), pp. 21-36.

[54] Allan Drazen, "The Political Business Cycle After 25 Years," *NBER Macroeconomics Annual*, vol. 15 (2000), pp. 75-117.

[55] Alberto Alesina and Guido Tabellini, "A Positive Theory of Fiscal Deficits and Government Debt," *Review of Economic Studies*, vol. 57, July 1990, pp. 403-414; Torsten Persson and Lars E. O. Svensson, "Why a Stubborn Conservative Would Run a Deficit: Policy with Time-Inconsistent Preferences," *Quarterly Journal of Economics*, vol. 104 (May 1989), pp. 325-345.

[56] The European Union's Growth and Stability Pact was created as part of negotiations leading to the 1992 Maastricht Treaty. See Anthony Annett, Jörg Decressin, and Michael Deppler, "Reforming the Stability and Growth Pact," IMF Discussion Paper, February 2005, available at http://www.imf.org/external/pbs/ft/pdp/2005/pdp02.pdf.

[57] Alex Cukierman and Allan H. Meltzer, "A Political Theory of Government Debt and Deficits in a Neo-Ricardian Framework," *American Economic Review*, vol. 79, no. 4 (September 1989).

[58] Andrew Samwick, Dartmouth College, "How to Advise on Fiscal Policy," *Vox Baby*, July 6, 2007, available at http://voxbaby.blogspot.com/2007/07/how-to-advise-on-fiscal-policy.html.

[59] This example is closely related to the overlapping generations model. For a comprehensive exposition and analysis see David Gale, "Pure Exchange Equilibrium of Dynamic Economic Models," *Journal of Economic Theory*, vol. 5 (1973), pp. 12-36.

[60] Goetzmann and Ibbotson found that the real rate of return on U.S. Treasury bills from 1924-2004 was less than 1% per year. See Table II in William N. Goetzmann and Roger G. Ibbotson, "History and the Equity Risk Premium," Yale School of Management working paper, October 2005, available at http://eco n.ucsb.edu/conferences/equity05/papers/ Goetzmann.pdf.

[61] For a defense of pay-as-you-go financing, see Peter Diamond, "Social Security," *American Economic Review*, vol. 94, no.1 (March 2004), pp. 1-24.

[62] Laurence J. Kotlikoff and Scott Burns, *The Coming Generational Storm* (Cambridge, Mass.: MIT Press, 2004).

[63] Alan J. Auerbach, Jagadeesh Gokhale, and Laurence J. Kotlikoff, "The 1995 Budget and Health Care Reform: A Generational Perspective," *Economic Review*, Federal Reserve Bank of Cleveland, issue QI, 1994, pp. 20-30.

[64] Jagadeesh Gokhale, Benjamin Page, Joan Potter, and John Sturrock, "*Generational Accounts for the United States: An Update*," CBO Technical Paper Series, 2000.

[65] John B. Shoven and Sita N. Slavov, "Political Risk versus Market Risk in Social Security," April 2006, NBER Working Paper No. W12135, available at http://papers.ssrn.com/sol3/papers.cfm?abstract_id=896208.

[66] Altruistic impulses play an important role in many questions concerning intergenerational transfers. For an overview of recent research on the subject, see L.-A. Gérard-Varet, S.-C. Kolm and J. Mercier-Ythier (eds.), *Handbook of the Economics of Giving, Reciprocity and Altruism*, vol. 1, (Amsterdam: North Holland, 2006).

[67] For a discussion of the relationship between the fiscal gap, generational accounting, accrual accounting, and other ways of accounting for government, see Alan J. Auerbach, William G. Gale, Peter R. Orszag, and Samara Potter, "Budget Blues: The Fiscal Outlook and Options for Reform," in Henry Aaron, James Lindsay, and Pietro Nivola, eds., *Agenda for the Nation* (Washington: Brookings Institution, 2003), pp. 109-143.

[68] U.S. Congressional Budget Office, *The Budget and Economic Outlook, An Update*, August 2009, available at http://www.cbo.gov/ftpdocs/105xx/doc10521/08-25-BudgetUpdate.pdf.

[69] The CBO baseline assumes that all expiring tax cuts will not be extended and that discretionary spending remains at its current level. The alternative fiscal scenario extends expiring tax cuts and uses Congress's past behavior as an indicator of future actions to predict future spending levels.

[70] U.S. Congressional Budget Office, *Long Term Budget Outlook*, June 2009, available at http://www.cbo.gov/ftpdocs/ 102xx/doc10297/06-25-LTBO.pdf.

[71] Alan J. Auerbach and William G. Gale, "An Update on the Economic and Fiscal Crises: 2009 and Beyond," working paper, September 2009.

[72] U.S. Treasury, *Major Foreign Holders of Treasury Securities*, November 17, 2009, available at http://www.ustreas.gov/tic/mfh.txt.

[73] CRS Report RL32462, *Foreign Investment in U.S. Securities*, by James K. Jackson.

In: Economic Policies in a Time of Financial Crisis
Editor: Heather D. Perkins
ISBN: 978-1-61122-686-7

Chapter 6

Foreign Ownership of U.S. Financial Assets: Implications of a Withdrawal

James K. Jackson

Summary

This chapter provides an overview of the role foreign investment plays in the U.S. economy and an assessment of possible actions a foreign investor or a group of foreign investors might choose to take to liquidate their investments in the United States. Concerns over the potential impact of disinvestment have grown as national governments have become more active investors in the U.S. economy and as innovation in creating financial instruments has increased volatility in financial markets. Such concerns seem out of step with the experience of the 2008-2009 financial crisis, during which the dollar became the preferred safe haven investment for foreign investors. If some foreign investors were to liquidate their holdings, these actions could affect the U.S. economy in a number of ways due to the role foreign investment plays in the United States and due to the current mix of economic policies the United States has chosen. The impact of any such action on the economy would also depend on the overall condition and performance of the economy and the financial markets. If the economy were experiencing a strong rate of economic growth, the impact of a foreign withdrawal likely would be minimal, especially given the dynamic nature of credit markets. If a withdrawal occurred when the economy were not experiencing a robust rate of growth or if credit financial markets were under duress, the withdrawal could have a stronger effect on the economy.

The particular course of action foreign investors might choose to take and the overall strength and performance of the economy at the time of their actions could affect the economy in different ways. Congress likely would become involved as a result of its direct role in making economic policy and its oversight role over the Federal Reserve. In addition, the actions of foreign investors could complicate domestic economic policymaking. Foreign investors who decide to liquidate their holdings of one particular type of investment would normally need to look for other types of assets to acquire. While there are a multitude of possible strategies foreign investors could pursue, this analysis assesses the impact of four of the most likely strategies a single large foreign investor or a group of foreign investors could choose to employ to reduce or withdraw entirely their holdings of U.S. financial assets:

- A rapid liquidation of U.S. Treasury securities.
- A shift in the make-up of foreign investors' portfolios among various dollar-denominated assets.
- A rapid shift from dollar-denominated assets to assets denominated in other currencies.
- A slow shift in the make-up of future accumulations of assets away from dollar-denominated assets to assets denominated in currencies other than the dollar.

OVERVIEW

Foreign capital inflows are playing an important role in the economy. Such inflows bridge the gap between U.S. supplies and demands for credit, thereby allowing consumers and businesses to finance purchases at interest rates that are lower than they would be without overseas capital inflows. Similarly, capital inflows allow federal, state, and local governments to finance their budget deficits at rates that are lower then they would be otherwise. These foreign capital inflows allow the Nation to support expenditures exceeding its current output level and finance its trade deficit. A sharp reduction in those inflows likely would complicate domestic efforts at making and conducting economic policies.

To date, the world economy has benefitted from the stimulus provided by the nation's combination of fiscal and monetary policies and trade deficit. Foreign investors now hold slightly less more 55% of the publicly held and publicly traded U.S. Treasury securities, 26% of corporate bonds, and about 12% of U.S. corporate stocks.[1] The large foreign accumulation of U.S. securities has spurred some observers to argue that this foreign presence in U.S. financial markets increases the risk of a financial crisis, whether as a result of the uncoordinated actions of market participants or by a coordinated withdrawal from U.S. financial markets by foreign investors for economic or political reasons. Concerns are also growing that over the long run U.S. economic policies and the accompanying large deficit in its international trade accounts could have a negative impact on global economic developments, especially for the economically less developed countries.

Some observers are concerned that a foreign investor with significant holdings in the United States or a group of foreign investors could engage in an abrupt and large-scale liquidation of dollar-denominated securities, particularly a sell-off of U.S. Treasury securities. These observers argue that the vast sums of dollars held and managed by some foreign governments, termed sovereign wealth funds, raise the prospects of such a coordinated withdrawal, because the funds potentially increase the ability of foreign governments to instigate a rapid withdrawal. It is uncertain, though, what types of events could provoke a coordinated withdrawal from U.S. securities markets. Indeed, during the recent financial crisis, dollar-denominated assets were the preferred safe haven investment of foreign investors. Although unlikely, a coordinated withdrawal from U.S. financial markets potentially could be staged by foreign investors for economic or political reasons or it could arise as a result of an uncoordinated correction in market prices. Also, concerns over the ability of the federal government to service its foreign debt and a loss of confidence in the ability of national U.S. policy makers to conduct economic policies that are perceived abroad as prudent and stabilizing could spur some foreign investors to reassess their estimates of the risks involved in holding dollar-denominated assets. In other cases, international linkages that connect national capital markets could be the conduit through which events in one market are quickly spread to other markets and ignite an abrupt, seemingly uncoordinated, withdrawal of capital.

A liquidation of capital could be limited to one segment of the credit markets as one foreign investor or a group of foreign investors attempted to adjust the composition of their portfolios. A withdrawal also could mark a major shift in investment strategies by foreign investors as they shifted away from dollar-denominated securities. Short of a financial crisis, events that cause some foreign investors to adjust their portfolios likely would have short-run negative effects on U.S. interest rates and on the international exchange value of the dollar. However, should a large group of foreign investors make a permanent shift in their strategies to limit or to reduce their purchases of U.S. securities, such actions likely would complicate efforts to finance budget deficits. Given the current mix of economic policies, the loss of capital inflows would affect U.S. interest rates, domestic investment, and the long-term rate of growth of the economy unless there is an accompanying shift in the national rate of saving. Such a loss of capital inflows would be especially troublesome if it occurred during a time when concerns over the rate of growth in the economy were increasing. During periods when the rate of economic growth is slowing, the Federal Reserve generally resorts to reducing interest rates to stimulate the economy. However, the loss of capital inflows would tend to push the Federal Reserve to raise interest rates to attract more capital inflows. Congress likely would find itself embroiled in any such economic or financial crisis through its direct role in conducting fiscal policy and in its indirect role in the conduct of monetary policy through its supervisory responsibility over the Federal Reserve.

Some observers are also concerned that the financial crisis has damaged the international financial system and raise concerns about the U.S. leadership role. The rapid expansion of market activity through the consolidation of equity exchanges and the development of complex financial instruments and hybrid securities that are traded across national borders has raised additional concerns that financial innovations have outpaced the efforts of regulators. Some observers argue that improvements in the financial system that arise from greater market efficiencies by spreading risk across national borders may be blunted, because the underlying risks of certain widely traded financial instruments have become more difficult to assess. Some also argue that the recent financial crisis demonstrate the risks that a domestic financial crisis pose for the global economy because such crises can spread across national borders due to the rapid internationalization of financial services. Others note that by expanding into financial activities that were not part of the original core business of financial services, providers have become exposed to new and additional types of risk for which they are not well prepared. According to the IMF, "there is little empirical evidence to date to determine whether cross-border diversification of financial institutions reduces or increases firm-specific or systemic vulnerabilities."[2]

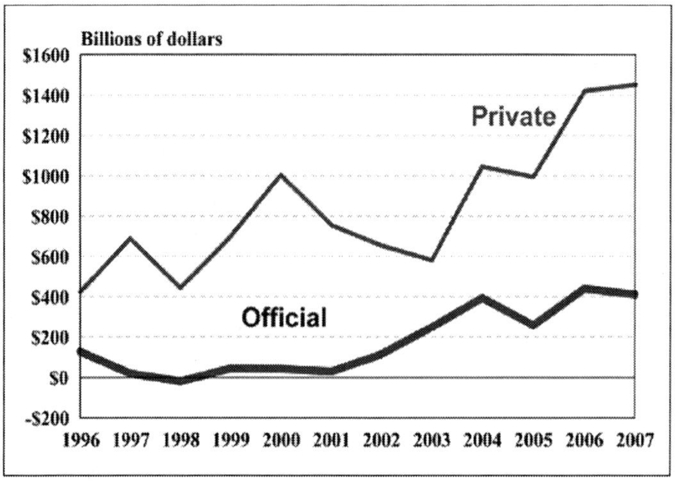

Source: Department of Commerce

Figure 1. Foreign Private and Official Capital Inflows Into the United States, 1996-2007

FOREIGN INVESTMENT IN THE U.S. ECONOMY

Capital flows are highly liquid, can respond abruptly to changes in economic and financial conditions, and exercise a primary influence on exchange rates and through those rates onto global flows of goods and services. As indicated in Figure 1, these capital inflows are composed of official inflows, primarily foreign governments' purchases of U.S. Treasury securities, and private inflows composed of portfolio investment, which includes foreigners' purchases of U.S. Treasury and corporate securities, financial liabilities, and direct investment in U.S. businesses and real estate. In 1996, total foreign capital inflows to the United States reached over $551 billion, but by 2000 foreign capital inflows totaled more than $1 trillion, as indicated in Table 1. Such inflows were reduced in 2001 and 2002 as the growth rate of the U.S. economy slowed, but grew to over $2 trillion in 2007 as the rate of economic growth improved. Private capital inflows comprise more than three-fourths of the total capital inflows, with foreign purchases of corporate securities, stocks and bonds being the main components of these inflows. In 2007, official inflows attributed to foreign governments accounted for 22% of total foreign capital inflows, down slightly from the share recorded in 2006. This pattern shifted sharply in 2008 as private capital inflows fell as the financial crisis reduced private access to capital markets. Foreign officials, however, remained steady as foreign governments attempted to stabilize financial markets.

Economists generally attribute the rise in foreign investment in the United States to comparatively favorable returns on investments relative to risk, a surplus of saving in other areas of the world, the well-developed U.S. financial system, and the overall stability of the U.S. economy. These net capital inflows (inflows net of outflows) bridge the gap in the United States between the amount of credit demanded and the domestic supply of funds, likely keeping U.S. interest rates below the level they would have reached without the foreign capital. These capital inflows also allow the United States to support expenditures exceeding its current output level and finance its trade deficit, because foreigners are willing to "lend" to the United States in the form of exchanging goods, represented by U.S. imports, for such U.S. assets as stocks, bonds, and U.S. Treasury securities. Such inflows, however, put upward pressure on the dollar, which tends to push up the price of U.S. exports relative to its imports and to reduce the overall level of exports. Furthermore, foreign investment in the U.S. economy drains off some of the income earned on the foreign-owned assets that otherwise would accrue to the U.S. economy as foreign investors repatriate their earnings back home.

Table 1. Capital Inflows to the United States, 1997-2008 (in Billions of Dollars)

Year	Total	Official assets	Private assets					
			Total	Direct investment	Treasury securities	Corporate securities	U.S. currency	Other
1997	704.5	19.0	685.4	105.6	130.4	161.4	22.4	265.5
1998	420.8	-19.9	440.7	179.0	28.6	156.3	13.8	62.9
1999	742.2	43.5	698.7	289.4	-44.5	298.8	22.4	130.5
2000	1,038.2	42.8	995.5	321.3	-70.0	459.9	-3.4	287.6
2001	782.9	28.1	754.8	167.0	-14.4	393.9	23.8	184.5
2002	795.2	115.9	679.2	84.4	100.4	283.3	18.9	192.3
2003	858.3	278.1	580.2	63.8	91.5	220.7	10.6	193.7
2004	1,533.2	397.8	1,135.4	146.0	93.6	381.5	13.3	501.1
2005	1,247.3	259.3	988.1	112.6	132.3	450.4	8.4	284.3
2006	2,065.2	487.9	1,577.2	243.2	-58.2	683.2	2.2	706.8
2007	2,129.5	480.9	1,648.5	275.8	66.8	605.7	-10.7	711.0
2008	534.1	487.0	47.1	319.7	196.6	-126.7	29.2	-371.8

Source: Weinberg, Douglas B., U.S. International Transactions Second Quarter of 2009, *Survey of Current Business*, October 2009, p. 75.

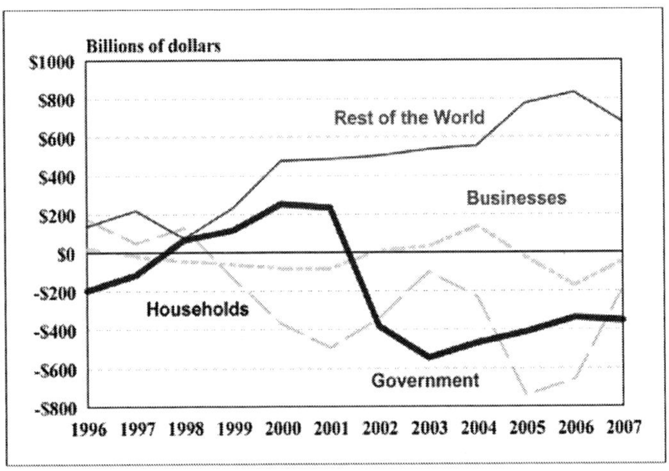

Source: Federal Reserve

Figure 2. Flows of Funds in the U.S. Economy, 1996-2007

Flow of Funds in the U.S. Economy

Figure 2 shows the net flow of funds in the U.S. economy. The flow of funds accounts measure financial flows across sectors of the economy, tracking funds as they move from those sectors that supply the capital through intermediaries to sectors that use the capital to acquire physical and financial assets.[3] The net flows show the overall financial position by sector, whether that sector is a net supplier or a net user of financial capital in the economy. Because the demand for funds in the economy as a whole must equal the supply of funds, a deficit in one sector must be offset by a surplus in another sector.

Generally, the household sector, or individuals, provides funds to the economy, because individuals save part of their income, while the business sector uses those funds to invest in plant and equipment that, in turn, serve as the building blocks for the production of additional goods and services. The government sector (the combination of federal, state, and local governments) can be either a net supplier of funds or a net user, depending on whether the sector is running a surplus or a deficit, respectively. The interplay within the economy between saving and investment, or the supply and uses of funds, tends to affect domestic interest rates, which move to equate the demand and supply of funds. Shifts in the interest rate also tend to attract capital from abroad, denoted by the rest of the world (ROW) in **Table 2**.

As **Table 2** indicates, from 1996 through 1998, the household sector ran a net surplus, or provided net savings to the economy. The business sector also provided net surplus funds in 1996, or businesses earned more in profits than they invested. The government sector, primarily the federal government, experienced net deficits, which decreased until 1998, when the federal government and state and local governments experienced financial surpluses. Capital inflows from the rest of the world rose and fell during this period, depending on the combination of household saving, business sector saving and investment, and the extent of the deficit or surplus in the government sector.

Starting in 1999, the household sector began dissaving, as individuals spent more than they earned. Part of this dissaving was offset by the government sector, which experienced a surplus from 1998 to 2001. As a result of the large household dissaving, however, the economy as a whole experienced a gap between domestic saving and investment that was filled with large capital inflows. Those inflows were particularly large in nominal terms from 2000 to 2006, as household dissaving continued and as government sector surpluses turned to historically large deficits in nominal terms. Such inflows likely kept interest rates below the level they would have reached without the inflows, but they added to pressures on the international exchange value of the dollar.

In 2007, 2008 and 2009, the household has saved at rates not experienced in recent periods as the financial crisis and economic recession spurred households to save and businesses to build up their balance sheets. This saving has been offset by the large deficits experienced by state, local, and the federal governments as the economic recession and the drop in property values had reduced government revenue. Similarly, capital inflows have declined, reflecting the higher level of domestic saving.

As the flow of funds data indicate, foreign capital inflows augment domestic U.S. sources of capital, which in turn keep U.S. interest rates lower than they would be without the foreign capital. Indeed, economists generally argue that it is this interplay between the demand for and the supply of credit in the economy that drives the broad inflows and outflows of capital. As U.S. demands for capital outstrip domestic sources of funds, domestic interest rates rise relative to those abroad, which tends to draw capital away from other countries to the United States.

Foreign and Domestic Sources of Funds

The United States also has benefitted from a surplus of saving over investment in many areas of the world that has provided a supply of funds and accommodated the overall shortfall of saving in the country. This surplus of saving has been available to the United States because foreigners have remained willing to loan that saving to the United States in the form of acquiring U.S. assets, which have accommodated the growing current account deficits. Over the past decade, the United States experienced a decline in its rate of saving and an increase in the rate of domestic investment. The large increase in the nation's current account deficit would not have been possible without the accommodating inflows of foreign capital.

Foreign capital inflows, while important, do not fully replace or compensate for a lack of domestic sources of capital. Capital mobility has increased sharply over the last 20 years, but economic analysis shows that a nation's rate of capital formation, or domestic investment, seems to be linked primarily to its domestic rate of saving. This phenomenon was first presented in a paper published in 1980 by Martin Feldstein and Charles Horioka.[4] The Feldstein-Horioka paper maintained that despite the dramatic growth in capital flows between nations, international capital mobility remains somewhat limited so that a nation's rate of domestic investment is linked to its domestic rate of saving.[5]

Table 2. Flow of Funds of the U.S. Economy, 1996-2008 (in Billions of Dollars)

Year	Households	Businesses	Government			ROW
			Total	State and Local	Federal	
1996	175.2	19.8	-196.8	-1.2	-195.6	137.9
1997	47.4	-18.3	-116.6	-47.5	-69.1	219.6
1998	128.0	-45.7	64.8	48.8	16.0	75.0
1999	-132.7	-62.6	115.3	9.9	105.4	231.7
2000	-371.0	-82.9	252.5	54.5	198.0	476.3
2001	-494.4	-82.9	233.4	35.4	198.0	485.4
2002	-343.4	8.7	-382.6	-95.6	-287.0	501.7
2003	-101.8	30.3	-546.3	-70.4	-475.9	535.4
2004	-230.6	136.8	-468.6	-32.9	-435.7	554.4
2005	-445.2	-44.8	-374.0	7.6	-381.6	712.1
2006	-530.3	-201.5	-188.4	78.6	-267.0	805.2
2007	112.5	-272.1	-323.4	13.5	-336.9	661.7
2008	666.9	-172.3	-769.8	-39.0	-730.8	506.0
I 2009	558.7	76.6	-1,164.8	-134.7	-1,030.1	138.7
II 2009	178.2	166.3	-1,700.4	-236.5	-1,463.9	230.3
III 2009	1,371.0	334.1	-1,358.3	-142.4	-1,215.9	172.2

Source: Board of Governors of the Federal Reserve System, Flow of Funds Accounts of the United States, Flows and Outstandings Third Quarter 2009, December 5, 2009.

Foreign Capital and the Value of the Dollar

Liberalized capital flows and floating exchange rates have greatly expanded the amount of capital flows between countries. These capital transactions are undertaken in response to commercial incentives or political considerations that are independent of the overall balance of payments or of particular accounts. As a result of these transactions, national economies have become more closely linked, the process some refer to as "globalization." The data in Table 3 provide selected indicators of the relative sizes of the various capital markets in various countries and regions and the relative importance of international foreign exchange markets. In 2008, these markets amounted to over $500 trillion, or more than 30 times the size of the U.S. economy. Worldwide, foreign exchange and interest rate derivatives, which are the most widely used hedges against movements in currencies, were valued at $486 trillion in 2008, 78% larger than the combined total of all public and private bonds, equities, and bank assets. For the United States, such derivatives total nearly three times as much as all U.S. bonds, equities, and bank assets.

Another aspect of capital mobility and capital inflows is the impact such capital flows have on the international exchange value of the dollar. Demand for U.S. assets, such as financial securities, translates into demand for the dollar, because U.S. securities are denominated in dollars. As demand for the dollar rises or falls according to overall demand for dollar-denominated assets, the value of the dollar changes. These exchange rate changes, in turn, have secondary effects on the prices of U.S. and foreign goods, which tend to alter the U.S. trade balance. At times, foreign governments have moved aggressively in international capital markets to acquire the dollar directly or to acquire Treasury securities in order to strengthen the value of the dollar against particular currencies.

Also, the dollar is heavily traded in financial markets around the globe and, at times, plays the role of a global currency. Disruptions in this role have important implications for the United States and for the smooth functioning of the international financial system. This prominent role means that the exchange value of the dollar often acts as a mechanism for transmitting economic and political news and events across national borders. While such a role helps facilitate a broad range of international economic and financial activities, it also means that the dollar's exchange value can vary greatly on a daily or weekly basis as it is buffeted by international events.[6]

A triennial survey of the world's leading central banks conducted by the Bank for International Settlements in April 2007 indicates that the *daily* trading of foreign currencies through traditional foreign exchange markets[7] totals more than $3.2 trillion, up sharply from the $1.9 trillion reported in the previous survey conducted in 2004. In addition to the traditional foreign exchange market, the over-the-counter (OTC)[8] foreign exchange derivatives market reported that daily turnover of interest rate and non-traditional foreign exchange derivatives contracts reached $2.1 trillion in April 2007. The combined amount of $5.3 trillion for daily foreign exchange trading in the traditional and OTC markets is more than three times the *annual* amount of U.S. exports of goods and services. The data also indicate that 86.3% of the global foreign exchange turnover is in U.S. dollars, slightly lower than the 88.7% share reported in a similar survey conducted in 2004.[9]

Table 3. Selected Indicators of the Size of the Global Capital Markets, 2008 (in Billions of U.S. Dollars)

	Gross Domestic Product (GDP)	Total Official Reserves	Bonds, Equities, and Bank Assets				Exchange Market Derivatives		
			Total	Stock Market Capitalization	Debt Securities	Bank Assets	Total	OTC Foreign Exchange Derivatives	OTC Interest Rate Derivatives
World	60,917.3	6,787.8	214,424.0	33,513.1	83,529.6	97,381.4	485,973.0	48,775.0	437,198.0
European Union	17,037.4	278.4	46,802.4	7,262.8	29,137.0	46,802.4	N.A.	N.A.	N.A.
Euro Area	13,538.4	167.7	32,510.8	4,984.7	23,793.3	32,510.8	160,646.0	20,653.0	160,646.0
United States	14,441.4	66.6	56,391.8	11,737.6	30,657.7	13,996.5	194,904.0	40,737.0	154,167.0
Japan Emerging	4,910.7	1,009.4	24,714.4	3,209.0	11,478.4	10,027.0	68,889.0	11,438.0	57,451.0
markets	20,605.9	4,286.8	34,394.2	8,558.9	7,815.4	18,020.0	N.A.	N.A.	N.A.

Source: *Global Financial Stability Report*, International Monetary Fund, December 2009. Statistical Appendix, Table 3. Quarterly Review, Bank for International Settlements, December 2009, Tables 20b and 21b.

Note: Total derivatives does not include equity and commodity-linked derivatives.

In the U.S. foreign exchange market, the value of the dollar is followed closely by multinational firms, international banks, and investors who are attempting to offset some of the inherent risks involved with foreign exchange trading. On a daily basis, turnover in the U.S. foreign exchange market[10] averages $664 billion; similar transactions in the U.S. foreign exchange derivative markets[11] average $607 billion, nearly double the amount reported in a similar survey conducted in 2004.[12] Foreigners also buy and sell U.S. corporate bonds and stocks and U.S. Treasury securities. Foreigners now own slightly less than 50% of the total amount of outstanding U.S. Treasury securities that are publicly held and traded.[13]

WITHDRAWAL OF FOREIGN INVESTMENT

This section analyzes four possible strategies a single large foreign investor or a group of foreign investors could employ to reduce or withdraw entirely their holdings of financial assets in the United States. These strategies include

- a rapid liquidation of U.S. Treasury securities,
- a shift in the make-up of foreign investors' portfolios among various dollar-denominated assets,
- a rapid shift from dollar-denominated assets to assets denominated in other currencies, and
- a slow shift in the make-up of future accumulations of assets away from dollar-denominated assets to assets denominated in currencies other than the dollar.

Sudden Withdrawal from U.S. Treasury Securities

The large holdings of U.S. Treasury securities by foreign governments have led some observers to consider the prospect of a withdrawal from the U.S. Treasury securities market by a single foreign government. At the first hint that a foreign government was attempting to liquidate all or even a large part of its holdings of U.S. Treasury securities, the price of such Treasury securities likely would plummet in U.S. securities markets and the market rate of interest would rise, perhaps appreciably, in the first few hours or days. For instance, on November 7, 2007, a report, which was later repudiated, asserted that Chinese officials were considering shifting some of China's foreign currency reserves, reportedly worth $1.4 trillion, in dollars and in such dollar-denominated assets as Treasury securities, out of dollar-denominated securities. Acting on the report, investors sold securities and the dollar. As a result, the broad Dow Jones industrial average plunged 360 points in one day and the dollar sank against other major currencies.[14] In response to the fall in the exchange value of the dollar, indexes of equities markets in Europe and Japan also fell.

Such cross-border spill-over effects are not new, but potentially have become more pervasive as a result of the broad linkages that have been forged among the once-disparate national financial systems. As an example, concerns in U.S. capital markets in early June 2006 over prospects that a rise in consumer prices and in the core inflation rate would push the Federal Reserve to raise key U.S. interest rates sparked a drop in prices in U.S. capital and equity markets where inflation concerns quickly spread to markets in Europe and Asia as equity prices fell in those markets as well.[15]

If a foreign investor with large U.S. holdings or a group of foreign investors attempted to launch a withdrawal from U.S. Treasury securities, investors and other market participants would calculate quickly the expected effects of those intended actions on market prices, interest rates, and the exchange value of the dollar and would then act swiftly on those anticipated effects. As a result, the prices of Treasury securities likely would drop sharply, while interest rates would rise, because the price of such securities is inversely related to the interest rate. In addition, the dollar likely would fall in value relative to other currencies, because the shift away from dollar-denominated assets would increase demand for and the prices of other currencies relative to the dollar. Consequently, the drop in the price of Treasury securities and the drop in the exchange value of the dollar would significantly discount the value of any Treasury securities that would be sold and sharply reduce the proceeds for any investor participating in such a sell-off. As a result, the potentially large financial losses that would attend an attempt to liquidate assets rapidly are likely to dissuade most investors from employing such a strategy.

The drop in the prices of Treasury securities and the decline in the exchange value of the dollar, however, probably would be short-lived. Foreign investors selling Treasury Securities presumably would do so in order to acquire non-dollar-denominated assets. Such a shift in demand from U.S.

Treasury securities to other foreign securities would drive up the prices of those securities and the exchange value of foreign currencies. As a result, the lower prices for Treasury securities and for the dollar would offer other investors arbitrage and investment opportunities to acquire assets that investors likely would deem to be temporarily undervalued. As a result, investors likely would move to acquire Treasury securities and the dollar, which means that demand would increase for both the low-priced Treasury securities and the lower-valued dollar, which would drive up the prices of both assets. Such a response could significantly blunt, or even entirely reverse, the initial drop in prices of the securities and of the dollar. Given the dynamic nature of finance and credit markets and the instantaneous communication of information, such actions likely would occur within a very short time frame.

For instance, fears spread rapidly after the terrorist attacks on New York and Washington on September 11, 2001, that foreigners would curtail their purchases of U.S. financial assets and reduce the total inflow of capital into the U.S. economy. Following the attacks, foreign governments and private investors did reduce their purchases of Treasury securities from pre-attack levels and the value of the dollar fell relative to other major currencies. These effects were fully reversed within 30 days, however, as currency traders forged a short-lived agreement not to profit from the attacks and the Federal Reserve undertook actions on its own and in concert with central bankers and financial ministers around the globe to ensure the smooth operation of the international financial markets.[16] Similarly, the Federal Reserve likely would not be expected to sit by idly while foreign investors attempted a coordinated withdrawal from U.S. equity markets, if those actions threatened to undermine the stability of the markets.

The overall performance of the U.S. economy at the time of any attempted withdrawal would also influence the economic effect of the withdrawal. For instance, if the U.S. economy were experiencing a robust rate of economic growth, the impact of a withdrawal by foreign investors likely would be minimal, both in the short run and in the long run. However, if such a withdrawal were to occur at a time when the U.S. economy were not experiencing a robust rate of economic growth, or if the U.S. credit and financial markets were under duress, such a withdrawal may well have a more pervasive effect by undermining investors' confidence in the stability and performance of the markets and could result in higher interest rates and a lower exchange value of the dollar over the short run and prolong the adjustment process. In addition, actions that change foreign investors' assessment of the underlying risks of the financial system or that undermine foreign investors' confidence in the stability of the financial system could prod some foreign investors to reassess the composition of their portfolios.

For instance, at the time of the rumored Chinese withdrawal from U.S. securities, U.S. financial markets already were strained by concerns over the impact of record oil prices and potentially large losses associated with sub-prime mortgaged-backed securities. As a result, the Dow Jones industrial average of U.S. stocks moved erratically through the end of November 2007. By the end of November 2007, the Dow was down nearly 290 points from where it had been following the loss of 360 points on November 7, 2007.

Diversify Portfolios among Dollar-Denominated Assets

Another possible course of action some foreign investors could pursue would be to diversify abruptly the composition of their portfolios by replacing a sizeable portion of their holdings of U.S. Treasury securities with other dollar-denominated assets. As foreign investors traded Treasury securities for other assets, the price of Treasury securities would decline and the prices of other assets would rise as demand shifted away from Treasury securities and toward other dollar-denominated assets. Because total demand for dollar-denominated assets would remain constant, there likely would be little movement in the exchange value of the dollar, but the shift of demand would alter the relative prices of various domestic assets. Such shifts in demand are not a rare occurrence, but happen frequently as investors change their evaluations of the relative value of corporate equities, corporate bonds, and Treasury securities and in response to changes in economic policies and actions by the Federal Reserve.

If foreign investors attempt to alter abruptly the composition of their portfolios away from Treasury securities, the prices of such securities would fall and the prices of corporate bonds and equities would rise, reflecting the shift in demand. If investors perceived this shift in demand and, therefore, the shift in prices, as a one-time adjustment in the composition of foreign investors' portfolios, some investors likely would take advantage of the rise in prices in equities and bonds to sell their holdings and take their profits at what likely would be perceived to be overvalued prices and, conversely, buy Treasury securities at what they would view as temporarily undervalued prices. After these adjustments, market prices likely would settle at prices that would be close to or equal to those that had existed prior to the original shift in demand by foreign investors.

Shift away from Dollar-Denominated Assets

Another course of action some foreign investors could pursue would be to pare down their holdings of dollar-denominated assets through a relatively swift liquidation of part of their holdings of dollar-denominated assets. In this case, a single foreign investor or a group of foreign investors would sell off part of their holdings of such dollar-denominated assets as corporate stocks and bonds or Treasury securities and possibly even direct investments (investments in U.S. businesses and real estate), although selling direct investments in this manner seems less likely given the generally long-run strategies investors use in acquiring them. If some foreign investors attempted to accomplish such a readjustment in their portfolios quickly by liquidating a portion of their holdings of corporate stocks and bonds and of Treasury securities, the prices of those assets would fall, given the current pervasive role foreign investors play in most U.S. financial markets.

In addition, because foreign investors would be liquidating their dollar-denominated assets in order to acquire assets denominated in other currencies, the exchange value of the dollar would fall relative to the price of foreign currencies. The drop in the prices of dollar-denominated equities and bonds combined with the lower exchange value of the dollar would erode the expected profits of any investor selling such securities and likely would attract the interest of other foreign investors, who presumably could liquidate their now higher-priced foreign securities and leverage their now higher-valued foreign currency to acquire dollar-denominated assets. Furthermore, U.S. multinational firms may well take advantage of the higher-valued foreign currency to repatriate part of the profits of their foreign affiliates, which would boost the balance sheet of their U.S. parent company, possibly even using the repatriated profits to acquire their own stock. Such repatriated profits likely would put upward pressure on the exchange value of the dollar, because foreign earnings would have to be converted into dollars before they were repatriated. Similarly, foreign firms operating in the United States likely would retain their profits rather than suffering a loss in value by translating those profits into higher priced foreign currencies in order to repatriate their profits back to their foreign parent company. Presumably, such profits could be used to augment investments within the United States.

Slow Shift away from Dollar-Denominated Assets

Finally, some foreign investors could decide to shift away from dollar-denominated assets by engaging in a long-term shift in the rate at which they accumulate such assets. Such a strategy would have the benefit of avoiding the large short-run shifts in the prices of financial assets and in the exchange value of the dollar that would attend any attempt by a group of foreign investors to make a rapid adjustment in the composition of their portfolios. A decrease in the inflow of capital from abroad would reduce the domestic availability of capital and place upward pressure on credit and financial assets as interest rates would rise to equate the demand and supply of credit. For the U.S. economy as a whole, a long-term shift away from dollar-denominated assets by foreign investors could have a slightly negative impact on the economy over the long run given the current mix of economic policies. A reduction in the inflow of foreign investment would tend to push down the prices of stocks and bonds and push up interest rates since those wanting credit would be competing for a smaller pool of funds. The price of Treasury securities would fall as the Federal government would be required to raise interest rates in order to attract domestic and foreign investors to acquire Treasury securities, which would raise the cost of financing the Federal government's budget deficit.

In addition, the shift from dollar-denominated assets would tend to push up the exchange value of foreign currencies relative to that of the dollar because an increase in demand for foreign assets would also raise demand for foreign currencies. The lower-valued dollar would raise the price of U.S. imports, particularly of raw materials and manufactured goods, which would put upward pressure on consumer and wholesale prices and tend to affect most negatively those sectors of the economy that are especially sensitive to movements in interest rates: the housing and automobile sectors. The decline in the international exchange value of the dollar also would tend to favor those industries and sectors of the economy that export. As long as the international exchange value of the dollar remained relatively low compared with other currencies, the exported goods sectors of the economy likely would expand by attracting more capital and labor and the imported goods sector of the economy would decline, assuming that all other things in the economy remained constant.

CONCLUSIONS

It is not uncommon for investors to adjust the composition of their portfolios as economic and financial conditions change. Given the recent surge in foreign investors' accumulation of dollars and dollar-denominated assets, it is not unreasonable to expect that from time to time they will also attempt to adjust the composition of their portfolios between corporate stocks and bonds, U.S. Treasury securities, and direct investments in U.S. businesses and real estate. A long-term shift away from dollar-denominated assets, however, could have a negative effect on the long-term rate of investment, productively, and the rate of growth in the U.S. economy. Such a shift in the value of the dollar would tend over the long run to benefit the exported goods sector of the economy, but it could also complicate efforts to conduct domestic economic policies. Although there are numerous other currencies that might attract investors, the dollar continues to be the most widely traded currency around the globe, which means it likely will retain its desirability as an investment asset and as a medium of exchange for some time to come. Also, the vast and deep capital markets in the United States combined with the highly developed banking and legal systems continue to make investments in U.S. financial assets attractive to foreign investors, despite short-run changes in perceptions of risk or economic performance.

Should a foreign investor with large financial holdings in the United States or a group of investors attempt to liquidate abruptly their holdings of assets such as Treasury securities, they would experience a severe loss in the value of those assets first as they attempted to sell their large holds in the market and then as they attempted to convert their dollar holdings into other currencies. As a result of these losses, it seems unlikely that a foreign investor with large holdings or a group of foreign investors would attempt to liquidate their securities quickly. A more likely course of action would be for foreign investors to adjust the composition of their portfolios slowly over time.

If only one or a few foreign investors engaged in a strategy to liquidate part of their U.S. financial holdings, their actions alone are likely to have a limited impact on the economy over the short run, because market forces would be expected to adjust to attract other foreign investors to replace those who had withdrawn. However, if a broad range of foreign investors, for whatever reason, decided to reduce their holdings of dollar-denominated assets, interest rates in the United States likely would rise in response to market forces that would place them above the level where they would have been if the foreign capital inflows had remained at their higher levels. A higher level of interest rates would lead some firms to reduce their level of borrowing and investing and spur some households to curtail their consumption, especially of such interest sensitive products as housing and automobiles, which usually are financed over long periods of time. Over the long run, the lower level of investment by firms could be expected to result in a lower rate of growth in productivity and, therefore, in a lower rate of growth in the economy.

In addition, if foreign investors were to attempt an abrupt adjustment to the composition of their portfolios that disrupted the financial markets or the broader economy, the Federal Reserve would not be expected to stand idly by on the sidelines. In such circumstances, the Federal Reserve has shown some agility in intervening on its own to stabilize credit markets and to move in coordination with other central banks. On December 11, 2007, for instance, the Federal Reserve decreased the federal funds rate and the discount rate on loans between banks by a quarter of a percentage point to ease credit conditions. Then, on December 12, 2007, the Federal Reserve announced that it would make $40 billion and perhaps more available to commercial banks in short-term loans to ease domestic liquidity issues and another $24 billion available to European central banks that had become so concerned about potential losses from U.S. mortgage-backed securities that they had begun to hoard cash and were unwilling to make loans to each other except at unusually high interest rate premiums.[17] Such willingness on the part of the Federal Reserve to intervene in the financial markets to ensure stability likely makes a prolonged financial crisis arising from a liquidation of financial assets by one foreign investor or a group of foreign investors unlikely, even if those investors are foreign governments.

End Notes

[1] For more information, see CRS Report RL32964, *The United States as a Net Debtor Nation: Overview of the International Investment Position.*

[2] Op. cit., *Global Financial Stability Report*, p. 107.

[3] Teplin, Albert M., the U.S. Flows of Funds Accounts and Their Uses, *Federal Reserve Bulletin*, July 2001, pp. 431-441.

[4] Feldstein, Martin, and Charles Horioka, Domestic Saving and International Capital Flows, *The Economic Journal*, June, 1980, pp. 314-329; Feldstein, Martin, *Aspects of Global Economic Integration: Outlook for the Future.* NBER Working Paper 7899, September 2000, pp. 9-12.

[5] Developments in capital markets have improved capital mobility since the Feldstein-Horioka paper was published and have led some economists to question Feldstein and Horioka's conclusion concerning the lack of perfect capital mobility. (Ghosh, Atish R., International Capital Mobility Amongst the Major Industrialized Countries: Too Little or Too Much?, *The Economic Journal,* January 1995, pp. 107-128.) Indeed, some authors argue that short-term capital flows among the major developed economies are highly liquid, perhaps too liquid, and seem to be driven as much by short-term economic events and speculation as they are by longer term economic trends.

[6] Samuelson, Robert J., "Dangers in a Dollar on the Edge," *The Washington Post*, December 8, 2006, p. A39.

[7] Traditional foreign exchange markets are organized exchanges which trade primarily in foreign exchange futures and options contracts where the terms and condition of the contracts are standardized.

[8] The over-the-counter foreign exchange derivatives market is an informal market consisting of dealers who custom-tailor agreements to meet the specific needs regarding maturity, payments intervals, or other terms that allow the contracts to meet specific requirements for risk.

[9] *Triennial Central Bank Survey: Foreign Exchange and Derivatives Market Activity in 2007.* Bank for International Settlement, September 2007, pp. 1-2. A copy of the report is available at http://www.bis.org/publ/rpfx07.pdf.

[10] Defined as foreign exchange transactions in the spot and forward exchange markets and foreign exchange swaps. A spot transaction is defined as a single transaction involving the exchange of two currencies at a rate agreed upon on the date of the contract; a foreign exchange swap is a multi-part transaction that involves the exchange of two currencies on a specified date at a rate agreed upon at the time of the conclusion of the contract and then a reverse exchange of the same two currencies at a date further in the future at a rate generally different from the rate applied to the first transaction.

[11] Defined as transactions in foreign reserve accounts, interest rate swaps, cross currency interest rate swaps, and foreign exchange and interest rate options. A currency swap commits two counterparties to exchange streams of interest payments in different currencies for an agreed upon period of time and usually to exchange principal amounts in different currencies as a pre-agreed exchange rate; a currency option conveys the right to buy or sell a currency with another currency as a specified rate during a specified period.

[12] *The Foreign Exchange and Interest Rate Derivatives Markets: Turnover in the United States April 2007.* The Federal Reserve Bank of New York, April, 2004. pp. 1-2. A copy of the report is available at http://www.newyorkfed.org/ markets/triennial/fx_survey.pdf.

[13] *Treasury Bulletin,* March 2007, Table OFS-2, p. 48.

[14] Grynbaum, Michael M., and Peter S. Goodman, Markets and Dollar Sink as Slowdown Worry Increases. *The New York Times,* November 8, 2007.

[15] Masters, Brooke A., Pondering the Bear Necessities, *The Washington Post*, June 7, 2006, p. D1; Samuelson, Robert J., Global Capital On the Run, *The Washington Post*, June 14, 2006, p. A23.

[16] For more information, see CRS Report RS21102, *International Capital Flows Following the September 11 Attacks*, by James K. Jackson.

[17] Federal Reserve Press Release, December 12, 2007; Irwin, Neal, "Fed to Team With Central Banks on Credit," *The Washington Post*, December 12, 2007; Norris, Floyd, and Vikas Bajaj, "Fed Joins Other Banks to add Cash," *The New York Times*, December 12, 2007.

In: Economic Policies in a Time of Financial Crisis
Editor: Heather D. Perkins
ISBN: 978-1-61122-686-7

Chapter 7

INFLATION: CAUSES, COSTS, AND CURRENT STATUS

Marc Labonte

SUMMARY

Since the end of World War II, the United States has experienced almost continuous inflation—the general rise in the price of goods and services. It would be difficult to find a similar period in American history before that war. Indeed, prior to World War II, the United States often experienced long periods of deflation. It is worth noting that the Consumer Price Index (CPI) in 1941 was virtually at the same level as in 1807.

During the last two economic expansions, March 1991-March 2001 and November 2001-December 2007, the inflation rate remained low by the standards of previous decades, and has remained low since this recession began. This is true regardless of which index is used to calculate the rate at which the price of goods and services rose. A low inflation rate is especially significant since the U.S. economy was fully employed, if not over fully employed, according to many estimates for the last three years of the 1991-2001 expansion and during 2006-2007. Yet, contrary to expectations, the inflation rate accelerated only modestly. Keeping an economy moving along a full employment path without igniting a burst of inflation is a difficult policy task.

Because labor costs make up nearly two-thirds of total production costs, the rate at which they rise is often regarded as an indication of future inflation at the retail level. They tended to rise in the latter stage of the 1991-2001 expansion and to moderate during the subsequent contraction, recovery, and expansion that ended in December 2007.

Rather than measure inflation by using the rate at which prices overall are rising, some economists prefer a measure that reflects primarily the systematic factors that raise prices. This yields the "underlying" or "core" rate of inflation. Price increases over this period have been especially sharp in food and energy, which are not included in the core rate.

Why should the United States be concerned about inflation? This study reports the distilled knowledge of economists on the real cost to an economy from inflation. These are remarkably more varied than the outlays for "shoe leather," long reported to be the major cost of inflation ("shoe leather" being a shorthand term for the resources that have to be expended on less efficient methods of exchanges).

The costs of inflation are related to its rate, the uncertainty it engenders, whether it is anticipated, and the degree to which contracts and the tax system are indexed. A major cost is related to the inefficient utilization of resources because economic agents mistake changes in nominal variables for changes in real variables and act accordingly (the so-called signal problem). Inflation in the United States during the post-World War II era may not have been high enough for this cost to be significant.

INTRODUCTION

Inflation—the general rise in the prices of goods and services—is one of the differentiating characteristics of the U.S. economy in the post-World War II era. Except for 1949, 1955, and 2009, the prices of goods and services have, on average, risen each year since 1945. The cumulative effect of this inflation is staggering: the price level has risen more than 1000% since the end of World War II.[1] Inflation rose in the 1960s, peaked in the 1970s and early 1980s, and has been generally low since then.

This was not true in the pre-World War II period. On the eve of that war, 1941, the U.S. price level was virtually the same as in 1807. During the periods from 1846 to 1861 and 1884 to 1909, the United States experienced a near constant price level. And in the 15 years from 1865 through 1879, the price level either remained constant or declined. The principal periods of inflation between 1800 and 1941 were associated with wars and the discoveries of gold and silver both here and abroad (and with increased efficiencies in extracting both metals).

INFLATION DEFINED

Inflation can be defined as a sustained or continuous rise in the general price level or, alternatively, as a sustained or continuous fall in the value of money. Several things should be noted about this definition. First, inflation refers to the movement in the general level of prices. It does not refer to changes in one price relative to other prices. These changes are common even when the overall level of prices is stable.[2] Second, the prices are those of goods and services, not assets. Third, the rise in the price level must be somewhat substantial and continue over a period longer than a day, week, or month.[3]

CAUSES OF INFLATION

There has been practically no period in American history in which a significant change in the price level has occurred that was not simultaneously accompanied by a corresponding change in the supply of money.[4] This has led to a widely held view that "inflation is always and everywhere a monetary phenomenon resulting from and accompanied by a rise in the quantity of money relative to output."[5]

Although this view is generally accepted, it is, in fact, consistent with two quite different views as to the cause of inflation.

In one view a more rapid rate of money growth plays an active role in inflation and results either from mistaken policies of the Federal Reserve or because the Federal Reserve subordinates itself to the fiscal requirements of the federal government and finances budget deficits through money creation. Examples of Federal Reserve policies that are likely to produce inflation are those that fix rates of interest too low or that support unrealistic foreign exchange values of the dollar. According to this view, the control of inflation rests with the Federal Reserve (Fed) and depends upon its willingness to limit the growth in the money supply.[6] Because of this relationship, some economists are concerned about the rapid growth in the portion of the money supply controlled by the Fed (called the monetary base) from 2008 to 2009, although to date the rise in the monetary base has not been accompanied by a proportionate increase in the broader money supply, mainly because of the large slack in the economy at the time.[7]

An alternative view comes in several versions. They have in common a belief that the major upward pressure on prices comes from activities which would produce a fall in real output. A favorite candidate is the attempt by organized labor to obtain increases in real wages. Other activities include the monopolistic pricing behavior of OPEC, major crop failures or changes in the terms of international trade produced by a decline in the foreign exchange value of the dollar. The decline in real output that these activities produce will, in general, lead to rises in unemployment. To prevent unemployment from increasing, in one version of this alternative, the Federal Reserve is seen to pump up demand by easing the growth of money and credit. In the process it ratifies the rise in the price level. Thus, in this version, while a growth in the money supply is necessary to ratify the upward movement in the price level, it is not the cause of the rise in prices.

It is interesting to speculate what would happen if the Federal Reserve refused to expand demand in the face of the rise in unemployment. Presumably, after a protracted period, the additional unemployment would lead to a fall in wages, costs, and other prices. Over the longer run, output would return to its previous level or growth path, the price level would fall back to its previous level and only relative prices and wages would be different. Thus, while the Federal Reserve has the power to curb inflation, it is unlikely to exercise this power in the face of a large run up in unemployment.

In another extreme variant, what the Federal Reserve does is really irrelevant. Should it refuse to expand what is conventionally called money to pump up demand in the presence of these developments that reduce output, money substitutes under the guise of credit will emerge that will allow demand to grow and the price increases to be ratified. This variation, interestingly, precludes excessive money growth from causing inflation, for it also holds that the Federal

Reserve cannot force too much money on the economy. Inflation, then, cannot be a case in which too much money is chasing too few goods.[8]

The first two explanations for inflation find many adherents among American economists, whereas the third is more common among some British economists.

The Relationship between Inflation and Unemployment

In most years, inflation tends to rise when unemployment falls, and vice versa. Economic theory explains this relationship in terms of a full employment rate of unemployment, also called the natural rate of unemployment or the non-accelerating inflation rate of unemployment (NAIRU).[9] Whenever the actual unemployment rate is above the full employment rate, total spending in the economy will fall, and the resultant slack will cause the inflation rate to fall (since there is less demand for goods and services). As the inflation rate falls, the expected rate of inflation should also fall if economic agents believe the government is sincere in its efforts to end inflation (i.e., that the government will not reverse its policy in the face of rising unemployment). As inflation expectations fall so will wage demands, and falling wage demands will bring about a lower unemployment rate (since employers will have more demand for labor when labor costs fall). Ultimately, the economy will move back to full employment at a zero inflation rate or a stable price level. Thus, the important steps in the sequence are (1) a convincing government policy to reduce the inflation rate to zero; (2) toleration of an above normal rate of unemployment; and (3) the adjustment of inflation expectations and wage demands to the lower rate of inflation. In practice, policymakers have shown a preference for stimulating the economy before inflation hits zero, so that unemployment returns to the full employment rate faster. As a result, most recessions have featured a falling but still positive inflation rate.

Inflation and Expectations

Economists believe that expectations of future inflation play an important role in the relationship between inflation and unemployment. To illustrate why, consider the example of tightening monetary policy (raising short-term interest rates) to reduce the inflation rate. Higher interest rates reduce spending on interest-sensitive goods, such as business investment spending, consumer durables, and housing. As spending on these goods declines, so will employment in the sectors producing these goods. If inflation expectations are low, the overall decline in spending and employment will put downward pressure on prices, as discussed in the previous section. But if inflation expectations are high, prices will respond less quickly to the same decline in spending and employment. As a result, spending and employment would have to fall further and longer to produce the same decline in prices. Whether inflation expectations are high or low will depend importantly on the perceived credibility of the Fed's commitment to maintaining low inflation. If businesses and workers do not believe that the Fed will stick with a policy of tighter monetary policy when faced with higher unemployment, they may not be willing to lower their price demands and wage demands, respectively.

The Economic Costs of Inflation

Economists often discuss jointly the costs to an economy from unemployment and inflation because, for much of the period since the late 1950s, it was generally believed that a long-run tradeoff existed between the two.[10] While the cost of unemployment was well articulated, the cost of inflation was relegated to "shoe leather."[11]

The high U.S. inflation rate of the late 1960s, 1970s, and early 1980s caused economists to rethink the costs of inflation to an economy. What follows is a distillation of those efforts.

Describing the costs to an economy from inflation can be confusing for several reasons. First and foremost there is the confusion over the cost to the economy versus the cost to specific individuals. Costs to individuals may not impose a burden on the economy because they are in the nature of a redistribution of either income and/or wealth. What is lost by some is gained by others. Nevertheless, some of these redistributions can have real effects.

Second, some of the costs of inflation are permanent in the sense that so long as the inflation continues the costs will be incurred. Others are only transitory and arise as the economy moves from one inflation rate to another or because the rate of inflation itself is variable.

Third, some costs are incurred only because the inflation is unanticipated while other costs arise even when the inflation is fully anticipated. Finally, some costs occur only because of the absence for one reason or another of appropriate safeguards: for example, the absence of indexed contracts.

Inflation Costs in a Fully Indexed Economy

As an introduction to understanding the costs imposed on an economy by inflation, consider first an economy that is completely indexed for inflation. Thus every conceivable contract is adjusted for changes in the price level including those for debt (bonds and mortgages) and wages and salaries; where taxes are imposed only on real returns to assets, where tax brackets, fines and all payments imposed by law are indexed, where the exchange rate is free to vary and there are no legal restrictions imposed on interest rates, etc.

In this economy, the distinction between anticipated and unanticipated inflation is unimportant except if the inflation rate is high and the indexed adjustments are not continuous. Then real costs can occur. However, for analytical purposes, assume that all individuals perfectly anticipated the inflation and that the indexed adjustments are continuous.

In this economy, inflation can impose only two real costs: the less efficient arrangement of transactions that result from holding smaller money balances and the necessity to change posted prices more frequently (the so-called menu costs).

The first of these, entailing the rearrangement of transactions due to the higher costs of holding money, is the one cost uniformly identified in the text books as "the cost of inflation." It is worth considering what is involved.

Both individuals and businesses hold money balances because it allows each to arrange transactions in an optimum or least cost way (e.g., for business this involves paying employees, holding inventories, billing customers, maintaining working balances, etc.) and to provide security against an uncertain future. Holding wealth or assets in a money form, however, is not costless. A measure of the so-called opportunity cost is the expected rate of inflation, a cost that rises because wealth can be held in alternative forms whose price or value rises with inflation.

When inflation occurs or when the rate of inflation rises, holding money becomes more costly. Individuals and businesses then attempt to get by with less money (for businesses this may mean billing customers more frequently, paying employees more frequently, etc.). This means that least cost transactions patterns are no longer least cost. The new patterns are less efficient—they use more time or more resources to effect a given transaction. In addition, holding smaller real money balances also reduces the security money provides against an uncertain future.

The magnitude of this cost has been reduced in the United States in recent years because financial institutions can now pay interest on a variety of deposits that function as money. Thus, the primary cost of inflation on money holding applies to currency on which no interest is paid. To the extent, however, that financial institutions are slow to raise interest rates in tandem with inflation, deposit holders will economize on holding deposits and arrange transactions less efficiently, thereby imposing a short-run cost on the economy.

The other cost imposed by inflation in a fully indexed economy is the so-called menu cost, which involves the extra time and resources that are used in adjusting prices more frequently in an environment where prices are rising. These additional costs are incurred mainly with goods and services that are sold in nonauction markets. It does not apply to auction markets where prices change more or less continuously in response to shifts in supply and demand.

Inflation Costs in a Partially Indexed Economy

Inflation Anticipated

Very few economies are fully indexed, even those in which inflation is severe. In the United States, indexation is incomplete. As such, inflation can impose costs even if it is fully anticipated. A case in point involves the arrangements for levying taxes. Taxes are levied in several instances on nominal as opposed to real income. As a result, the interaction of inflation and taxation can impose real effects on an economy by altering the incentives to work, save, and invest. Several examples should suffice to explain what is involved.

First, consider an individual who, in a non-inflationary period, earns a real rate of interest of 5% and who pays taxes of 30% on this income. The aftertax real rate of interest is 3.5%, that is, [5%–(30% x 5%)]. Now, assume that a 10% rate of inflation is expected over the one-year term of the loan. As a result, the market rate of interest rises to 15% (composed of a real rate of 5% and an expected inflation rate of 10%). At a tax rate of 30%, the aftertax rate of return falls to 0.5%.[12] To the extent that saving is responsive to the real aftertax rate of return, taxing nominal yields, as is done in the United States, distorts the incentive for individuals to save.[13] (The existing empirical evidence for the United States suggests that private sector saving is quite insensitive to the aftertax rate of return.)

Second, consider what happens to the real aftertax rate of return on business capital during an inflation. For tax purposes, the depreciation of business plant and equipment is based on actual or historic costs. During an inflation, charging depreciation based on historic cost raises the nominal profits of businesses and the basis on which corporate profits taxes are levied. As a result, the aftertax real rate of return falls and this discourages businesses from adding to their stock of plant, equipment, and structures—the bases for future economic growth.[14 15]

Third, to the extent that income tax brackets are not indexed or not indexed completely, inflation in a progressive income tax system can reduce the real aftertax income for wage and salary earners over time, distorting the incentives to work.

During the 1980s, the U.S. tax code was rewritten to adjust the tax brackets for inflation as well as to reduce the level and progressivity of the federal income tax. As a result, inflation has a much reduced interaction with federal taxes in reducing aftertax real income.

Several private sector practices also interact with inflation to produce real economic effects. The first is the continuation of level payment nominal mortgages for financing housing. This practice front loads the real cost of a mortgage during an inflation and, as a result, it discourages the purchase of homes, especially by younger first-time buyers.

Second, business firms continue to record all data in terms of the dollar even though the real purchasing power of this important unit of measure varies considerably over time. This practice has the potential for distorting the real profitability of business over time as well as the valuation of other relevant magnitudes. Since these nominal magnitudes are frequently used as the basis for borrowing and lending decisions, they have the potential for seriously distorting resource allocations.[16]

Inflation Unanticipated

In this section, the real effects of inflation are analyzed in an environment where it is unanticipated and where the economy relies on nominal or unindexed contracts. In this situation, an important effect of inflation is to redistribute both income and wealth. It would be a mistake, however, to conclude that because gainers and losers cancel, there can be no real effects from inflation.

To see one such real effect, consider what happens to the interest bearing public debt. Inflation reduces the real value of the public debt and with it the real value of the wealth of the private sector, the ultimate owners of most of that debt. Thus, inflation redistributes wealth from the private to the public sector. But who constitutes the public sector? These are the taxpayers who also happen to be the members of the private sector, some of whom own the debt.

Thus, redistribution reduces the real value of the taxes needed to service this debt, and the reduction is most beneficial for the younger workers in the current population and for future generations. As a result of the fall in real tax burden, their real disposable income rises, both today and in the future. They are thus able to save more while older workers and retirees will, no doubt, have to reduce their consumption, for while they are faced with a large wealth loss, they gain very little from the reduced tax burden. Thus, the redistribution of wealth between the private and the public sectors is really a redistribution between generations that could have an effect on the rate of capital formation.

Perhaps the most serious effect of unanticipated inflation in a market economy is its potential to make the price system malfunction and misallocate resources. Those who live in market economies are apt to take its functioning for granted. They may fail to appreciate or understand the vital role that prices perform in such a system. As standard textbooks in economics teach, the price system determines what is produced, how it is produced, and to whom the output is distributed.

For the price system to perform these functions efficiently, producers must be able to discern a change in real or relative prices from a change in nominal prices which essentially leaves all relative prices unchanged. Only with the former will it be profitable to alter production. A similar phenomenon holds for workers. A rise in money wages may bring forth a greater quantity of labor time if workers are convinced that this is a rise in real wages, that is, money wages relative to prices.[17]

It is easier for producers and workers to discern these changes in real prices and wages if the price level is stable or if the inflation rate is constant. It is more difficult when the rate of inflation is rising and/or more variable. Under these circumstances market economies are apt to have "signal" problems. That is, producers and workers mistake changes in nominal prices and wages for changes in corresponding real magnitudes and act accordingly. The resulting changes in output and labor time are inefficient and would not have occurred but for the mistakes in perception. Some economists, including Fed Chairman Ben Bernanke, have argued that low and stable inflation is conducive to higher long-term economic growth.[18] A "signal extraction" problem may not have arisen in the United States, however, since rates of inflation have been relatively low and stable.

Inflation and Uncertainty

Empirical studies completed in the 1970s support the view that inflation is associated with greater uncertainty about future prices and that the degree of uncertainty rises with the rate of inflation.[19]

Rising uncertainty about future prices is believed to produce several possible "real" effects. First, individuals appear to shift from buying assets denominated in nominal terms (e.g., bonds) to so-called real assets such as residential structures, land, precious metals, art work, etc. Because some of these assets are in fairly fixed supply, the resulting capital gain produced by the shift could conceivably raise private sector wealth by a sufficient amount to cause a fall in the saving rate. Second, to compensate for the perceived greater uncertainty, lenders appear to require a greater real reward for supplying funds for investment. Third, contracts tend to be shortened.

The first two developments lead to rising real interest rates, which tend to reduce the rate of investment and capital formation. The third development leads businessmen to prefer shorter lived assets.

Can a Little Inflation "Grease the Wheels" of the Economy?

A few prominent economists have broken with the mainstream view that inflation should be kept to a minimum. They have argued that moderate rates of inflation, in the 3%-5% range rather than the 1%-3% range, might be useful for smoother economic adjustment.[20] In a downturn, economic output falls because of "price stickiness"—prices and wages cannot adjust quickly enough to maintain full employment, so total spending falls below the productive capacity of the economy. These economists argue that with a higher average rate of inflation, adjustment would happen more quickly because real wage or price cuts would be possible while avoiding nominal wage cuts. For example, a worker might resist a 2% nominal cut in his wages when inflation is zero, but accept a 3% nominal wage increase when inflation is 5%. In both cases, real wages would have adjusted downward by 2%, but the latter example would have possibly occurred more quickly. Inherent in this view is that individuals suffer from some "money illusion" at moderate rates of inflation (i.e., a 2% real wage cut is accepted because the 3% nominal increase is not seen as a cut.) The existence of "money illusion" is inconsistent with anticipated inflation, and is only possible if inflation is insignificant; there is significant evidence that individuals in high inflation economies are highly sensitive to the inflation rate.[21]

Another argument made for targeting a higher (but still moderate) inflation rate is that deflation (falling prices) is a more serious problem than inflation, with Japan as an example of a country stuck in a long period of deflation and sluggish economic growth. A higher average inflation rate makes it less likely that a country would slide into deflation during a downturn. The reason that it could be hard to escape deflation is related to the "zero bound" on monetary policy.[22] The Federal Reserve can only reduce short-term interest rates to zero when it is stimulating the economy, but sometimes, as was the case in 2008, further stimulus is needed to end a recession. With a higher average rate of inflation, average interest rates would also be expected to be higher. Higher average interest rates would be further from the zero bound on average, so that the Federal Reserve could undertake more stimulus before hitting the zero bound. This argument neglects the fact that the Fed can undertake (and has recently undertaken[23]) unconventional monetary policy actions and expansionary fiscal policy to further stimulate the economy at the zero bound.

ECONOMIC COSTS OF INFLATION: SUMMARY

What is the cost of inflation? It is customary in textbooks to answer this question in terms of a situation where the rate of inflation is anticipated by all market participants who can either continuously re-contract or in which everyone is protected from inflation through indexation. In this world the cost to an economy from inflation is the increased resource cost from conducting transactions with reduced holdings of money—popularly termed "shoe leather" costs. If the inflation is serious, this cost is by no means trivial.[24]

However, inflations are seldom perfectly anticipated. In this situation, perhaps the most serious real effect comes from the ability of rising prices to jam the price signals that are so important to the smooth and efficient functioning of a market economy. Evidence suggests that this may not have been a problem for the United States in the post-World War II era.

In general, the cost of inflation to an economy will be larger the higher the rate of inflation, the more variable the rate, the less it is anticipated, the greater is the uncertainty it causes, and the less indexed is the economy.

THE MEASUREMENT OF INFLATION

Changes in the Prices of Goods and Services

There is no single measurement of inflation. The rise in the general level of prices, the essence of inflation, is measured by using a price index that aggregates the price of different goods and services. Ideally, the price index used should be broad based and one in which the individual prices are weighted to indicate their importance to the economy. Many different price indexes are available in the United States that measure different types of inflation rates.

For purposes of this chapter, two separate price indexes are used. The first is very broad based and derived from the measurement of the nation's gross domestic product (GDP), covering price changes of consumption, investment, government, and traded goods. The other is the Consumer Price Index (CPI), which prices a "market basket" of goods and services purchased by an urban family, a market basket whose individual items are weighted by how much the urban family spent on them in a base year period—currently 1982-1984. Inflation rates according to the two measures are usually similar. Inflation, according to the CPI, was very low (usually below 2%) in the 1950s and early 1960s, began rising in the late 1960s, was relatively high in the 1970s and early 1980s (rising above 10% in 1974 and 1979-1981), began falling in the mid-1980s, and generally remained in the 2%-3% range in the 1990s and 2000s.[25] Inflation tends to rise over the course of an economic expansion and decline during an economic recession, for reasons discussed above (see "The Relationship Between Inflation and Unemployment").

Current CPI data can be accessed at http://www.bls.gov/news.release/pdf/cpi.pdf.

Current data for the GDP price deflator can be accessed at http://www.bea.gov/news releases/ national/gdp/gdpnewsrelease.htm.

THE UNDERLYING OR CORE RATE OF INFLATION

When comparing purchasing power over two time periods, the overall (referred to as "headline") inflation rate is the relevant measure. Comparisons over time of wages, wealth, rates of return, government transfers such as Social Security payments, and so on should all use a headline measure of inflation, because all of these concepts depend on a broad measure of inflation. Although the headline rate of inflation can provide much useful information to policymakers on the state of the economy, it can also be misleading since it responds to both systematic and random forces. The latter can best be understood by reference to the food component of the CPI. An unusual cold spell in Florida in January that damages a substantial part of the fresh produce crop can send food prices and the CPI soaring. A similar effect can be produced by an unusually wet summer in the Midwest. Alternatively, an unusually good combination of rain and sunshine can produce a bountiful harvest and lower prices. Energy prices are also susceptible to such random effects associated with events such as turmoil in major oil producing nations.

To minimize the confusing signals that could arise from the use of the actual rate of inflation, some economists prefer to use a price index that reflects basically only systematic forces to measure inflation. For some economists, this can be achieved by using the CPI less its food and energy components. (It should be noted that food and energy represent about 25% of the current CPI.) Others want to use a moving average either of the CPI itself or of the current CPI less its food and energy components. The use of a moving average is based on the belief that if there are random factors that influence the actual inflation rate, they have an average value of zero. Hence, the use of a moving average should minimize their influence. Others prefer a more complicated measure that trims off whatever prices have changed most in that period.[26]

Policymakers, particularly at the Federal Reserve, often refer to core inflation in their policy decisions. Some policymakers prefer to use core inflation to predict future overall inflation because food and energy price volatility makes it difficult to discern trends from the overall inflation rate. A drawback of an over-reliance on core inflation, however, is that an extended period of rapidly rising food or energy prices could cause all other prices to accelerate. A focus on core may cause policymakers to fail to react to such a rise in inflation until it is too late. This scenario may have occurred in the last decade. Since CPI less food and energy was higher than headline CPI in each year of the decade except 2002 and 2009, a focus on core inflation may have led policymakers to wait too long to tighten policy in the expansion. Furthermore, several studies have failed to find core inflation to be a good forecaster of future inflation, casting doubt on the very rationale for relying on it.[27]

Current data for the CPI less food and energy can be accessed at http://www.bls.gov /news.release/ pdf/cpi.pdf.

Changes in Labor Costs

Because labor costs comprise nearly two-thirds of the value of final output, some economists believe that they are an important determinant of the rate of inflation. However, changes in the rate of growth of labor costs must be read with care. Wage increases can be driven by productivity increases, tight labor markets, inflation, or fears of inflation. One way to determine the force or forces driving wage increases is to examine what happens to per-unit labor costs. To this end, two major measures of labor cost are available, a comprehensive measure of wage and benefit costs, the *employment cost index,* and *per-unit labor costs in the nonfarm business sector.*

The growth rate of both measures of labor cost generally showed a tendency to accelerate during the expansions of the 1980s and 1990s as labor markets tightened. Subsequent recessions and growing unemployment had a depressing effect on the rise in both measures. During the expansion beginning in 2002, the rate of increase in both measures was fairly comparable to the inflation rate (meaning real wage growth was low) even as the unemployment rate fell.

Current data for the employment cost index can be accessed at http://www.bls.gov/ne ws.release/ pdf/eci.pdf.

Current data for per unit labor costs can be accessed at http://www.bls. gov/news.release/pdf/ prod2.pdf.

Conclusion

Inflation can impose a real cost on society in terms of the efficiency with which the exchange mechanism works, by distorting the incentives to save, invest, and work, and by providing incorrect signals that needlessly alter production and work effort. Because of this, policymakers should be concerned with the ongoing rate of inflation and any tendency for it to accelerate. An additional reason for concern arises because efforts to reduce the rate of inflation have often been associated with economic downturns. It should not be forgotten that the double-digit inflation of the early 1980s was reduced only through an economic downturn during which the unemployment rate rose to its highest level since the Great Depression of the 1930s. It is argued that the tendency for the inflation rate to accelerate in the late 1980s was a major reason why the Federal Reserve tightened monetary policy, which was also an important factor causing the recession of 1990-1991. Inflationary developments subsequent to that recession have been encouraging. The inflation rate has shown either no or only a modest tendency to rise as unemployment came down. Using various measures, the inflation rate since 1993 was low by standards of the preceding decade. Nonetheless, inflation has risen modestly preceding the 2001 and 2009 recessions, illustrating that this is still an important measure to watch for evaluating the state of the economy. Given the relationship between inflation and the money supply, some economists are concerned that the rapid growth in the portion of the money supply controlled by the Fed from 2008-2009 could cause rapid inflation. To date, those concerns have not been realized, primarily because of the large slack in the economy.

End Notes

[1] In this and the following paragraph, all changes in the price level are as measured by the Consumer Price Index.

[2] Especially troublesome for the definition of inflation is how to define a rise in the price of an important commodity such as oil. Since it enters as an important input into the production process as well as being a final product, it may cause many other individual prices to rise. Is this a rise in relative prices or is it more appropriately defined as inflation? Economists differ on how to describe this phenomenon. Some blame OPEC for the inflation of the 1970s and early 1980s. Others treat this as a rise in relative prices and attribute the inflation of the period to misplaced policies of the Federal Reserve.

[3] The words "somewhat substantial" cannot be defined precisely. All of the major price indexes have a number of shortcomings, such as only imperfectly correcting for changes in the quality of the goods and services contained in the index. For that reason, relatively low rates for inflation (e.g., plus or minus 2% or less) are often taken to be equivalent to price level stability.

[4] Perhaps the only exception to this statement is the inflation during the Korean War of 1950-1953.

[5] Milton Friedman, *What Price Guideposts in Guidelines: Formal Controls of the Marketplace*, Aliber, Robert and George Schultz, ed. (University of Chicago Press, 1966), p. 18.

[6] For more information, see CRS Report RL30354, *Monetary Policy and the Federal Reserve: Current Policy and Conditions*, by Marc Labonte.

[7] For more information on the 2008-2009 increase in the monetary base, see CRS Report RL34427, *Financial Turmoil: Federal Reserve Policy Responses*, by Marc Labonte.

[8] This view is commonly held by economists associated with the late Nicholas Kaldor and systematically explained by him in "Monetarism and U.K. Monetary Policy," *Cambridge Journal of Economics*, vol. 4 (1980), pp. 293-318.

[9] For more information, see CRS Report RL30391, *Inflation and Unemployment: What is the Connection?*, by Brian W. Cashell.

[10] A comprehensive discussion of the costs of inflation can be found in Fischer, Stanley, and Franco Modigliani, "Towards an Understanding of the Real Effects and Costs of Inflation," *Weltwirtschaftliches Archiv*, vol. 114, no. 4 (1978), pp. 736-787.

[11] Before financial institutions could pay explicit interest on deposits that function as money, economists believed that individuals and businesses would shift their wealth into savings-type deposits on which interest was paid. Because of this, they would have to make more frequent trips to banks to obtain money. This involved primarily a cost of shoe leather, as shoes wore out more frequently because of the increased number of trips. Hence the often expressed view that the primary cost of inflation to an economy was "shoe leather." More generally, it refers to the resources devoted to avoiding anticipated inflation.

[12] The after-tax real rate is equal to: 15% - 4.5% (which is 30% of 15%) = after-tax nominal yield of 10.5% - 10.0% inflation = 0.5% real after-tax yield.

[13] The possibility arises that the interaction of inflation and the taxation of nominal rates of return will produce negative aftertax real rates of return.

[14] The taxation of nominal profits may also encourage business to opt for shorter-lived capital during an inflation. In addition, since interest expenses are deductible for tax purposes, inflation encourages businesses to finance expansion by the use of debt as opposed to equity. This can impart an element of instability to the financial structure of the economy.

[15] Inflation can also influence some public decision-making because it leads to a misrepresentation of the reported statistics on which these decisions are made. Specifically, the Federal budget deficit tends to be overstated because the inflation premium in interest rates that represents the repayment of principal, is reported as interest expense in both the federal budget accounts and the GNP accounts. To the extent that public concern centers on the current operating outlays of the federal government, true interest outlays are considerably less than currently reported in the budget and, thus, the current operating deficit is much smaller than reported in the federal budget document.

[16] These distortions could be minimized if the dollar was defined as a real unit of account (e.g., defined in terms of a standard basket of commodities). Several proposals for doing so have been put forth. See Warren L. Coats, Jr., *In Search of Monetary Anchor: A "New" Monetary Standard*, IMF Working Paper, 1989.

[17] The key word in this explanation is "may," for a rise in real wages has both a substitution and an income effect. The substitution effect will cause workers to substitute work for leisure while the rise in real income will make leisure a more attractive option to working. Whether the quantity of labor time increases or decreases as the real wage rises will depend on which effect is stronger.

[18] Ben Bernanke Testimony Before the Committee on Banking, Housing, and Urban Affairs, U.S. Senate November 15, 2005.

[19] There are numerous studies that provide support for this view. Some are cited in the references in the Fischer and Modigliani study on which this section is based.

[20] See, for example, George A. Akerlof, William T. Dickens, George L. Perry, *The Macroeconomics of Low Inflation*, Brookings Papers on Economic Activity, Vol. 1996, No. 1 (1996), pp. 1-76. Laurence Ball, *Testimony Before the House Committee on Financial Services,* March 25, 2010.

[21] While proponents of a higher but still moderate inflation target would not deny that there would be higher "shoe leather" costs associated with such a proposal, they would argue that the higher costs would not be great enough to outweigh the benefits.

[22] See, for example, Olivier Blanchard et al., "Rethinking Macroeconomic Policy," International Monetary Fund, *Staff Position Note 10/3*, February 2010.

[23] For more information on recent unconventional monetary actions, see CRS Report RL34427, *Financial Turmoil: Federal Reserve Policy Responses*, by Marc Labonte.

[24] It should be noted that this is not a one-time cost. The costs will be incurred as long as the inflation continues.

[25] Given that the CPI imperfectly measures the "true" rate of inflation, a stable price level or a "true" zero rate of inflation is thought to prevail when the inflation rate as measured by the CPI falls within a range of from 0.5% to 2.0%—this being the possible range of error in the current CPI.

[26] Economists have tried to find the best measure of core inflation according to different criteria. See Timothy Cogley, "A Simple Adaptive Measure of Core Inflation," *Journal of Money, Credit and Banking,* vol. 34, no. 1, February 2002, pp. 94-113; Danny Quah and Shaun P. Vahey, "Measuring Core Inflation," *The Economic Journal,* vol. 105, no. 432, September 1995, pp. 1130-1144; Michael Bryan and Stephen Cecchetti, "Measuring Core Inflation," in N. Gregory Mankiw, ed., *Monetary Policy*, (Chicago: University of Chicago Press, 1994), p. 195; Todd Clark, "Comparing Measures of Core Inflation," Federal Reserve Bank of Kansas City, *Economic Review*, 2002:2, p. 5.

[27] See Robert Rich and Charles Steindel, "A Review of Core Inflation and an Evaluation of Its Measures," Federal Reserve Bank of New York, staff report no. 236, December 2005. This study examines the forecasting power of inflation less food and energy, as well as alternative definitions of core inflation that have been proposed by others, and found that "no core measure does an outstanding job forecasting [headline] CPI inflation...we find no strong evidence to suggest that a selected core measure will be able to retain its usefulness as a tool to forecast inflation for any given period...." Todd Clark, "Comparing Measures of Core Inflation," Federal Reserve Bank of Kansas City, *Economic Review*, 2002:2, p. 5. This study did not find a statistically significant relationship between core inflation and future headline inflation, although the relationship becomes significant when limited to a more recent time period. Michael Bryan and Stephen Cecchetti, "Measuring Core Inflation,"

in N. Gregory Mankiw, ed., *Monetary Policy* (Chicago: University of Chicago Press, 1994), p. 195; and Julie Smith, "Weighted Median Inflation: Is This Core Inflation?" *Journal of Money, Credit, and Banking*, April 2004, vol. 36, no. 2, p. 253. Both of these studies compared the forecasting ability of many measures of inflation, and concluded that headline inflation is a better predictor of future headline inflation than core inflation and weighted median measure of inflation performed best. Frederic Mishkin, "Headline versus Core Inflation in the Conduct of Monetary Policy," speech at the Business Cycles, International Transmission and Macroeconomic Policies Conference, Montreal, Canada, October 20, 2007. This study used the Fed's macro model of the U.S. economy to show that when the Fed reacts to changes in headline inflation instead of core inflation, future inflation will be slightly less volatile, but unemployment will be significantly more volatile.

In: Economic Policies in a Time of Financial Crisis
Editor: Heather D. Perkins

ISBN: 978-1-61122-686-7

Chapter 8

MONETARY POLICY AND THE FEDERAL RESERVE: CURRENT POLICY AND CONDITIONS

Marc Labonte

SUMMARY

The Federal Reserve (Fed) defines monetary policy as the actions it undertakes to influence the availability and cost of money and credit to help promote its congressionally mandated goals, achieving a stable price level and maximum sustainable economic growth. Since the expectations of market participants play an important role in determining prices and growth, monetary policy can also be defined to include the directives, policies, statements, and actions of the Fed that influence how the future is perceived. In addition, the Fed acts as a "lender of last resort" to the nation's financial system, meaning that it ensures its sustainability, solvency, and integrity. This role has become of great importance with the onset of the financial crisis in the summer of 2007.

Traditionally, the Fed has had three means for achieving its goals: open market operations involving the purchase and sale of U.S. Treasury securities, the discount rate charged to banks who borrow from the Fed, and reserve requirements that governed the proportion of deposits that must be held either as vault cash or as a deposit at the Federal Reserve. Historically, open market operations have been the primary means for executing monetary policy. Recently, in response to the financial crisis, direct lending has become important once again and the Fed has created a number of new ways for injecting reserves, credit, and liquidity into the banking system, as well as making loans to firms that are not banks. As financial conditions normalize, the Fed is moving back to a more traditional reliance on open market operations.

The Fed conducts open market operations by setting an interest rate target that it believes will allow it to achieve price stability and maximum sustainable growth. The interest rate targeted is the federal funds rate, the price at which banks buy and sell reserves on an overnight basis. This rate is linked to other short term rates and these, in turn, influence longer term interest rates. Interest rates affect interest-sensitive spending – business capital spending on plant and equipment, household spending on consumer durables, and residential investment.

In the short run, monetary policy can be used to stimulate or slow aggregate spending. While monetary policy is charged with promoting maximum sustainable economic growth, it does so only indirectly in the long run by maintaining a stable price level since the direct effect of monetary policy is primarily on the rate of inflation. A low and stable rate of inflation through the business cycle promotes price transparency and, thereby, sounder economic decisions by households and businesses.

The Fed has frequently changed the federal funds target to match changes in expected economic conditions. Between January 3, 2001, and June 25, 2003, the target rate was reduced to 1% from 6½%. This policy was reversed on June 30, 2004, and in 17 equal increments ending on June 29, 2006, the target rate was raised to 5¼%. No additional changes were made until September 18, 2007, when, in a series of 10 moves, the target was reduced to a range of 0% to 1/4% on December 16, 2008, where it now remains. Since then, the Fed has added liquidity to the financial system beyond what is needed to meet its federal funds target through direct lending and, more recently, purchases of Treasury and government sponsored enterprise (GSE) securities. This practice is sometimes referred to as quantitative easing.

For more information on the Fed's crisis-response actions, see CRS Report RL34427, *Financial Turmoil: Federal Reserve Policy Responses*, by Marc Labonte. Legislative changes to the Fed's duties and authority related to financial regulatory reform can be found in CRS Report R40877, *Financial Regulatory Reform: Systemic Risk and the Federal Reserve*, by Marc Labonte.

INTRODUCTION

The Federal Reserve's (Fed's) responsibilities as the nation's central bank fall into four main categories: monetary policy, ensuring financial stability through the lender of last resort function, supervision of bank holding companies, and providing payment system services to financial firms and the government. This chapter will discuss the first two areas of responsibility.

The Fed defines monetary policy as the actions it undertakes to influence the availability and cost of money and credit to promote the goals mandated by Congress: a stable price level and maximum sustainable economic growth. Since the expectations of households as consumers and businesses as the purchasers of capital goods exert an important influence on the major portion of spending in the United States, and these expectations are influenced in important ways by the actions of the Fed, a broader definition of monetary policy would include the directives, policies, statements, forecasts of the economy, and other actions by the Fed, especially those made by or associated with the chairman of its Board of Governors, the nation's central banker.[1]

In addition, governments have traditionally assigned to a central bank the role of "lender of last resort" to the nation's financial system. This role means that the Federal Reserve is responsible for ensuring the sustainability, solvency, and continued functioning of the nation's financial system as a whole, although this does not necessarily extend to any individual financial institution. Thus, in times of financial stress or crisis, the Fed is responsible for ensuring that financial intermediation does not come to a halt. Historically, Federal Reserve intervention has been limited to the banking system. Indeed, the impetus for the founding of the Fed was an outgrowth of the financial panic of 1907. During its nearly 100 year history, the Federal Reserve has rarely been called upon to perform this role. It is now widely regarded as having failed to perform it during the collapse of the U.S. banking system in the contraction of 1929-1933. However, the financial crisis that began in the summer of 2007 with the bursting of the "housing price bubble," has placed this role front and center. The Fed has responded in the conventional way by making massive additions of reserves available to depository institutions (primarily commercial banks) through the purchase of U.S. Treasury securities and allowing banks to discount large amounts of eligible paper. In addition, it has created a number of additional ways to make credit available to a broader range of financial institutions as well as making loans directly to non-financial firms. These innovations are still evolving and several are authorized only in "unusual and exigent circumstances."[2]

Thus, the Federal Reserve has a monetary policy function and a financial stability function. Its monetary policy function is one of aggregate demand management. The availability and cost of credit are used to manage aggregate demand in such a way as to promote a stable price level and through it maximum sustainable growth. Its second function is as "lender of last resort" to the nation's financial system.

This chapter will examine the traditional execution of monetary policy. The "lender of last resort" role since 2007 is examined in CRS Report RL34427, *Financial Turmoil: Federal Reserve Policy Responses*, by Marc Labonte. Legislative changes to the Fed's duties and authority related to financial regulatory reform can be found in CRS Report R40877, *Financial Regulatory Reform: Systemic Risk and the Federal Reserve*, by Marc Labonte.

How Does the Federal Reserve Execute Monetary Policy?

The Federal Reserve has traditionally relied on three means to conduct monetary policy and they are used to alter the reserves available to depository institutions. These institutions are required to maintain reserves in the form of vault cash (currency) or as a deposit at the Fed against their deposit liabilities, primarily checking, saving, and time (CDs). The size of these reserves places a ceiling on the amount of deposits that financial institutions can have outstanding and deposit liabilities are related to the amount of assets these institutions can acquire. These assets are often called "credit" since they represent loans made to businesses and households, among others.

If the Federal Reserve wishes to expand money and credit, it has three ways to do so. The primary method is called open market operations and it involves the Fed buying and selling existing U.S. Treasury securities (or those that have been already issued and sold to private investors). Should it buy securities, it does so with the equivalent of newly issued currency (Federal Reserve notes). This expands the reserve base and the ability of depository institutions to make loans and expand money and credit. The reverse is true if the Fed decides to sell securities from its portfolio. The Fed can also change reserve requirements, meaning that a given amount of reserves will now support more or less deposits and, in the process, this will affect the lending capability of financial institutions. (This tool is rarely used today.)

Finally, the Fed permits certain depository institutions to borrow from it directly on a temporary basis. That is, these institutions can "discount" at the Fed some of their own assets to provide a temporary means for obtaining reserves. Discounts are usually on an overnight basis. For this privilege they are charged an interest rate called, appropriately, the discount rate. Direct lending, from the discount window and other recently created lending facilities, was negligible until late 2007, but has been an important source of reserves since then.[3]

Because the Fed defines monetary policy as the actions it undertakes to influence the availability and cost of money and credit, this suggests two ways to measure the stance of monetary policy. One is to look at the cost of money and credit as measured by the rate of interest relative to inflation (or inflation projections), while the other is to look at the growth of money and credit itself. Thus, one can look at either interest rates or the growth in the supply of money and credit in coming to a conclusion about the current stance of monetary policy, that is, whether it is expansionary, contractionary, or neutral.

Since the great inflation of the 1970s, most central banks have preferred to formulate monetary policy more in terms of the cost of money and credit rather than on their supply.[4] The Federal Reserve thus conducts monetary policy by focusing on the cost of money and credit as proxied by an interest rate. In particular, it targets a very short term interest rate known as the federal funds rate. This rate is determined in the overnight market for reserves of depository institutions. At the end of a given period, usually a day, depository institutions must calculate how many dollars of reserves they want to hold against their reservable liabilities (deposits).[5] Some institutions may discover a reserve shortage (too few reservable assets relative to those it wants to hold) while others may have had reservable assets in excess of their wants. A market exists in which these reserves can be bought and sold on an overnight basis. The interest rate in this market is called the federal funds rate. It is this rate that the Fed uses as a target for conducting monetary policy. If it wishes to expand money and credit, it will lower the target which encourages more lending activity and, thus, demand in the economy. To support this lower target, the Fed must stand ready to buy more U.S. Treasury securities. Conversely, if it wishes to tighten money and credit, it will raise the target and remove as many reserves from depository institutions as are necessary to accomplish its ends. This will require the sale of treasuries from its portfolio of assets.[6]

The federal funds rate is linked to the interest rates that banks and other financial institutions charge for loans – or the provision of credit. Thus, while the Fed may directly influence only a very short term interest rate, this rate influences other longer term rates. However, this relationship is far from being on a one-to-one basis since the longer term market rates are influenced not only by what the Fed is doing today, but what it is expected to do in the future and what inflation is expected to be in the future. This highlights the importance of expectations in explaining market interest rates. For that reason, there is a growing body of literature that urges the Federal Reserve to be very transparent in explaining what its policy is and will be and making a commitment to adhere to that policy. In fact, the Fed has responded to this literature and is increasingly transparent in explaining its policies and what they are expected to accomplish.

Using market interest rates as an indicator of monetary policy is fraught with danger, however. The interest rate that is essential to decisions made by households and businesses to buy capital goods is what economists call the "real" interest rate. It is often proxied by subtracting from the market interest rate the actual or expected rate of inflation. The real rate is largely independent of the amount of money and credit since over the longer run, it is determined by the interaction of saving and investment (or the demand for capital goods). The internationalization of capital markets means that for most developed countries the relevant saving and investment that determines the real interest rate is on a global basis. Thus, real rates in the United States depend not only on our national saving and investment, but on the saving and investment of other countries as well. For that reason national interest rates will be influenced by international credit conditions and business cycles.

THE IMPORTANCE OF MONETARY POLICY

It has been said the "money matters" and the case for this statement can be made in at least two different contexts. In one, monetary policy is compared with fiscal policy and, given the current international financial system with flexible exchange rates and a high degree of capital mobility between countries, the ability of changes in monetary policy to affect aggregate demand is great compared with fiscal policy. In the other context, changes in monetary policy have the potential to bring about major changes in the growth of GDP and employment only in the *short run.* Most economists do not believe that this holds true over the *longer run.* Over the more extended horizon, monetary policy has its primary effect on the rate of inflation. A brief discussion of the two contexts summarized above follows.

Monetary vs. Fiscal Policy

The standard open economy macroeconomic model makes a compelling case for the relative importance of monetary policy in a world whose financial arrangements involve the use of flexible exchange rates and where capital is highly mobile between countries. To see this, fiscal and monetary expansion will be contrasted.

Allow the full employment budget deficit to rise (or the full-employment surplus to fall) through either a tax rate cut or a rise in appropriated expenditures. While the increase in this budget deficit (or fall in surplus) raises aggregate demand, it also reduces national saving. The fall in the supply of saving relative to domestic investment demand causes domestic interest rates (both real and market) to rise relative to those in other financial centers. The rise in domestic interest rates makes U.S. financial assets more attractive to foreigners. They, in turn, increase the demand for dollars in foreign exchange markets to acquire the wherewithal to purchase U.S. assets. The increased demand for dollars causes the dollar to appreciate. Dollar appreciation then reduces the cost of foreign goods and services to Americans and raises the price of American goods and services to foreigners. As a result, U.S. spending on imports tends to rise and foreign spending on U.S. exports tends to fall. Thus, any expansionary effects on domestic demand from the larger budget deficit tends to be offset in part or total by a reduced foreign trade surplus or a larger foreign trade deficit.[7]

Monetary policy stimulus (as shown by a reduction in the target rate for federal funds) initially serves to lower U.S. interest rates (both real and market) relative to those in other financial centers. Foreign financial assets become more attractive to U.S. investors, the supply of dollars on the foreign exchange markets rises as U.S. investors attempt to acquire foreign currencies to buy foreign assets, and the dollar depreciates. Dollar depreciation then makes foreign goods and services more expensive to Americans and American goods and services cheaper to foreigners. As a result, the United States spends less on imports and foreigners spend more on U.S. exports. A falling foreign trade deficit or rising trade surplus thus reinforces any stimulus to domestic demand that comes from lower U.S. interest rates.

The implication from the standard open economy macroeconomic model is that monetary policy is more powerful than fiscal policy in influencing GDP growth and employment given current international financial arrangements.[8]

Short Run vs. Longer Run

The analysis above suggests that a more expansive monetary policy can cause domestic demand to expand. An examination of U.S. economic history will show that money and credit induced demand expansions can have a positive effect on U.S. GDP growth and total employment. This same history, however, also suggests that over the longer run, a more rapid rate of growth of money and credit is largely dissipated in a more rapid rate of inflation with little if any lasting effect on real GDP and employment.

Economists have two explanations for this paradoxical behavior. First, they note that, in the short run, many economies have an elaborate system of contracts (both implicit and explicit) that makes it difficult in a short period for significant adjustments to take place in wages and prices in response to a more rapid growth of money and credit. Second, they note that expectations for one reason or another are slow to adjust to the longer run consequences of major changes in monetary policy. This slow adjustment also adds rigidities to wages and prices. Because of these rigidities, changes in the growth of money and credit that change aggregate demand can have a large initial effect on output and employment. Over the longer run, as contracts are renegotiated and expectations adjust, wages and prices rise in response to the change in demand and much of the change in output and employment is undone. Thus, monetary policy can matter in the short run but be fairly neutral for GDP growth and employment in the longer run.[9]

It is noteworthy that in societies where high rates of inflation are endemic, the short run may be very short indeed. During the final stages of very rapid inflations, called hyperinflation, the ability of more rapid rates of growth of money and credit to alter GDP growth and employment is virtually nonexistent, if not negative.

The Recent and Current Stance of Monetary Policy

Following the 2001 recession, unemployment continued rising until mid-2003. Fearful that the economy would slip back into recession, the Fed kept the federal funds rate extremely low.[10] The federal funds target reached a low of 1% by mid-2003. As the expansion gathered momentum and prices began to rise, the federal funds target was slowly increased in a series of moves to 5¼% in mid-2006. Short-term interest rates followed and by the end of 2006, the yield curve (the relationship between short- and long-term interest rates) became inverted, with shorter term rates higher than longer term rates. [11]

It is now argued by many economists that the financial crisis was, at least in part, due to Federal Reserve policy to ensure that the then-ongoing expansion continued. In particular, critics now claim that the low short-term rates prevailing from 2001 through 2004 caused an increased demand for housing leading to a "price bubble." The shift in financing housing from fixed to variable rate mortgages made this sector of the economy increasingly vulnerable to movements in short-term interest rates. One consequence of the tightening of monetary policy, critics now claim, was to burst this "price bubble" (a bubble that was also due, in part, to lax lending standards that were subject to regulation by the Fed and others). The net result was the onset of a financial crisis affecting not only depository institutions, but other segments of the financial sector involved with housing finance as the delinquency rates on home mortgages rose to record numbers and the subsequent losses of financial institutions made national headlines. The contagious nature of this development was soon obvious as other types of loans and credit became adversely affected. This, in turn, spilled over into the broader economy as the lack of credit soon had a negative effect on both production and aggregate demand. In December 2007, the economy entered a recession.

As the magnitude of the financial crisis, as well as its international scope, became apparent, the Fed responded to the expected economic slump by reducing the federal funds target and the discount rate. Beginning on September 18, 2007, and ending on December 16, 2008, the target was reduced from 5¼% to a range between 0% and ¼%.

What began to concern the monetary authorities is that liquidity provided to the banking system was not reaching other parts of the financial system. It would appear that the traditional transmission mechanism for monetary policy is not working. To circumvent this problem, the Fed began to employ a little used emergency provision, Section 13(3) of the Federal Reserve Act,[12] that allows it to make loans to other financial institutions and to non-financial firms as well.

The magnitude of direct lending has been large. Total borrowing from the Federal Reserve during November 2007 was $366 million. In mid-November 2008, it reached a high of $725 billion. Direct lending did not fall below $100 billion until March 2009. The worsening of the crisis in September 2008 was accompanied by an unprecedented increase in the reserves of depository institutions. They increased from about $44.6 billion in August 2008 to $167 billion at the end of 2008 to $1,139 billion at the end of 2009. This is clearly not a "business as usual" monetary policy, but something quite extraordinary, sometimes referred to as "quantitative easing." Quantitative easing can be defined as increasing the reserves of the banking system beyond the amount needed to meet the Fed's interest rate target.

With direct lending falling as financial conditions normalize, the Fed found other tools to maintain the current level of liquidity in the financial system. On March 17, 2009, the FOMC announced plans for a massive purchase of agency and Treasury securities in excess of $1.0 trillion to further ease credit market conditions and stimulate spending. (Agency securities are here defined as securities of Fannie Mae, Freddie Mac, and Ginnie Mae.) These purchases were completed by the end of March 2010. Once the economy returns to normal, the task facing the Fed will be to remove this huge amount of credit from the financial system quickly enough to prevent inflation from taking hold.

It should not go unnoticed that a potential complication for the conduct of monetary policy emerges when the federal funds rate is at or near zero, its floor, as it is now. A zero federal funds rate does not constrain the Federal Reserve from supplying additional reserves and liquidity to the financial system, as the Fed is now doing through purchases of Treasury and agency securities. Whether the additional reserves will be lent out, resulting in lower market interest rates and an expansion of new spending, as posited in the text book explanation of how monetary policy works, is another story. Recent experience is not reassuring, as excess bank reserves held at the Fed have remained unusually high.[13]

Congressional Oversight and the Near-Term Goals of Monetary Policy

Congress has delegated monetary policy decisions to the Fed but retains oversight responsibilities. The primary form of congressional oversight of the Federal Reserve is the semiannual hearings with the Senate Committee on Banking, Housing, and Urban Affairs and the House Committee on Financial Services. At these hearings, which take place in February and July, the Fed Chairman presents the Fed's *Monetary Policy Report to the Congress*, testifies, and responds to questions from committee members. These hearings and reporting requirements were established by the Full Employment Act of 1978 (P.L. 95-523, 92 Stat 1897), also known as the Humphrey-Hawkins Act, and renewed in the American Homeownership and Economic Opportunity Act of 2000 (P.L. 106-569).

The semiannual *Monetary Policy Report* presents a review of recent economic and monetary policy developments, as well as economic projections for three years. Since monetary policy plays an important role in determining economic outcomes, these projections can be viewed as the Fed's perceptions of how today's monetary policy stance will influence future economic conditions. To increase the transparency of monetary policy, the Fed in 2007 began to publicly provide additional forecasts. They now appear quarterly.

The Federal Reserve's Mandate and Its Independence

The Constitution grants Congress the power to "coin money, and regulate the value thereof.... " However, operational responsibility for making U.S. monetary policy has been delegated by Congress to the Fed. Congress is still responsible for oversight, setting the Fed's mandate and approving the President's nominations for the Fed's Board of Governors, but several institutional features grant it significant "independence" from the political process.[14] The Federal Reserve system is quasi-public in structure: it is owned by its member banks. The governors are appointed to staggered 14-year terms, and can only be removed by Congress for cause. It is self-funded and does not receive appropriations. While it must follow its congressional mandate, it has been granted broad *discretion* to interpret and carry out that mandate as it sees fit on a day-to-day basis. Most economists argue that good monetary policy depends on independence because it reduces the temptation to raise inflation in the long run in order to lower unemployment in the short run. Researchers have made cross-country comparisons to try to make the case that countries with independent central banks are more likely to have low inflation rates and better economic performance.[15]

As a practical matter, the Fed's mandate can be seen as a further source of political independence by giving it broad policy discretion. The Federal Reserve Act of 1977 (P.L. 95-188, 91 Stat. 1387) charged the Fed with "the goals of maximum employment, stable prices, and moderate long-term interest rates." Note that the Fed controls none of these three indicators directly; it controls only overnight interest rates. Because it has only one instrument at its disposal and three goals, there will be times when the goals will be at odds with each other, and the Fed will have to choose to pursue one at the expense of the other two. Critics have argued that the ambiguity inherent in the current mandate makes for less than optimal transparency and accountability. It may also strengthen political independence if it allows the Fed to deflect congressional criticism by pointing, at any given time, to whatever goal justifies its current policy stance.

The most popular alternative to the current mandate is to replace it with a single mandate of price stability. Under this proposal, the Fed would typically be given (or, under the version mooted by Chairman Bernanke, give itself) a numerical inflation target, and would then be required to set monetary policy with the goal of meeting the target on an ongoing basis.[16] Proponents of inflation targeting say that maximum employment and moderate interest rates are not meaningful policy goals because monetary policy has no long-term influence over either one. They argue a mandate that is focused on keeping inflation low would deliver better economic results and improve transparency and oversight.[17] Opponents, including former Chairman Greenspan, say that the flexibility inherent in the current system has served the United States well in the past 25 years, delivering both low inflation and economic stability, and there is little reason to fix a system that is not broken. They argue that some focus on employment is appropriate given that monetary policy has powerful short-term effects on it, and that too great a focus on inflation could lead to an overly volatile business cycle. Various forms of inflation targeting have been adopted abroad.[18]

Another policy proposal that has gained prominence during the financial crisis is a removal of the statutory restrictions on Government Accountability Office (GAO) audits of the Fed. Currently, GAO cannot audit Fed actions related to monetary policy, including emergency lending activities.[19] Various proposals have been put forth to remove all audit restrictions or audit restrictions related to emergency lending. Another goal of some has been to require the Fed to disclose the identities of borrowers, which are currently kept confidential. Proponents of these proposals cite the need for more information to aid Congress in its oversight duties, while opponents predict that audits would have a negative effect on Fed independence and disclosing borrowers could cause runs on those institutions.[20]

Appendix A. Federal Reserve and the Discount Rate

The Federal Reserve has preferred to conduct monetary policy primarily through its target for the federal funds rate. This method has allowed the Federal Reserve to adopt an activist stance in the conduct of monetary policy. The Board of Governors controls another interest rate, the discount rate. Financial institutions can borrow on a temporary basis directly from the Fed at this rate through the Fed's discount window. The Board can either grant or deny the loan. The initiation of the loan, however, is at the discretion of the borrowing financial institution. In this sense, the Fed is passive in the process. Although the discount rate has long been a tool of central banking, the discount window has not been used much in the United States over the past several decades until market turmoil in 2008 gave it a more prominent role. Financial institutions prefer to borrow overnight in the federal funds market because they can obtain what they need without having to subject their borrowing needs to the purview of the Fed.[21] In conducting monetary policy, the Board has moved the discount rate in sympathy with the federal funds target.

Until 2003, the discount rate was set slightly below the federal funds target, and the Fed used moral suasion to discourage healthy banks from profiting from this low rate. To reduce the need for moral suasion, lending rules were altered in early 2003. Since that time, the discount rate has been set above the federal funds rate target and is now a penalty rate. However, following the financial crisis, the Fed has not discouraged banks in their use of the discount window.

APPENDIX B. FEDERAL RESERVE AND THE MONETARY AGGREGATES

Because the amount of money in circulation is an important determinant of money spending, it might appear to some as curious that the Fed does not target the money supply in the conduct of monetary policy. Such a target has not been popular with the Fed. However, the Fed did define several measures of money (designating them, ultimately, as M1, M2, and M3), published data on them on a monthly basis, and set growth rate ranges for each on a annual basis.

Early on, the Fed encountered problems with its defined measures of money. These monetary aggregates were not stably and predictably related to money spending (in the technical language of the economist, the demand for these measures of money was unstable). Hence, their usefulness as a target for monetary policy was questionable and deemed inferior to using an interest rate target. This the Fed ultimately recognized, and the Fed de-emphasized the importance of the aggregates in the 1990s.[22] In the Monetary Policy Report submitted to Congress on July 20, 2000, the Board of Governors stated:

> At its June meeting, the FOMC did not establish ranges for the growth of money and debt in 2000 and 2001. The legal requirement to establish and to announce such ranges had expired, and owing to uncertainties about the behavior of the velocities of debt and money, these ranges for many years have not provided useful benchmarks for the conduct of monetary policy. Nevertheless, the FOMC believes that the behavior of money and credit will continue to have value for gauging economic and financial conditions....

Even this view of the usefulness of the aggregates changed. The Board of Governors announced in November 2005 that beginning in March 23, 2006, it would no longer publish data on M3. In the words of the Board: "... publication of M3 was judged to be no longer generating sufficient benefit in the analysis of the economy or of the financial sector to justify the costs of publication."[23]

End Notes

[1] For a discussion of the important role played by expectations in formulation and execution of monetary policy, see Santomero, Anthony M. "Great Expectations: The Role of Beliefs in Economics and Monetary Policy." *Business Review,* Federal Reserve Bank of Philadelphia. Second Quarter 2004, pp. 1-6, and Sellon, Gordon H.,

Jr., "Expectations and the Monetary Policy Transmission Mechanism", *Economic Review*. Federal Reserve Bank of Kansas City, Fourth Quarter 2004, pp. 4-42.

[2] For a discussion of the current financial crisis, its origins, and the innovations by the Federal Reserve, see CRS Report RL34730, *Troubled Asset Relief Program: Legislation and Treasury Implementation*, by Baird Webel and Edward V. Murphyand CRS Report RL34427, *Financial Turmoil: Federal Reserve Policy Responses*, by Marc Labonte. For historical perspective on Federal Reserve's dealing in non-government debt, see Wheelock, David C. "Conducting Monetary Policy Without Government Debt: The Fed's Early Years. *Review*, Federal Reserve Bank of St. Louis. May/June 2002, pp. 1-14.

[3] For a more complete discussion of the role of the discount rate in Federal Reserve policy, see **Appendix A**.

[4] For a discussion of why the Federal Reserve does not conduct monetary policy by targeting the monetary aggregates, see **Appendix B**.

[5] Depository institutions are obligated by law to hold some fraction of their deposit liabilities as reserves. In addition, they are also likely to hold additional or excess reserves based on certain risk assessments they make about their portfolios and liabilities. Until very recently these reserves were non-income earning assets. The Fed now pays interest on both types of reserves. It is too early to assess how this shift in policy will affect bank reserve holdings.

[6] For a technical discussion of how this is actually done, see Edwards, Cheryl L., "Open Market Operations in the 1990s," *Federal Reserve Bulletin*, November 1997, pp. 859-872.

[7] It is important to note that this explanation requires the *full employment or structural* budget deficit to rise. Budget deficits produced by a fall in income, or *cyclical* deficits need not produce these results.

[8] It might be thought that this highly stylized account of monetary and fiscal policy is irrelevant to a world whose financial institutions and practices are undergoing rapid change. For a contrary view, see Sellon, Gordon H., Jr., "The Changing U.S. Financial System: Some Implications for the Monetary Transmission Mechanism," *Economic Review*, Federal Reserve Bank of Kansas City, First Quarter 2002, pp. 5-36.

[9] Two interesting papers bearing on what monetary policy can accomplish by two former officials of the Federal Reserve are Santomero, Anthony M. "What Monetary Policy Can and Cannot Do", *Business Review*, Federal Reserve Bank of Philadelphia, First Quarter 2002, pp. 1-4, and Mishkin, Frederic S. "What Should Central Banks Do?, *Review*, Federal Reserve Bank of St. Louis, November/December 2000, pp. 1-14.

[10] Historical and current targets for the federal funds rate can be found at http://www.federalreserve.gov/fomc/fundsrate.htm.

[11] Yield curve inversions pose potentially difficult problems for depository institutions since they squeeze their profitability and possibly undermine their capital structure. The reason for this is that depository institutions generally lend long and borrow short. Thus, their borrowing (their ability to attract and retain deposits which are the source of their funds) costs are very sensitive to movements in short term interest rates. Since they lend long, only a fraction of their assets, their new loans, are affected by movements in longer term rates. Thus, when short term rates rise relative to long term rates, depository institutions find their costs rising sharply as they struggle to retain and attract deposits, while the gross earnings from their assets rise only slowly – the classic case of a profit squeeze. In fact, if losses ensue, they undermine the capital base of these institutions setting in motion the possibility of failure. In any case, an inverted yield curve generally has negative effects on credit creation and is often a leading indicator of an impending economic downturn (see CRS Report RS22371, *The Pattern of Interest Rates: Does It Signal an Impending Recession?*, by Marc Labonte and Gail E. Makinen.

[12] 12 U.S.C. 343.

[13] For a recent discussion of this issue by the president of the Federal Reserve Bank of St. Louis, see Bullard, Thomas. *Effective Monetary Policy in a Low Interest Rate Environment*, The Henry Thornton Lecture, Cass Business School, London (March 24, 2009).

[14] For more information, see CRS Report RL31056, *Economics of Federal Reserve Independence*, by Marc Labonte.

[15] For a review of the research and criticisms, see CRS Report RL31955, *Central Bank Independence and Economic Performance: What Does the Evidence Show?*, by Marc Labonte and Gail E. Makinen.

[16] See CRS Report 98-16, *Should the Federal Reserve Adopt an Inflation Target?*, by Marc Labonte.

[17] In a recent speech, Fed Vice Chairman Donald Kohn reports that the Fed Governors and Reserve Bank presidents continue "to discuss whether an explicit numerical objective for inflation would be beneficial. Under current circumstances, those benefits would include underscoring our understanding that our legislative mandate for promoting price stability encompasses both preventing inflation from falling too low in the near term and from rising too far as the economy recovers." See *Monetary Policy in the Financial Crisis*, a Conference in Honor of Dewey Daane, Nashville, Tennessee, April 18, 2009.

[18] See CRS Report RL31702, *Price Stability (Inflation Targeting) as the Sole Goal of Monetary Policy: The International Experience*, by Marc Labonte and Gail E. Makinen.

[19] Currently, GAO can (and does) audit the Fed's regulatory and payment system duties. S. 896, which was signed into law on May 20, 2009 (P.L. 111-22), allows GAO audits of "any action taken by the Board under ... Section 13(3) of the Federal Reserve Act with respect to a single and specific partnership or corporation." This

would allow GAO audits of the Maiden Lane facilities and the asset guarantees of Citigroup and Bank of America, but would maintain audit restrictions on non-emergency activities and broadly accessed emergency lending facilities.

[20] The current legislative status of these proposals can be found in CRS Report R40877, *Financial Regulatory Reform: Systemic Risk and the Federal Reserve*, by Marc Labonte.

[21] A certain stigma was once attached to using the discount window to obtain reserves. Since banks "borrow" from their depositors to acquire assets, it was thought to be a sign of unsound banking to also borrow from the Federal Reserve.

[22] For a discussion of their usefulness in the conduct of monetary policy, see CRS Report RL31416, *Monetary Aggregates: Their Use in the Conduct of Monetary Policy*, by Marc Labonte; Dotsey, Michael, Carl Lanta, and Lawrence Santucci, "Is Money Useful in the Conduct of Monetary Policy? *Quarterly Review,* Federal Reserve Bank of Richmond, Vol. 86, No. 4 (Fall 2000), pp. 23-48, and Meyer, Laurence H. "The 2001 Homer Jones Memorial Lecture," Washington University, St. Louis, Missouri, March 28, 2001. When this lecture was given, Laurence Meyer was a governor of the Federal Reserve.

[23] *Monetary Policy Report to the Congress*, February 15, 2006, p. 22.

In: Economic Policies in a Time of Financial Crisis
Editor: Heather D. Perkins

ISBN: 978-1-61122-686-7

Chapter 9

ONGOING GOVERNMENT ASSISTANCE FOR AMERICAN INTERNATIONAL GROUP (AIG)

Baird Webel

SUMMARY

In the beginning of 2008, American International Group (AIG) was one of the world's largest insurers, generally considered to be financially sound with an AA credit rating. By the end of the year, it had undergone a near bankruptcy and had been forced to seek up to $173.4 billion in financial assistance from the U.S. government. The CEO had been replaced at the government's behest, executive compensation was under limits, and shareholders in AIG had been nearly wiped out as their equity was diluted by a new 79.9% stake held by the government. The government assistance to AIG has been largely ad hoc. The overarching AIG holding company was regulated by the Office of Thrift Supervision (OTS), but because the company was primarily an insurer, it was largely outside of the normal Federal Reserve (Fed) facilities that lend to thrifts facing liquidity difficulties. AIG was also outside of the normal receivership provisions that apply to banking institutions. Had AIG not been effectively deemed "too big to fail" and given assistance by the government, bankruptcy seemed a near certainty in September 2008.

The losses that led to AIG's essential failure resulted largely from two sources: the state-regulated AIG insurance subsidiaries' securities lending program and the AIG Financial Products (AIGFP) subsidiary, a largely unregulated subsidiary that specialized in financial derivatives. The transactions that led to the immediate losses were dealt with relatively quickly in 2008, albeit with significant outlay of government funds. Although the securities lending program was relatively straightforward to discontinue, the AIGFP derivative operations extended well beyond the transactions that caused the immediate losses and are taking longer to wind down. The overall AIGFP derivative portfolio remains significant, as AIG reported approximately $940.7 billion in notional net value of derivatives at the end of 2009.

The government assistance to AIG began with an $85 billion loan from the Fed in September 2008. This loan was on relatively onerous terms with a high interest rate and required a handover of 79.9% of the equity in AIG to the government. As AIG's financial position weakened, several rounds of additional funding were provided to AIG and the terms were loosened to some degree. The current major restructuring of the assistance to AIG was announced in March 2009 and comprises (1) $47.3 billion (of up to $68.8 billion) in capital injections through preferred share purchases by the Treasury; (2) $25.3 billion (of up to $35 billion) in extraordinary loans from the Fed; (3) $24.8 billion in Fed loans retired by equity interests provided to the government by AIG; (4) $2.3 billion in Fed loans through the Commercial Paper Funding Facility; and (5) $43.8 billion (of up to $52.5 billion) in Fed loans for troubled asset purchases—assets that are now owned by the government.

Congress has held several hearings specifically focusing on the intervention in AIG. Congressional attention and anger has been focused on perceived corporate profligacy, particularly bonuses for AIG employees. Bills that would place specific taxes on or otherwise restrict such bonuses include H.R. 1586, passed by the House on March 19, 2009; S. 651, introduced on the same day; and H.R. 1664, passed by the House on April 1, 2009.

The future of AIG and the ultimate government cost of the intervention are unclear. Recently announced asset sales by AIG may repay all of the Fed loans, but this would leave the Troubled Asset Relief Program (TARP) preferred shares outstanding. Recent estimates of the losses on the TARP funding range from $9 billion to $49 billion.

INTRODUCTION

In 2007, American International Group (AIG) was the fifth-largest insurer in the world with $110 billion overall revenues. In the United States, it ranked second in property/casualty insurance premiums ($37.7 billion/7.5% market share) and first in life insurance premiums ($53.0 billion/8.9%). For particular lines, AIG ranked first in surplus lines, ninth in private passenger auto, first in overall commercial lines (fifth in commercial auto), and fourth in mortgage guaranty. It was outside the top 10 in homeowners insurance.[1] According to the National Association of Insurance Commissioners, AIG had more than 70 state-regulated insurance subsidiaries in the United States, with more than 175 non-insurance or foreign entities under the general holding company.

Although AIG is generally identified as an insurance company, the parent entity of the various subsidiaries is a thrift holding company and thus falls under the general supervision of the Office of Thrift Supervision (OTS). The individual regulation of the subsidiaries is done according to the function of that subsidiary—for example, insurance subsidiaries are regulated by state insurance regulators, and bank subsidiaries are regulated by the appropriate banking regulator. This functional regulatory structure was enacted in the Gramm-Leach-Bliley Act of 1999.[2]

In the fall of 2008, facing losses on various operations, AIG experienced a significant decline in its stock price and downgrades from the major credit rating agencies.[3] These downgrades led to immediate demands for significant amounts of collateral (approximately $14 billion to $15 billion in collateral payments, according to contemporary press reports).[4] As financial demands on the company mounted, bankruptcy appeared a possibility, as occurred with Lehman Brothers. Fears about the spillover effects from such a failure brought calls for government action to avert such a failure. Many feared that AIG was "too big to fail"[5] due to the potential for widespread disruption to financial markets resulting from such a failure. The New York Insurance Superintendent, primary regulator of many of the AIG insurance subsidiaries, led an effort to allow access by the parent holding company and other subsidiaries of up to $20 billion in cash from AIG's insurance subsidiaries, which were perceived as solvent and relatively liquid. Ultimately, this transfer did not take place; instead, the Federal Reserve (Fed) approved an up to $85 billion loan in September 2008, as detailed below.

CURRENT STATUS OF GOVERNMENT ASSISTANCE TO AIG

As AIG's financial position weakened after September, several rounds of additional funding were provided to AIG and the terms were loosened to some degree (see "Forms of Assistance for AIG" below for more complete discussion of the changes to AIG's assistance). The latest major restructuring of the assistance to AIG was announced in March 2009. As currently structured, the assistance to AIG comprises

- $47.5 billion (of up to $68.8 billion) in capital injections through preferred share purchases by the Treasury's Troubled Asset Relief Program (TARP);[6]
- $24.8 billion (of up to $35 billion) in extraordinary loans from the Fed;[7]
- $25 billion in Fed loans retired by equity interests in AIG subsidiaries AIA Group Limited (AIA) and American Life Insurance Company (ALICO);[8]
- $2.3 billion in Fed loans through the Commercial Paper Funding Facility (CPFF);[9] and
- $43.8 billion (of up to $52.5 billion) in Fed loans for troubled asset purchases—assets that are now owned by the government.[10]

On March 1, 2010, AIG announced that an agreement had been reached to sell AIA to the Prudential PLC[11] for approximately $35.5 billion, which includes $25 billion in cash and $10.5 billion in securities. Assuming completion of this sale, the Fed would receive approximately $16 billion immediately because of its previous equity stake in AIA. AIG indicated that the remaining $9 billion in cash and the ultimate proceeds of the securities would be used to pay down some of the outstanding loan from the Fed.[12]

On March 8, 2010, AIG announced that an agreement had been reached to sell ALICO to MetLife for approximately $15.5 billion, including $6.8 billion in cash and $8.7 billion in securities. Assuming completion of this sale, the Fed would likely receive all of the cash as well as an additional $2.2 billion in securities because of its previous $9 billion equity stake in ALICO. The remaining securities would be sold over time with the proceeds being used to pay down a portion of the outstanding loan from the Fed.[13]

These announced asset sales will likely take several months to complete and will not be reflected in the announced totals from government assistance to AIG until completion. A summary of current amounts outstanding is presented in Table 1.

Table 1. Summary of Assistance to AIG

Program	Maximum Amount of Current Government Assistance	Latest Reported Amount Outstanding	Recompense to the Government/Value of Current Holdings
TARP Share Purchase	$69.8 billion	$47.5 billion (Feb. 28, 2010)	10% dividend; warrants for 2% of AIG equity
Federal Reserve Loan	$35 billion	$24.8 billion (Mar. 10, 2010)	3 month LIBOR+3%; 77.9% of AIG equity
Retired Federal Reserve Loan	$25 billion	$25.3 billion (Mar. 10, 2010)	$25.3 billion
Commercial Paper Funding Facility	$2.3 billion	$2.3 billion (Feb. 17, 2010) $15.3 billion	three-month overnight index swap (OIS) rate+1%; OIS+3% $15.6 billion
Maiden Lane II	$19.5 billion	(Mar. 10, 2010) $17.3 billion	(Dec. 31, 2009) $22.4 billion
Maiden Lane III	$24.3 billion	(Mar. 10, 2010)	(Dec. 31, 2009)

Source: Federal Reserve, U.S. Treasury, AIG 10-Q and 10-K Statements.

Notes: Dividend paid on shares under TARP is subject to the AIG board approval. Outstanding amounts for Federal Reserve loans and LLCs include interest and dividends due. The loan amounts to Maiden Lane II and III are from these entities to the Fed, and are not to be repaid by AIG.

ULTIMATE COST OF ASSISTANCE TO AIG?

Because the assistance to AIG has come in the form of asset purchases and loans, which have resulted in equity stakes in AIG, the ultimate cost to the government of the AIG rescue will depend critically on the future value of these assets. The Federal Reserve assistance to AIG appears to be on track to be repaid without loss to the Fed. If the sales of ALICO and AIA go through as currently reported, the proceeds of these sales would be approximately enough to repay the extraordinary loans made by the Fed. The current estimated values of the Maiden Lane II and III LLCs are also approximately sufficient to repay the loans to the Fed, and the CPFF amount has been dropping and will be repaid shortly, as the program's term has expired.

If the Fed loans are indeed repaid, the ultimate cost of the intervention in AIG would largely be determined by the outcome of the outstanding assistance under TARP, currently approximately $45.3 billion, and the value of the approximately 80% equity interest in the company held by the government. Current estimates of the value of the TARP preferred shares are for significant losses on these instruments, although precise values vary significantly. As of September 30, 2009, the Treasury estimated that the value of its holdings of TARP preferred shares was only $13.2 billion on the then-outstanding balance of $43.2 billion. In January 2010, the Congressional Budget Office estimated a net cost of $9 billion for the TARP assistance to AIG, whereas the Office of Management and Budget estimated a net cost of $49.9 billion.

The value of the government common equity interests in AIG is equally uncertain. As of March 5, 2009, the market value of the shares being traded on the open market was approximately $3.8 billion. If the approximately 80% of the company held by the government is valued equally to the 20% that is trading, the government's common equity interests would be worth approximately $15 billion. It should be noted that a government move to sell its equity interest would likely have a significant impact on AIG's share price.

LEGAL AUTHORITY FOR ASSISTANCE TO AIG

According to the Fed, its assistance to AIG is authorized under Section 13(3) of the Federal Reserve Act,[14] the same emergency authorization used for numerous other Fed actions in the ongoing financial crisis. This emergency authorization was needed because the Federal Reserve cannot normally lend to a financial firm that is neither a depository institution nor a primary dealer. Following amendments passed in 2008, the Fed is required to report on emergency loans under Section 13(3).[15]

Treasury assistance to AIG has occurred under Section 101 of the Emergency Economic Stabilization Act (EESA),[16] which authorizes the purchase of "troubled assets" by the Treasury. Part (B) of the act's definition of "troubled assets" defines such assets as "any other financial instrument that the Secretary, after consultation with the Chairman of the Board of Governors of the Federal Reserve System, determines the purchase of which is necessary to promote financial market stability." Treasury is required to report on its transactions under the EESA.[17]

SOURCES OF AIG LOSSES

AIG, as most financial institutions, suffered losses on a wide variety of financial instruments because of the widespread market downturn. The exceptional losses resulting in essential failure of AIG arose primarily from two sources: the derivative activities of the AIG Financial Products (AIGFP) subsidiary and the securities lending activities managed by AIG Investments with securities largely from the AIG insurance subsidiaries.

AIG Financial Products

The AIGFP subsidiary is headquartered in Connecticut with major operations in London. According to AIG's website, it was "founded in 1987 as one of the first companies in the United States focused principally on OTC [over the counter] derivatives markets."[18] In recent years, AIGFP began writing credit default swaps (CDS), particularly on mortgage-related securities. CDS can act essentially as insurance policies on securities, typically requiring the company selling the CDS to pay off the claims on these CDS if there is a default or specified credit event involving the security.[19] AIGFP's portfolio of CDS at the end of 2007 had a notional value of approximately $500 billion, including around $60 billion in CDS on securities linked to subprime loans. By August of 2008, approximately 64% of the subprime-linked securities backed by AIG had been downgraded and six were in default.[20]

As over-the-counter derivatives, CDS can take any form desired by the two parties writing the contracts in question. In typical CDS contracts, collateral requirements are placed on CDS sellers such that, even before default occurs, the seller may be required to post cash collateral as either the seller's financial condition weakens or the likelihood of default increases. AIG was forced to post increasing collateral on the CDS written by AIGFP. These collateral calls were an important factor driving the need for a rescue in September 2008, and a primary motivation for the Fed's creation of the Maiden Lane III Limited Liability Corporation (LLC) in the November 2008 restructuring of the AIG intervention (see "Collateralized Debt Obligations/Maiden Lane III" below for more details on these interventions).

AIG Securities Lending Program

Securities lending is a not uncommon practice where the holder of a security agrees to lend a security to another party.[21] Such transactions are, like CDS, done over the counter rather than on exchanges, and thus can take almost any form desired by the two parties. Typically, the borrower of the security provides some form of collateral, often cash, which the lender invests to further profit from the transaction. The timing aspects of the transactions, such as when and how loaned securities are returned, are up to the contract specifics negotiated by the two parties.

Although managed centrally by AIG Investments, the securities used in AIG's securities lending originated primarily from its state-regulated insurance subsidiaries. As of June 30, 2008, 71% of the loaned securities came from AIG's U.S. life insurers and retirement services and 4% came from AIG's U.S. property/casualty insurers. In return for lending securities, AIG typically received cash collateral worth between 100% and 102% of the loaned securities and then invested this cash until the loaned securities were returned, at which point the cash collateral was to be returned. In mid-2008, AIG's total liability for the return of securities lending collateral equaled $75.1 billion. The market value of the investments made by AIG with this collateral (largely in mortgage-backed securities) totaled only $59.5 billion.[22] As AIG suffered downgrades and increased market skepticism during the fall of 2008, increasing numbers of AIG's counterparties in securities lending agreements returned the original securities and expected the return of their cash collateral. This demand for cash led to the Securities Borrowing Facility, announced by the Fed on October 8, 2008, and the creation of the Maiden Lane II LLC in November 2008, as detailed below in "Residential Mortgage-Backed Securities/Maiden Lane II."

FORMS OF ASSISTANCE FOR AIG

Initial Loan

On September 16, 2008, the Fed announced, after consultation with the Treasury Department, that it would lend up to $85 billion to AIG over the next two years. Drawing from the loan facility would only occur at the discretion of the Fed. A new CEO was installed after the initial intervention and Fed staff was put on site with the company to oversee operations. The interest rate on the funds drawn from the Fed was 8.5 percentage points above the London Interbank Offered Rate (LIBOR), a rate that banks charge to lend to each other. AIG also had to pay a flat 8.5% interest rate on any funds that it is does not draw from the facility. The government received warrants that, if exercised, would give the government a 79.9% ownership stake in AIG. Three independent trustees were to be named by the Fed to oversee the firm for the duration of the loan. The trustees for the AIG Credit Trust were announced on January 16, 2009.[23]

This lending facility (and its successors) is secured by the assets of AIG's holding company and non-regulated subsidiaries.[24] In other words, the Fed could seize AIG's assets if AIG fails to honor the terms of the loan. This reduces the risk that the Fed and the taxpayers would suffer a loss. The risk still remains that if AIG turns out to be insolvent, its assets may be insufficient to cover the amount it had borrowed from the Fed.[25]

On September 18, the Fed announced that it had initially lent $28 billion of the $85 billion possible. This amount grew to approximately $61 billion on November 5, shortly before the restructuring of the loan discussed below in "Loan Restructuring."[26]

Securities Borrowing Facility[27]

On October 8, the Fed announced that it was expanding its assistance to AIG by swapping cash for up to $37.8 billion of AIG's investment-grade, fixed-income securities. These securities stemmed from the AIG securities lending program (described above). As some counterparties stopped participating in the lending program, AIG was forced to incur losses on its securities lending investments.[28] AIG needed liquidity from the Fed to cover these losses and counterparty withdrawals. This lending facility was to extend for nearly two years, until September 16, 2010, and advances from the securities borrowing facility to AIG paid an interest rate of 1% over the average overnight repo rate. As of November 5, 2008, $19.9 billion of the $37.8 billion remained outstanding.

Although this assistance resembles a typical collateralized loan (the Fed receives assets as collateral, and the borrower receives cash), the Fed characterized the agreement as a loan of securities from AIG to the Fed in exchange for cash collateral. It appears the arrangement was structured this way because New York insurance law prevents AIG from using the securities as collateral in a loan.[29]

Commercial Paper Funding Facility

The Commercial Paper Funding Facility (CPFF) was initially announced by the Fed on October 7, 2008, as a measure to restore liquidity in the commercial paper market. Through the CPFF, the Fed purchases both asset-backed and unsecured commercial paper. Rather than charging an interest rate, the Fed purchases the paper at a discount based on the three-month overnight index swap rate. Unsecured paper is discounted by 3%, whereas secured paper is discounted by 1%. Individual participants in this facility and the amounts accessed are not announced by the Fed.

AIG itself announced that, as of November 5, 2008, it had been authorized to issue up to $20.9 billion of commercial paper to the CPFF and had actually issued approximately $15.3 billion of this amount. Subsequent downgrades of AIG's airline leasing subsidiary (ILFC) reduced the maximum amount AIG could access from the CPFF to $15.2 billion in early January 2009. ILFC had approximately $1.7 billion outstanding to the CPFF when it was downgraded; this amount was repaid by January 28, 2009. As of February 17, 2010, the reported total outstanding was $2.3 billion.[30] CPFF purchase of commercial paper expired February 1, 2010, with maximum maturities extending 90 days from this point. Thus, all AIG borrowing from the CPFF must be repaid by April 30, 2010.

November 10, 2008, Revision of Assistance to AIG

On November 10, 2008, the Federal Reserve and the U.S. Treasury announced a restructuring of the federal intervention to support AIG. Following the initial loan, some, notably AIG's former CEO Maurice Greenberg, criticized the terms as overly harsh, arguing that the loan itself might be contributing to AIG's eventual failure as a company. As evidenced by the additional borrowing after the September 16 loan, AIG had continued to see cash flow out of the company. The revised agreement points to a fundamental trade-off between making the terms of the assistance undesirable enough to deter other firms from seeking government assistance and making the terms of assistance so punitive that they exacerbate the financial problems of the recipient firm. It also points to the risk that once a firm has been identified as too big to fail, government assistance to the firm can become open-ended, as the original amounts offered were quickly revised upward.

The revised agreement eased the payment terms for AIG and had three primary parts: (1) restructuring of the initial $85 billion loan, (2) a $40 billion direct capital injection, and (3) up to $52.5 billion purchases of troubled assets. Specific details follow. Separately, AIG continued to access the Fed commercial paper funding facility as described above.

Loan Restructuring

The Fed reduced the $85 billion loan facility to $60 billion, extended the time period to five years, and eased the financial terms considerably. Specifically, the interest rate on the amount outstanding was reduced by 5.5 percentage points (to LIBOR plus 3%), and the fee on undrawn funds was reduced by 7.75 percentage points (to 0.75%).

Troubled Asset Relief Program Direct Capital Injection

Through the Troubled Asset Relief Program (TARP), the Treasury purchased $40 billion in preferred shares of AIG. In addition to the preferred shares, the Treasury also received warrants for common shares equal to 2% of the outstanding AIG shares. AIG was the first announced non-bank to receive TARP funds. The $40 billion in preferred AIG shares held by the Treasury were slated to pay a 10% dividend per annum, accrued quarterly.[31] The amount of shares held in trust for the benefit of the U.S. Treasury under the previous Fed loan was also reduced to 77.9% so that the total government equity interest in AIG (trust shares plus warrants) remained 79.9% after the TARP intervention.

Executive Compensation Restrictions under TARP

By accepting TARP assistance, AIG is subject to the executive compensation standards for their senior executive officers (SEOs, generally the chief executive officer, the chief financial, and the three next most highly compensated officials) generally required under Section 111 of EESA. In addition to these general restrictions, Treasury imposed additional executive compensation restrictions on AIG that are more stringent than for other participants in TARP in recognition of the special assistance received by AIG.[32]

The TARP executive compensation restrictions were amended and strengthened by the 111th Congress in the American Recovery and Reinvestment Act of 2009,[33] which amended Section 111 of EESA to further limit executive compensation for financial institutions receiving assistance under that act, including AIG. Among other things, for applicable companies, the new language requires the adoption of standards by Treasury that

1. prohibit paying certain executives any bonus, retention or incentive compensation other than certain long-term restricted stock that has a value not greater than one-third of the total annual compensation of the employee receiving the stock (the determination of how many executives will be subject to these limitations depends on the amount of funds received by the TARP recipient);
2. require the recovery of any bonus, retention award or incentive compensation paid to SEOs and the next 20 most highly compensated employees based on earnings, revenues, gains or other criteria that are later found to be materially inaccurate;
3. prohibit any compensation plan that would encourage manipulation of the reported earnings of the firm to enhance the compensation of any of its employees;
4. prohibit the provision of "golden parachute" payment to an SEO and the next five most highly compensated employees for departure from a company for any reason, except for payments for services performed or benefits accrued; and
5. prohibit any compensation plan that would encourage manipulation of the reported earnings of the firm to enhance the compensation of any of its employees.

Although the new Section 111 (b)(1) of the amended EESA indicates that these standards are to apply to all TARP recipients until they repay TARP funding, later language (Section 111(b)(3)(iii)) specifically allows bonuses required to be paid under employment contracts executed before February 11, 2009, to go forward notwithstanding the new requirements. Treasury published an interim final rule implementing these requirements in June 2009 and the Special Master for TARP Executive Compensation released several specific determinations for AIG compensation.[34]

Purchase of Troubled Assets

Although P.L. 110-343 provided for Treasury purchase of troubled assets under TARP, the troubled asset purchases related to AIG were done by LLCs created and controlled by the Federal Reserve. This structure is similar to that created by the Fed to facilitate the purchase of Bear Stearns by JPMorgan Chase in March 2008. There are two LLCs set up for AIG—Maiden Lane II for residential mortgage-backed securities (RMBS) and Maiden Lane III for collateralized debt obligations (CDO).[35]

Residential Mortgage-Backed Securities/Maiden Lane II

Under the November 2008 restructuring, the RMBS LLC/Maiden Lane II could receive loans up to $22.5 billion by the Fed and $1 billion from AIG to purchase RMBS from AIG's securities lending portfolio. The previous $37.8 billion securities lending loan facility was repaid and terminated following the creation of this LLC. The Fed is credited with interest from its loan at a rate of LIBOR plus 1% for a term of six years, extendable by the Fed. The $1 billion loan from AIG is credited with interest at a rate of LIBOR plus 3%. The AIG loan, however, is subordinate to the Fed's. Any proceeds from Maiden Lane II are to be distributed in the following order: (1) operating expenses of the LLC, (2) principal due to the Fed, (3) interest due to the Fed, and (4) deferred payment and interest due to AIG. Should additional funds remain at the liquidation of the LLC, these remaining funds are to be shared by the Fed and AIG with AIG's insurance subsidiaries receiving one-sixth of the value.

The actual amount of Fed loan made to Maiden Lane II was $19.5 billion of the $22.5 billion maximum. Maiden Lane II purchased RMBS with this amount along with the $1 billion loan from AIG. The securities purchased had a face value of nearly double the purchase price ($39.3 billion).[36] As of February 24, 2010, outstanding loan principal plus interest owed to the Fed was $15.5 billion; the reported market value of the RMBS portfolio holdings was $15.5 billion as of December 31, 2009.[37]

Collateralized Debt Obligations/Maiden Lane III

Under the November 2008 restructuring, the CDO LLC/Maiden Lane III could receive loans up to $30 billion from the Fed and $5 billion from AIG to purchase CDOs on which AIG has written credit default swaps. The Fed and AIG are to be credited with interest from the loans at a rate of LIBOR plus 3% until the LLC is ultimately liquidated. The proceeds from Maiden Lane III are to be distributed in the following order: (1) operating expenses of the LLC, (2) principal due to the Fed, (3) interest due to the Fed, and (4) deferred payment and interest due to AIG. Should any funds remain after this distribution, they are to go two-thirds to the Fed and one-third to AIG.

The actual amount of the Fed loan to Maiden Lane III was $24.3 billion of the $30 billion maximum, while AIG loaned the LLC $5 billion. In addition to these loans, Maiden Lane III purchase of CDOs was also funded by approximately $35 billion in cash collateral previously posted to holders of CDS by AIGFP. In return for the use of this collateral, AIGFP received approximately $2.5 billion from the LLC. The total par value of CDOs purchased by Maiden Lane III was approximately $62.1 billion. At the same time that the CDOs were purchased, the CDS written on these CDOs were terminated, relieving financial pressure on AIG. The outstanding loan principal plus interest owed to the Fed was $17.7 billion as of February 24, 2010, whereas the reported market value of the CDO portfolio holdings was $22.4 billion as of December 31, 2009.[38]

March 2, 2009, Revision of Assistance to AIG

On March 2, 2009, the Treasury and Fed announced another revision of the financial assistance to AIG. On the same day, AIG announced a loss of more than $60 billion in the fourth quarter of 2008. In response to the poor results and ongoing financial turmoil, the ratings agencies were reportedly considering further downgrading AIG, which would most likely have resulted in further significant cash demands due to collateral calls.[39] According to the Treasury, AIG "continues to face significant challenges, driven by the rapid deterioration in certain financial markets in the last two months of the year and continued turbulence in the markets generally." The revised assistance is intended to "enhance the company's capital and liquidity in order to facilitate the orderly completion of the company's global divestiture program."[40]

The announced revised assistance includes the following:

- Exchange of the previous $40 billion in preferred shares purchased through the TARP program for $41.6 billion in preferred shares that more closely resemble common equity, thus improving AIG's financial position. Dividends paid on these new shares remain at 10%, but will be non-cumulative and only be paid as declared by AIG's Board of Directors. Should dividends not be paid for four consecutive quarters, the government would have the right to appoint at least two new directors to the board.
- Commitment of up to $29.8 billion[41] in additional preferred share purchases from TARP. When these share purchases may occur are at the discretion of AIG.
- Reduction of interest rate on the existing Fed loan facility by removing the current floor of 3.5% over the LIBOR portion of the rate. The rate will now simply be three-month LIBOR plus 3%, which was approximately 4.25% at the time.
- Limit on Fed revolving credit facility is to be reduced from $60 billion to as low as $25 billion.
- Up to $34.5 billion of the approximately $38 billion outstanding on the Fed credit facility is to be repaid by asset transfers from AIG to the Fed. Specifically, (1) $8.5 billion in ongoing life insurance cash flows will be securitized by AIG and transferred to the Fed; and (2) approximately $26 billion in equity interests in two of AIG's large foreign life insurance subsidiaries (ALICO and AIA) will be issued to the Fed. This effectively transfers a majority stake in these companies to the Fed, but the companies will still be managed by AIG.

A $25 billion repayment of the Fed loan through the transfer of equity interest worth $16 billion in AIA and $9 billion in ALICO was completed on December 1, 2009, with a corresponding reduction in the Fed loan maximum to $35 billion. According to AIG's 2009 annual 10-K filing with the SEC, the repayment through securitization of life insurance cash flows is no longer expected to occur.

WHO HAS BENEFITED FROM ASSISTANCE TO AIG?

Although billions of dollars in government assistance have gone to the AIG, in many cases, it can be argued that AIG has essentially acted as an intermediary for this assistance. In short order after drawing on government assistance, substantial funds flowed out of AIG to entities on the other side of AIG's financial transactions, such as securities lending or credit default swaps. If AIG had been allowed to fail and had entered bankruptcy, as was the case with Lehman Brothers, then these counterparties in many cases would have been treated as unsecured creditors and may have received relatively little for their claims.

Seen from this view, the true beneficiary of many of the federal funds that flowed to AIG was not AIG itself, but these counterparties. In the interest of transparency, many argued that these counterparties need to be identified, so that both Congress and taxpayers can judge the efficacy and fairness of the assistance to AIG. Until March 15, 2009, no such list of counterparties had been published by the Fed or AIG. Several Senators pressed Donald Kohn, the vice chairman of the Board of Governors of the Federal Reserve, on this point in a March 5, 2009, Senate hearing on AIG. Vice Chairman Kohn, however, expressed his judgment that "giving the names would undermine the stability of the company and could have serious knock-on effects to the rest of the financial markets and the government's efforts to stabilize them."[42] Ten days following the Senate hearing, on March 15, 2009, AIG released information detailing $52.0 billion of direct support to AIG that went to AIGFP related transactions, $27.1 billion in Maiden Lane III CDS-related transactions, and $43.7 billion in payments to securities lending counterparties.[43]

Questions about transparency and disclosure were brought forward again late in 2009 and early in 2010, particularly regarding the actions of the Federal Reserve Bank of New York, whose president was then Timothy Geithner, who is now the U.S. Treasury Secretary, relating to AIG SEC filings regarding the creation of the Maiden Lane entities. According to reports, staff at the Fed discouraged AIG from including details such as 100% payments to counterparties and the identification of counterparties in SEC filings in late 2008. During the subsequent months, AIG amended its SEC filings several times in response to the agency's request for more disclosure. Later, AIG asked the SEC to grant confidential treatment to the filings that would exclude them from public disclosure. On May 22, 2008, after a staff ruling that the filings met the necessary standard of "commercially sensitive information"—the SEC granted the AIG filings confidential treatment through November 25, 2018.[44] Several Members of Congress have raised questions about the Fed's intervention in the AIG disclosures and the House Committee on Government Reform and Oversight focused on this question in a hearing on January 27, 2010. Following this hearing, the information that had been granted confidential treatment was released publicly by Representative Darryl Issa.[45]

CONGRESSIONAL ACTION

Hearings

Congressional committees, including the House Oversight and Reform Committee, the House Financial Services Committee, and the Senate Banking, Housing, and Urban Affairs Committee, have held several hearings on AIG. Congressional attention (and anger) toward AIG has been focused on concerns regarding possible waste of taxpayer money through corporate profligacy and payment of employee bonuses. Transparency regarding the intervention and the ultimate future of AIG have also been of significant concern.

Table 2. Congressional Hearings Focusing on AIG

Date	Title	Committee
October 7, 2008	The Causes and Effects of the AIG Bailout	House Oversight and Government Reform
March 5, 2009	American International Group: Examining what went wrong, government intervention, and implications for future regulation	Senate Banking, Housing & Urban Affairs
March 18, 2009	American International Group's Impact on the Global Economy: Before, During, and After Federal Intervention	House Financial Services
March 24, 2009	Oversight of the Federal Government's Intervention at American International Group	House Financial Services
April 2, 2009	The Collapse and Federal Rescue of AIG and What it Means for the U.S. Economy	House Oversight and Government Reform
May 15, 2009	AIG: Where is the Taxpayer Money Going?	House Oversight and Government Reform
October 14, 2009	AIG Bonuses: Report of the Special Inspector General for the Troubled Asset Relief Program	House Oversight and Government Reform
January 27, 2010	The Federal Bailout of AIG	House Oversight and Government Reform

Source: CRS.

Legislation

Legislation regarding AIG has focused on issues surrounding executive compensation including the following:

H.R. 1586

This bill, "[t]o impose an additional tax on bonuses received from certain TARP recipients," was introduced by Representative Charles Rangel on March 18, 2009. It has been widely portrayed as responding to an outpouring of anger over the AIG bonuses. The House passed H.R. 1586 under suspension of the rules by a vote of 328-93 on March 19, 2009.

The bill would institute a tax of 90% on bonuses given by companies who have more than $5 billion in outstanding funding from TARP. In addition to AIG, several other companies would fall under this definition, including Bank of America, Citigroup, Goldman Sachs, JPMorgan Chase, Morgan Stanley, Wells Fargo, U.S. Bancorp, and General Motors. The bill also specifically included Fannie Mae and Freddie Mac by name. The 90% tax rate would only apply to bonus recipients with a household income greater than $250,000 for singles or married couples filing jointly or $125,000 for a married person filing separately.

H.Con.Res. 76

This Sense of the Congress resolution regarding "executive and employee bonuses paid by AIG and other companies assisted with taxpayer funds" was introduced March 19, 2009. It was brought up the same day under suspension of the rules, but failed to gain a two-thirds majority on a vote of 255-140.

S. 651

The Compensation Fairness Act of 2009 was introduced on March 19, 2009. It was placed on the legislative calendar but has not been acted on by the full Senate.

This bill would impose an excise tax of 35% on both the employee and the employer should "excessive" bonuses be paid out by recipients of federal economic assistance. Any retention bonus would be considered excessive, while non-retention bonuses would be excessive if they exceeded $50,000 with an exception for equity-based bonuses with a vesting period of at least three years. It would also apply a $1 million limit on nonqualified deferred compensation. These provisions would apply to Fannie Mae and Freddie Mac specifically, as well as to any recipient of federal assistance with more than $100 million of assistance outstanding.

H.R. 1664

This bill "[t]o amend the executive compensation provisions of the Emergency Economic Stabilization Act of 2008 to prohibit unreasonable and excessive compensation and compensation not based on performance standards," was introduced on March 23, 2009. It was amended and passed by the House on April 1, 2009, on a vote of 241-171.

As passed, it would prohibit institutions with outstanding capital obligations from TARP, as well as Fannie Mae, Freddie Mac, and the Federal Home Loan Banks, from making a compensation payment (other than a longevity bonus or a payment in the form of restricted stock) to any employee under an existing or new compensation arrangement, if (1) it provides for compensation that is "unreasonable or excessive," or (2) it results in any bonus or supplemental payment that is not directly based on performance. Defining both "unreasonable and excessive" and allowable performance-based measures would be done by the Treasury Secretary, with the approval of the agencies that make up the Federal Financial Institutions Examination Council, and in consultation with the chairperson of the Congressional Oversight Panel.

H.Res. 251

This resolution would direct the Secretary of the Treasury to transmit specified information regarding AIG to the House. It was introduced on March 17, 2009, and marked up on March 25, 2009, by the House Financial Services Committee. Although placed on the House Calendar when reported on April 23, 2009, it has not been considered by the full House.

H.Res. 251 would direct the Secretary to transmit information regarding (1) negotiations on possible break-up of AIG, (2) negotiations regarding additional TARP assistance, or (3) communications or authorization for payment of executive bonuses by AIG.

End Notes

[1] Statistics from *The I.I.I. Insurance Fact Book 2009*, (New York: Insurance Information Institute, 2009).

[2] P.L. 106-102, 113 Stat. 1338.

[3] In 2005, amid accounting irregularities that ultimately led to the resignation of then-CEO Maurice Greenberg, AIG was downgraded by S&P from AAA to AA+. Further downgrades followed in June 2005 and May 2008. In September 2008, S&P downgraded AIG to A-.

[4] See, for example, "U.S. to Take Over AIG in $85 Billion Bailout; Central Banks Inject Cash as Credit Dries Up," *Wall Street Journal*, September 17, 2008, pp. A1-A6.

[5] Institutions that are too big to fail are ones that are deemed to be big enough that their failure could create systemic risk, the risk that the financial system as a whole would cease to function smoothly. See CRS Report R40877, *Financial Regulatory Reform: Systemic Risk and the Federal Reserve*, by Marc Labonte and CRS Report R40417, *Macroprudential Oversight: Monitoring Systemic Risk in the Financial System*, by Darryl E. Getter for more information on systemic risk and "too big to fail."

[6] U.S. Treasury, *TARP Monthly 105(a) Report—February 2010*, March 10, 2010, pp.12-13, available at http://financialstability.gov/latest/reportsanddocs.html.

[7] Federal Reserve H.4.1 data release, *Factors Affecting Reserve Balances of Depository Institutions*, March 11, 2010, Table 1, available at http://www.federalreserve.gov/releases/h41/.

[8] Federal Reserve H.4.1 data release, *Factors Affecting Reserve Balances of Depository Institutions*, March 11, 2010, Table 9, available at http://www.federalreserve.gov/releases/h41/.

[9] American International Group, Inc., "Aig Reports Fourth Quarter and Full Year 2009 Results", press release, February 26, 2010, p. 5, available at http://phx.corporate-ir.net/External.File?item=UGFyZW50S UQ9MzM3MjR8Q2hpbGRJRD0tMXxUeXBlPTM=&t=1. The CPFF was closed to further borrowing on February 1, 2010.

[10] Federal Reserve H.4.1 data release, *Factors Affecting Reserve Balances of Depository Institutions*, March 11, 2010, Tables 5 and 6, available at http://www.federalreserve.gov/releases/h41/.

[11] Prudential PLC is a British insurer and not related to the large U.S. insurer Prudential Financial.

[12] AIG, "AIG to Sell AIA to Prudential for Approximately $35.5 Billion," press release, March 1, 2010, http://www.aigcorporate.com/newsroom/index.html.

[13] AIG, "AIG to Sell ALICO to MetLife for Approximately $15.5 Billion," press release, March 8, 2010, http://www.aigcorporate.com/newsroom/index.html.

[14] 12 U.S.C. 343.

[15] Section 13(3) reports can be found at http://www.federalreserve.gov/monetarypolicy/bst_reportsresources.htm.

[16] 12 U.S.C. 5211.

[17] TARP reports can be found at http://financialstability.gov/latest/reportsanddocs.html.

[18] See http://www.aig.com/AIG-Financial-Products-Corp_20_20258.html.

[19] For more information on CDS see CRS Report RS22932, *Credit Default Swaps: Frequently Asked Questions*, by Edward V. Murphy and Rena S. Miller.

[20] For examples, see "Goldman, Merrill Collect Billions after Fed's AIG Bailout Loans," Bloomberg, available at http://www.bloomberg.com/apps/news?pid=newsarchive&sid=aTzTYtlNHSG8 and "Behind Insurer's Crisis, Blind Eye to a Web of Risk," New York Times, September 27, p. A1.

[21] The International Securities Lending Association estimates that the global amount of loaned securities is greater than 1 trillion pounds (approximately $1.4 trillion).

[22] Statistics from American International Group, Inc., *Form 10-Q*, for the quarterly period ending June 30, 2008, pp. 111-112, available at http://media.corporate-ir.net/media_files/irol/76/76115/reports/Q210Q.pdf.

[23] See http://www.newyorkfed.org/newsevents/news/markets/2009/an090116.html.

[24] The regulated subsidiaries are primarily the state-chartered insurance subsidiaries. Thus, if AIG were to default on the loan, the Fed could seize the insurance subsidiary stock held by the holding company, but not the actual assets held by the insurance companies.

[25] If AIG is indeed too big to fail, however, it is unclear whether its assets could be seized in the event of non-payment without precipitating system-wide problems.

[26] Federal Reserve, "Factors Affecting Reserve Balances," Statistical Release H.4.1, September 18, 2008. See http://www.federalreserve.gov/releases/h41/20080918/; and "Report Pursuant to Section 129 of the Emergency Economic Stabilization Act of 2008: Restructuring of the Government's Financial Support to the American International Group, Inc. on November 10, 2008, p. 4. See http://www.federalreser ve.gov/monetarypolicy/files/ 129aigrestructure.pdf.

[27] Terms detailed by the Federal Reserve in "Report Pursuant to Section 129 of the Emergency Economic Stabilization Act of 2008: Securities Borrowing Facility for American International Group, Inc.," available at http://www.federalreserve.gov/monetarypolicy/files/129aigsecborrowfacility.pdf.

[28] Liam Pleven et al, "AIG Bailout Hit By New Cash Woes," *Wall Street Journal*, October 9, 2008, p. A1.

[29] N.Y. Ins. Law, Sec. 1410.

[30] American International Group, Inc., "Aig Reports Fourth Quarter and Full Year 2009 Results", press release, February 26, 2010, p. 5, available at http://phx.corporate-ir.net/External.File?item= UGFyZW50SUQ9M zM3MjR8Q2hpbGRJRD0tMXxUeXBlPTM=&t=1.

[31] Full details of the preferred shares can be found on the Treasury website at http://ustreas.gov/press/re leases/reports/ 111008aigtermsheet.pdf.

[32] U.S. Treasury, "Treasury to Invest in AIG Restructuring under the Emergency Economic Stabilization Act," hp-1261, November 10, 2008, available at http://www.ustreas.gov/press/releases/hp1261.htm.

[33] Section 7001 of P.L. 111-5.

[34] See "Executive Compensation" on the Treasury Financialstability.gov website available at http://www.financialstability.gov/about/executivecompensation.html.

[35] The headquarters of the Federal Reserve Bank of New York sits between Maiden Lane and Liberty Street in downtown New York City. [36] "Maiden Lane Transactions" on the webpage of the Federal Reserve Bank of New York, available at http://www.newyorkfed.org/markets/maidenlane2.html.

[37] Information on Maiden Lane II from the Federal Reserve, "Factors Affecting Reserve Balances," Statistical Release H.4.1, February 25, 2010, available at http://www.federalreserve.gov/releases/h41/Current/.

[38] Information on Maiden Lane III from the Federal Reserve, "Factors Affecting Reserve Balances," Statistical Release H.4.1, February 25, 2010, available at http://www.federalreserve.gov/releases/h41/Current/, and "Factors Affecting Efforts to Limit Payments to AIG Counterparties" Testimony of Thomas C. Baxter Jr. of the Federal Reserve Bank of New York, January 27, 2010, available at http://www.newyo rkfed.org/newsevents/speeches/2010/bax100127.html.

[39] See, for example, "A.I.G. Reports Loss of $61.7 Billion as U.S. Gives More Aid," New York Times, March 2, 2009, p. A1.

[40] U.S. Treasury, "U.S. Treasury and Federal Reserve Board Announce Participation in AIG Restructuring Plan," Press Release dated March 2, 2009.

[41] The amount was reduced from $30 billion following controversy over $165 million in employee bonuses paid to AIGFP employees in March 2009.

[42] Donald Kohn, answering a question by Senator Christopher Dodd, reported in Federal News Service's transcript of the March 5, 2008 hearing of the Senate Committee On Banking, Housing, And Urban Affairs on "American International Group: Examining What Went Wrong, Government Intervention, and Implications For Future Regulation."

[43] See http://www.aig.com/aigweb/internet/en/files/CounterpartyAttachments031809_tcm385-155645.pdf for a full listing of counterparties.

[44] For example, see "SEC May Keep Potentially Controversial AIG Actions Secret for a Decade," Best's *Insurance News*, January 12, 2010.

[45]See "Issa: AIG Investigation Just Getting Started," January 27, 2010, available at http://republicans.ov ersight.house.gov/index.php?option=com_content&view=article&id=518%3Aissa-aig-investigation-just-getting-started&catid=22&Itemid=1.

In: Economic Policies in a Time of Financial Crisis
Editor: Heather D. Perkins

ISBN: 978-1-61122-686-7

Chapter 10

POVERTY IN THE UNITED STATES: 2008

Thomas Gabe

SUMMARY

In 2008, 39.8 million people were counted as poor in the United States—an increase of 2.6 million persons from 2007, and nearly the largest number of persons counted as poor since 1960. The *poverty rate*, or percent of the population considered poor under the official definition, was reported at 13.2%; this is up from 12.5% in 2007, and is the highest rate since 1997. The recent increase in poverty reflects the worsening of economic conditions since the onset of the economic recession in December 2007. Many expect poverty to rise further next year, and it will likely remain comparatively high even after the economy begins to recover. The incidence of poverty varies widely across the population according to age, education, labor force attachment, family living arrangements, and area of residence, among other factors. Under the official poverty definition, an average family of four was considered poor in 2008 if its pre-tax cash income for the year was below $22,025.

The measure of poverty currently in use was developed nearly 50 years ago, and was adopted as the "official" U.S. statistical measure of poverty in 1969. Except for minor technical changes, and adjustments for price changes in the economy, the "poverty line" (i.e., the income thresholds by which families or individuals with incomes that fall below are deemed to be poor) is the same as that developed nearly a half century ago, reflecting a notion of economic need based on living standards that prevailed in the mid-1950s.

Moreover, poverty as it is currently measured only counts families' and individuals' pre-tax money income against the poverty line in determining whether or not they are poor. In-kind benefits, such as benefits under the Supplemental Nutrition Assistance Program (SNAP, formerly named the Food Stamp program) and housing assistance are not accounted for under the "official" poverty definition, nor are the effects of taxes or tax credits, such as the Earned Income Tax Credit (EITC) or Child Tax Credit (CTC). In this sense, the current "official" poverty measure fails to capture the effects of a variety of programs and policies specifically designed to address income poverty.

A congressionally commissioned study conducted by a National Academy of Sciences (NAS) panel of experts recommended, some 15 years ago, that a new U.S. poverty measure be developed, offering a number of specific recommendations. Bills introduced in the 111th Congress (H.R. 2909 and S. 1625) would instruct the Census Bureau to develop a new "modern" poverty measure, following NAS recommendations. More recently, under the Obama Administration, an initiative is underway for the Census Bureau to develop a Supplemental Poverty Measure (SPM) that would reflect many of the NAS panel's recommendations and be informed by research conducted on those recommendations over the past 15 years. This initiative aligns with many of the provisions in H.R. 2909 and S. 1625. Statistics based on the SPM, which has yet to be developed, are to accompany the Census Bureau's fall 2011 scheduled release of 2010 income and poverty statistics under the "official" measure. The new poverty measure is to be considered an "experimental" measure, to supplement the "official" poverty measure. The "official" statistical poverty measure would continue to be used by programs that use it as the basis for allocating funds under formula and matching grant programs. The Department of Health and Human Services (HHS) would continue to issue poverty income guidelines derived from "official" Census Bureau poverty thresholds. HHS poverty guidelines are used in determining individual and family income eligibility under a number of federal and state programs. *This CRS report will be updated on an annual basis, following release of U.S. Census Bureau annual income and poverty estimates.*

TRENDS IN POVERTY[1]

In 2008, the U.S. poverty rate was 13.2%, accounting for 39.8 million persons as having income below the official poverty line. The 2008 poverty rate was up from 12.5% in 2007, and was at the highest level it has been over the past 11 years. In 2008, 2.6 million more persons were counted as poor than the year before, and the number of poor in that year was the highest since 1960. (See **Figure 1.**) The recent increase in poverty reflects the effects of the economic recession that began in December 2007, and has not yet ended. Given that poverty tends to follow the economic cycle, tending to rise when the economy is faltering and fall when the economy is in sustained growth, the poverty rate and number of poor are expected by analysts to be even higher in 2009. Over the course of 2008, the unemployment rate increased from 4.9% (January 2008) to 7.2% (December 2008); by March 2010 (the latest data available at the time of this chapter), the unemployment rate was 9.7%, down from a most recent high of 10.2% in October 2009. Estimates of poverty in 2009 will not be available until the late summer of 2010, but given the most recent unemployment data, they will most certainly be higher than in 2008. Even after the economy begins to recover, poverty is expected to remain high, as poverty rates generally do not begin to fall until economic expansion is well underway. A strong economy during most of the 1990s is generally credited with the declines in poverty that occurred over the latter half of that decade, resulting in a record-tying, historical low poverty rate of 11.3% in 2000 (a rate statistically tied with the previous lowest recorded rate of 11.1% in 1973). The poverty rate increased each year from 2001 through 2004, a trend generally attributed to economic recession (March 2001 to November 2001), and failed to recede appreciably before the onset of the current recession.

Given the depth and projected duration of the current recession, by some estimates, it may be a decade or more before poverty rates recede to their 2007 pre-recession level.[2]

The longer-term secular trend in poverty has been affected by changes in household and family composition and by government income security and transfer programs. In 1959, over one-third (35.2%) of persons age 65 and over were poor, a rate well above that of children (26.9%). (See **Figure 2.**) In 2008, the aged poverty rate was 9.7%—a rate statistically tied with the historical low rate of 9.4% in 2006. Social security in combination with a maturing pension system has helped greatly to reduce the incidence of poverty among the aged over the years. The poverty rates of children were cut nearly in half from 1959 to 1969, reaching a historical low of 13.8% in 1969. Since reaching an all-time low, the growth in the number of single-parent families, which tend to have a high incidence of poverty, has contributed to higher rates of child poverty overall.

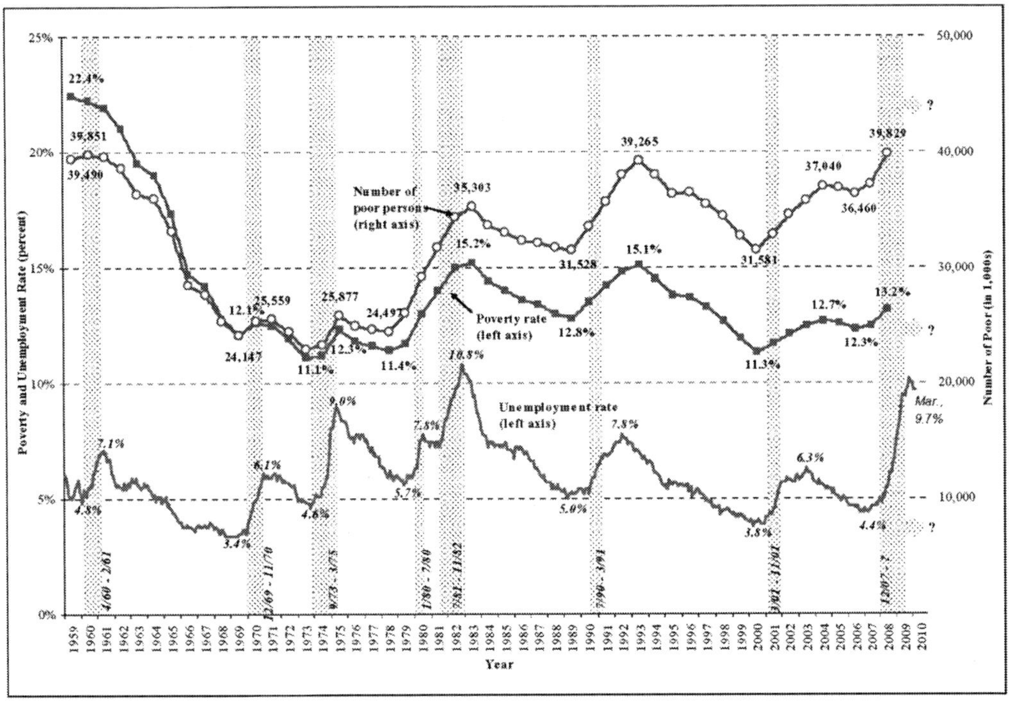

Source: Prepared by the Congressional Research Service (CRS) using U.S. Census Bureau, "Income, Poverty, and Health Insurance Coverage in the United States: 2008," Table B-1, Current Population Report P60-236, September 2009, available on the internet at http://www.census.gov/prod/2009pubs/p60-236.pdf. Unemployment rates are available on the internet at http://www.bls.gov/cps/. Recessionary periods defined by National Bureau of Economic Research Business Cycle Dating Committee: http://www.nber.org/cycles/main.html.

Figure 1. Trend in Poverty Rate and Number of Poor Persons: 1959-2008, and Unemployment Rate from January 1959 through March 2010 (recessionary periods marked in red)

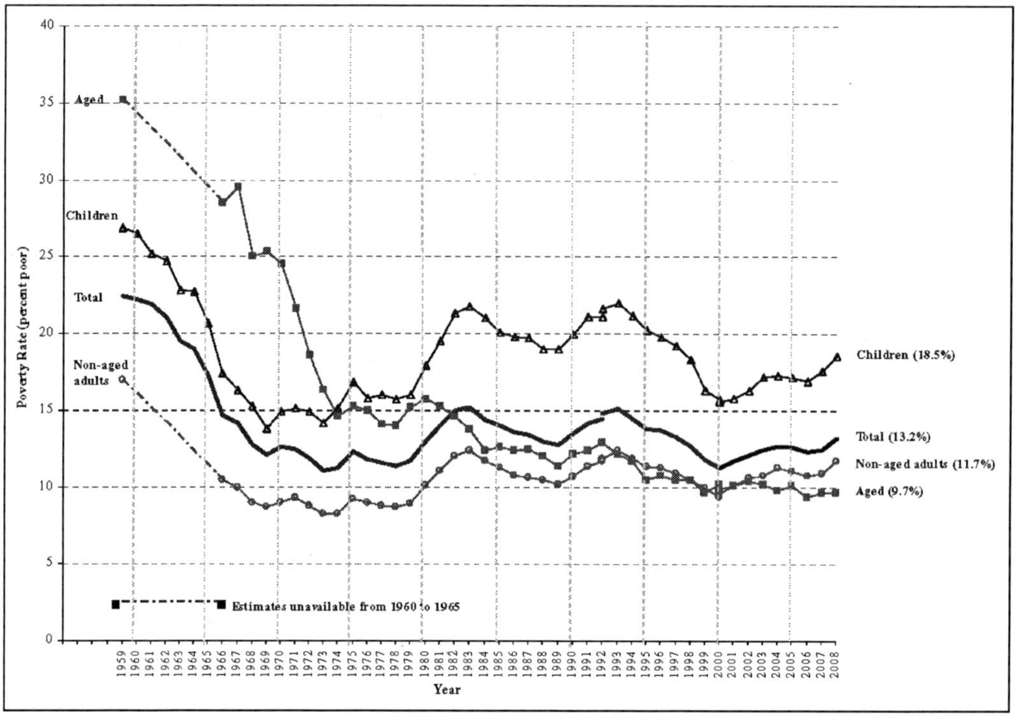

Source: Prepared by the Congressional Research Service using U.S. Census Bureau, "Income, Poverty, and Health Insurance Coverage in the United States: 2008," Tables B-1 and B-2, Current Population Report P60-236, September 2009, available at http://www.census.gov/prod/2009pubs/p60-236.pdf.

Figure 2. U.S. Poverty Rates by Age Group, 1959-2008

Cash welfare programs that target the poor, including many poor single-parent families, tend to lift few families' incomes above the poverty line, but in combination with other noncash aid, such programs help to reduce the depth of income and material deprivation poor families incur. Changes in cash welfare programs implemented since passage of the 1996 welfare reform law (Personal Responsibility and Work Opportunity Reconciliation Act (PRWORA), P.L. 104-193) continue to be assessed in terms of their possible impacts on economically vulnerable populations.[3] The welfare reform law ended the Aid to Families with Dependent Children (AFDC) program, replacing it with the Temporary Assistance for Needy Families (TANF) program.[4] Among other features, TANF sets a five-year lifetime limit on receipt of federally funded cash assistance (allowing lower limits at state option), imposes strong work requirements, and allows states to impose sanctions that reduce or deny benefits to families who fail to comply with program requirements.

Many forms of noncash assistance, such as food assistance under the Supplemental Nutrition Assistance Program (SNAP, formerly called the Food Stamp Program), and tax benefits, such as the Earned Income Tax Credit (EITC) for working families and the Child Tax Credit (CTC), are not counted as income under the official poverty measure. Many believe that these and other benefits should be included in a poverty measure so as to better reflect the effects of government programs on poverty.

DEFINITION OF POVERTY[5]

The Census Bureau's poverty thresholds form the basis for statistical estimates of poverty in the United States.[6] The thresholds reflect crude estimates of the amount of money individuals or families, of various size and composition, need per year to purchase a basket of goods and services deemed as "minimally adequate," according to the living standards of the early 1960s. The thresholds are updated each year for changes in consumer prices. In 2008, for example, the average poverty threshold for an individual living alone was $10,991; for a two-person family, $14,051; and for a family of four, $22,025.[7]

The current official U.S. poverty measure was developed in the early 1960s using data available at the time. It was based on the concept of a minimal standard of food consumption, derived from research that used data from the U.S. Department of Agriculture's (USDA) 1955 Food Consumption Survey. That research showed that the average U.S. family spent one-third of its pre-tax income on food. A standard of food adequacy was set by pricing out the USDA's Economy Food Plan—a bare-bones plan designed to provide a healthy diet for a temporary period when funds are low. An overall poverty income level was then set by multiplying the food plan by three, to correspond to the findings from the 1955 USDA Survey that an average family spent one-third of its pre-tax income on food and two-thirds on everything else.

The "official" U.S. poverty measure[8] has changed little since it was originally adopted in 1969, with the exception of annual adjustments for overall price changes in the economy, as measured by the Consumer Price Index for all Urban Consumers (CPI-U). Thus, the poverty line reflects a measure of economic need based on living standards that prevailed in the mid-1950s. It is often characterized as an "absolute" poverty measure, in that it is not adjusted to reflect changes in needs associated with improved standards of living that have occurred over the decades since the measure was first developed. If the same basic methodology developed in the early 1960s was applied today, the poverty thresholds would be at least 2 1/2-times higher than the current thresholds.[9]

Persons are considered poor, for statistical purposes, if their family's countable money income is below its corresponding poverty threshold. Annual poverty estimates are based on a Census Bureau household survey (Current Population Survey) conducted each March. The official definition of poverty counts most sources of money income received by families during the prior year (e.g., earnings, social security, pensions, cash public assistance, interest and dividends, alimony and child support, among others). For purposes of officially counting the poor, noncash benefits (such as the value of Medicare and Medicaid, public housing, or employer provided health care) and "near cash" benefits (e.g., food stamps, renamed Supplemental Assistance Nutrition (SNAP) benefits beginning in FY2009) are not counted as income, nor are tax payments subtracted from income, nor are tax credits added (e.g., Earned Income Tax Credit (EITC)).

There is mounting interest in including the value of noncash benefits and tax credits when assessing progress against poverty. These benefits represent a growing share of assistance to the poor. In FY2008, the federal government provided an estimated $33.6 billion in Food Stamp benefits, most of which went to poor households. The EITC program is the fastest growing form of cash aid for children. In FY2008, the Treasury paid an estimated $39.5 billion in EITC to families with relatively low earnings who owed no income tax. Neither

Food Stamp (SNAP) benefits nor the EITC are counted as income under the official poverty definition. The Census Bureau provides a variety of alternate measures of poverty, based on various combinations of cash, noncash, and after-tax income. These alternative measures are still considered experimental; none have displaced the official measure.

The *poverty rate* is the estimated percentage of the national population living alone or in families whose money income is below the poverty threshold. Under an alternate *experimental* definition of poverty, the poverty rate would be lower than under the *official* definition of poverty, based on pre-tax cash income. Using a more comprehensive definition of income measured against the poverty line (one which includes the value of noncash benefits and the effect of taxes), the estimated poverty rate would have been 10.2% in 2008,[10] as opposed to 13.2% under the official measure in 2008.

Major changes to the way in which poverty is defined and measured in the United States have been recommended by a congressionally commissioned study conducted by a National Academy of Sciences (NAS) panel of experts.[11] The NAS panel recommended that the poverty level be reset to take into account improvements in the U.S. standard of living that have occurred over the past 40-plus years (i.e., since the current poverty measure was originally devised). The Academy recommended that noncash benefits, taxes, and tax credits be counted with cash income, and that certain expenses (e.g., work-related child care expenses, housing, and out-of-pocket medical expenses) be deducted from income in determining families' poverty status. The effect of these, and other changes, would result in comparatively more working families and aged persons being counted as poor. The NAS panel also recommended that the poverty income levels be adjusted for area cost of living differences. The current poverty income thresholds are uniform across the 50 states and the District of Columbia. Most experts agree that the current measure underestimates the extent of poverty in high cost of living areas. If adopted, a cost of living adjustment to the poverty thresholds would result in comparatively higher levels of measured poverty in the Northeast and West, compared to the South and Midwest, than under the current measure.

A bill introduced by Representative McDermott, The Measuring American Poverty Act of 2009 (H.R. 2909[12]), and a companion bill introduced by Senator Dodd (S. 1625[13]) would instruct the Census Bureau to adopt many of the NAS recommendations as a new "modern" poverty measure. The legislation, if adopted, would result in a new "modern" poverty measure that would coexist with the current "official" poverty measure, and re-designate the current "official" measure as the "traditional" poverty measure. The new "modern" poverty measure would not affect programs that use poverty as a criterion for either determining eligibility or allocating funds, but would stand as an additional statistical indicator to measure the effects of programs on poverty.

More recently, the Department of Commerce announced that the Census Bureau, in cooperation with the Bureau of Labor Statistics (BLS), is preparing to develop a Supplemental Poverty Measure (SPM) designed to implement many of the NAS panel recommendations.[14] President Obama's Office of Management and Budget's (OMB) Chief Statistician formed a Technical Working Group[15], charged with developing a set of initial starting points to help the Census Bureau, in consultation with BLS, develop the new statistic. Observations from the Working Group are based on much of what has been learned over the past 15 years on developing data and methods to implement the NAS panel's recommendations, as well as on conceptual discussions about how best to estimate economic need.[16] The President's FY2011 budget proposal includes $5 million to assist the Census

Bureau in creating the new statistic, and $2.5 million for the Bureau of Labor Statistics to develop supplemental poverty thresholds to be used by the Census Bureau. Statistics based on the SPM, which is yet to be developed, are to accompany the Census Bureau's fall 2011 scheduled release of 2010 income and poverty statistics under the "official" measure.

The SPM would not replace the "official" poverty measure, as it would be considered an experimental measure. According to the Working Group, the SPM should be considered a "work in progress," as improvements in data and methods are made over time. The Working Group's observations serve as an initial starting point intended to assist the Census Bureau in developing the new statistical measure. Ultimately, the Census Bureau is responsible for the development and final decisions relating to the development and initial publication of the SPM, as well as for making improvements to the measure over time.

As noted above, the proposed new poverty measure is intended to supplement the "official" statistical measure of poverty currently in use. Used in conjunction with the "official" poverty measure, the SPM would help in assessing the effects of economic and social conditions and government programs and policies on individuals and families in ways not possible with the "official" measure. The "official" statistical poverty measure would continue to be used by programs that use it as the basis for allocating funds under formula and matching grant programs. Additionally, HHS poverty guidelines (footnote 6), used as a basis for determining income eligibility of individuals, families, and households for federal and state programs, would continue to be derived from the "official" statistical poverty measure.

POVERTY AMONG SELECTED GROUPS

Even during periods of general prosperity, poverty is concentrated among certain groups and in certain areas. Minorities, women and children, the very old, the unemployed, and those with low levels of educational attainment, low skills, or disability, among others, are especially prone to poverty.

Racial and Ethnic Minorities[17]

African Americans and Hispanics have poverty rates that exceed the white poverty rate by several times. In 2008, 24.7% of blacks (9.4 million) and 23.2% of Hispanics (11.0 million) had incomes below poverty, compared to 8.6% of non-Hispanic whites (17.0 million) and 11.8% of Asians (1.6 million). Although blacks represent only 12.6% of the total population, they make up 23.6% of the poor population; Hispanics, who represent 15.7% of the population, account for 27.6% of the poor. Poverty for all groups above, except blacks, increased from 2007 to 2008—the rate for blacks was statistically unchanged over the period.

Nativity and Citizenship Status[18]

In 2008, among the native-born population, 12.6% (33.3 million) were poor in 2008, up from 11.9% (31.1 million) in 2007. Among the foreign-born population, 17.8% (6.5 million) were poor in 2008, up from a respective 16.5% (6.2 million) in 2007. The poverty rate of naturalized citizens (10.2%) was lower than that of native-born citizens (12.6%) in 2008; both the rate and number of poor naturalized citizens was unchanged from 2007. In 2008, the poverty rate of noncitizens (23.3%) was nearly twice that of the native-born population (12.6%). In that year, the 5.0 million non-citizens who were counted as poor accounted for about one-in-seven of all poor persons (34.9 million). From 2007 to 2008, the poverty rate for non-citizens increased from 21.3% to 23.3%.

Children[19]

In 2008, 13.5 million children (18.5%) were poor—a statistically significant increase in the number of poor (up from 12.8 million) and the poverty rate (up from 17.6%) from 2007. The lowest recorded rate of child poverty was in 1969, when 13.8% of children were counted as poor. Children living in single female-headed families are especially prone to poverty. In 2008, a child living in a single female-headed family was well over four times more likely to be poor than a child living in a married-couple family. In 2008, 43.5% of all children living in single female-headed families were poor (statistically unchanged from 43.0% in 2007). In contrast, 9.9% of children living in married-couple families were poor, which represented a statistically significant increase from 2007, when 8.5% of such children were poor. The increased share of children who live in single female-headed families has contributed to the high overall child poverty rate. In 2008, 23.9% of children were living in single female-headed families, about double the share who lived in such families when the *overall* child poverty rate was at its historical low (1969). Among all poor children, well over half (56.2%) lived in single female-headed families in 2008.

In 2008, 34.4% of black children were poor (3.8 million), compared to 30.3% of Hispanic children (4.9 million) and 10.0% of white non-Hispanic children (4.1 million). Among children living in single female-headed families, the poverty rate for black and Hispanic children was identical at 51.9%; non-Hispanic white children in such families had a poverty rate of 31.7%. The poverty rate among Hispanic children who live in married-couple families (22.1%) was over twice that of black children (11.0%), and more than four times that of white non-Hispanic children (5.3%) who live in such families. Contributing to the high rate of overall black child poverty is the large share of black children who live in single female-headed families (55.0%) compared to Hispanic children (26.5%) or white non-Hispanic children (15.4%).

Adults with Low Education, Unemployment, or Disability

Adults with low education, those who are unemployed, or those who have a work-related disability are especially prone to poverty. In 2008, 34.7% of 25-34 year olds without a high school diploma were poor. Within the same age group, 16.7% of those whose highest level of educational attainment was a high school diploma were poor. In contrast, only 4.4% of 25-34 year olds with at least a bachelor's degree were found to be living below the poverty line. (About 12% of 25-34 year olds lack a high school diploma.) Among persons between the ages of 16 and 64 who were unemployed in March 2009, 20.8% were poor based on their families' incomes in 2008; among those who were employed, 6.0% were poor. In 2008, persons who had a work disability[20] represented 10.3% of the 16-64 year old population, and 26.1% of the poor population within this age range. Among those with a severe work disability, 33.6% were poor, compared to 14.1% of those with a less severe disability and 9.1% who reported having no work-related disability.

The Aged

The poverty rate of persons age 65 and older in 2008 was 9.7% (3.7 million poor). The poverty rate among the aged in 2008 was identical to that in 2007, and statistically tied with its historical low rate of 9.4% in 2006. Among those ages 75 and over, 11.2% were poor in 2008, compared to 8.4% of those ages 65 to 74. Although the aged poverty rate tends to be lower than the child poverty rate, many of the aged live just slightly above the poverty line. As measured by a slightly raised poverty standard (125% of the poverty threshold), 15.9% of the aged could be considered poor or "*near poor;*" 13.6% who are ages 65 to 74, and 18.7% who are 75 years of age and over could be considered poor or "near poor." In comparison, 25.0% of children (persons under age 18) could be considered poor or "near poor."

Receipt of Welfare among the Poor

In 2008, seven of every 10 persons who were poor (70.4%) lived in households that received any means-tested assistance during the year.[21] Such assistance could include cash aid, such as Temporary Assistance for Needy Families (TANF), Supplemental Security Income (SSI) payments, SNAP benefits (Food Stamps), Medicaid, subsidized housing, free or reduced price school lunches, and other programs. In 2008, only 19.6% of poor persons lived in households that received *cash aid*, 41.3% received Food Stamps, 57.9% lived in households where one or more household members were covered by Medicaid, and 15.8% lived in subsidized housing. Poor single-parent families with children are among those families most likely to receive cash aid. Among poor children who were living in single female-headed families, 28.2% were in households that received government cash aid in 2008. The share of poor children in single female-headed families receiving cash aid is well below historical levels. In 1993, 70.2% of these children's families received cash aid. In 1995, the year prior to passage of sweeping welfare changes under PRWORA, 65% of such children were in families receiving cash aid.

The Geography of Poverty

Poverty is more highly concentrated in some areas than in others; it is about twice as high in center cities than it is in suburban areas and nearly three times as high in the poorest states than it is in the least poor states.

Within metropolitan areas, the incidence of poverty in central city areas is considerably higher than in suburban areas, 17.7% versus 9.8%, respectively, in 2008. Nonmetropolitan areas had a poverty rate of 15.1%. In 2003 (the most recent year's data available for this comparison), over one-third (34.8%) of the nation's poor lived in neighborhoods of concentrated poverty (areas based on census tracts and minor civil divisions with a poverty rate of 20% or higher based on the *1990* census). Poor racial and ethnic minorities are more likely to live in areas of concentrated poverty than non-Hispanic whites. Among *poor* African Americans, 52.9% lived in areas of concentrated poverty, and among *poor* Hispanics, 47.5%. In contrast, 18.8% of *poor* non-Hispanic whites lived in areas of concentrated poverty. In 2008, poverty rates were lowest in the Northeast (11.6%), followed by the Midwest (12.4%), the West (12.4%) and the South (14.3%).

American Community Survey (ACS) State Poverty Estimates

Up to this point, the poverty statistics presented in this chapter come from the U.S. Census Bureau's Annual Social and Economic Supplement (ASEC) to the Current Population Survey (CPS). For purposes of producing state and sub-state poverty estimates, the Census Bureau now recommends using the American Community Survey (ACS)—because of its much larger sample size, the ACS produces estimates with a much smaller margin of statistical error than that of the ASEC/CPS. However, it should be noted that the ACS survey design differs from the ASEC/CPS in a variety of ways, and may produce somewhat different estimates than those obtained from the ASEC/CPS. The ASEC/CPS estimate that 13.2% of the nation's population was poor in 2008 was coincidently the same as that obtained for the 2008 ACS, although the two surveys were conducted at different times, and account for income reported over different periods. The ASEC/CPS estimates are based on a survey conducted in February through April 2009, and account for income reported for the previous year. In contrast, the ACS estimates are based on income information collected between January and December 2008, for the prior 12 months. For example, for the sample with data collected in January, the reference period is from January 2007 to December 2007, and for the sample with data collected in December, from December 2007 to November 2008. The ACS data consequently cover a time span of 23 months, with the data centered at mid-December 2007. ***The economic recession did not officially begin until December 2007, so the 2008 ACS data only partially capture its possible effects on poverty.***

Figure 3 shows estimated poverty rates for the United States and for each of the 50 states and the District of Columbia on the basis of the 2008 American Community Survey (ACS). In addition to the point estimates, the figure displays a 90% statistical confidence interval around each state's estimate, indicating the degree to which these estimates might be expected to vary based on sample size.[22] Although the states are sorted from lowest to highest by their respective poverty rate point estimates, the precise ranking of each state is not possible because of the depicted margin of error around each state's estimate. For example, New Hampshire would appear to have the lowest poverty rate (7.6%), but it overlaps statistically with Maryland (8.1%) and Alaska (8.4%). Mississippi stands out as having the highest poverty rate (21.26%) and is followed by Louisiana (17.3%), which is statistically tied with five other jurisdictions: Kentucky (17.3%), Arkansas (17.3%), the District of Columbia (17.2%), New Mexico (17.1%), and West Virginia (17.0%).

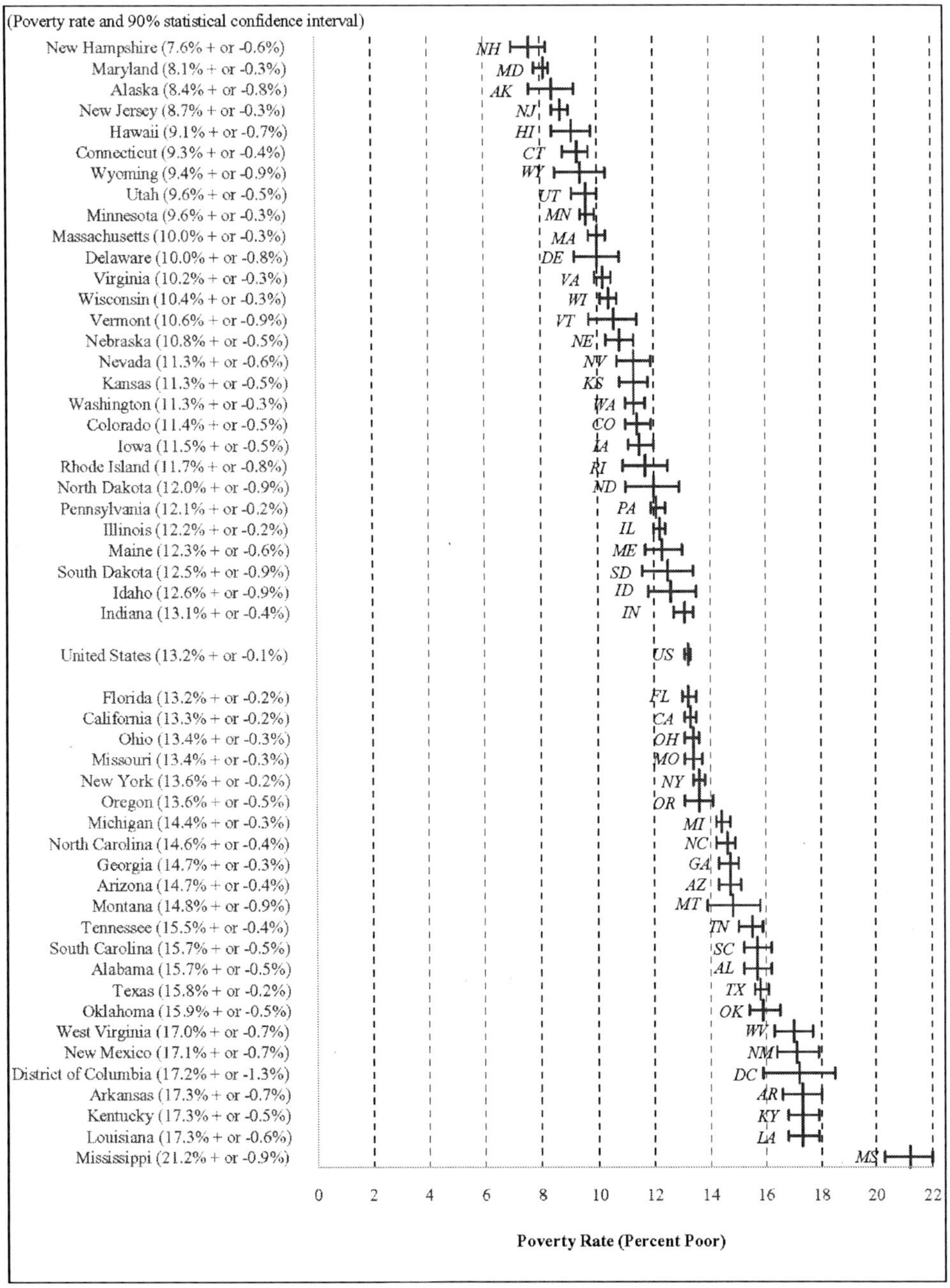

Source: Prepared by the Congressional Research Service on the basis of U.S. Census Bureau 2008 American Community Survey (ACS) data.

Figure 3. Poverty Rates for the 50 States and the District of Columbia: 2008 American Community Survey (ACS) Data

Table 1. Poverty Rates for the 50 States and the District of Columbia, 2002 to 2008 Estimates from the American Community Survey (ACS) (Percent Poor)

	Estimated Poverty Rate and Statistically Significant Differences over Previous Year							Change in Poverty Rates over Selected Periods and Statistically Significant Differences		
	2002	2003	2004	2005	2006[a]	2007[a]	2008[a]	2005 vs. 2002	2008 vs. 2006	2008 vs.2002[a]
United States	12.4	12.7▲	13.1▲	13.3▲	13.3	13.0▼	13.2▲	0.9▲	-0.1	0.8▲
Alabama	16.6	17.1	16.1	17.0▲	16.6	16.9	15.7▼	-0.1	-1.3▼	-0.9
Alaska	7.7	9.7▲	8.2▼	11.2▲	10.9	8.9▼	8.4	3.2▲	-2.8▼	0.7
Arizona	14.2	15.4▲	14.2	14.2	14.2	14.2	14.7	0.0	0.5	0.6
Arkansas	15.3	16.0	17.9▲	17.2	17.3	17.9	17.3	2.0▲	0.2	2.0▲
California	13.0	13.4	13.3	13.3	13.1	12.4▼	13.3▲	0.1	0.0	0.2
Colorado	9.7	9.8	11.1	11.1	12.0▲	12.0	11.4	2.3▲	0.4	1.7▲
Connecticut	7.5	8.1	7.6	8.3	8.3	7.9	9.3▲	0.8	1.0▲	1.8▲
Delaware	8.2	8.7	9.9	10.4	11.1	10.5	10.0	2.9▲	-0.4	1.8▲
District of Columbia	17.5	19.9▲	18.9	19.0	19.6	16.4▼	17.2	2.2	-1.8	-0.2
Florida	12.8	13.1	12.2▼	12.8▲	12.6	12.1▼	13.2▲	-0.2	0.4▲	0.4
Georgia	12.7	13.4	14.8▲	14.4	14.7	14.3	14.7	2.0▲	0.3	2.0▲
Hawaii	10.1	10.9	10.6	9.8	9.3	8.0▼	9.1▲	-0.8	-0.7	-1.0
Idaho	13.8	13.8	14.5	13.9	12.6▼	12.1	12.6	-1.2	-1.2▼	-1.2
Illinois	11.6	11.3	11.9	12.0	12.3	11.9	12.2	0.7▲	0.2	0.6
Indiana	10.9	10.6	10.8	12.2▲	12.7	12.3	13.1▲	1.8▲	0.9▲	2.2▲
Iowa	11.2	10.1	9.9	10.9▲	11.0	11.0	11.5	-0.2	0.7▲	0.3
Kansas	12.1	10.8	10.5	11.7▲	12.4	11.2▼	11.3	0.3	-0.4	-0.8
Kentucky	15.6	17.4	17.4	16.8	17.0	17.3	17.3	1.3▲	0.5	1.7▲
Louisiana	18.8	20.3	19.4	19.8	19.0	18.6	17.3▼	0.2	-2.4▼	-1.5▼
Maine	11.1	10.5	12.3▲	12.6	12.9	12.0	12.3	1.8▲	-0.3	1.2▲
Maryland	8.1	8.2	8.8	8.2	7.8	8.3	8.1	-0.3	-0.2	0.0

Table 1. (Continued)

	Estimated Poverty Rate and Statistically Significant Differences over Previous Year							Change in Poverty Rates over Selected Periods and Statistically Significant Differences		
	2002	2003	2004	2005	2006[a]	2007[a]	2008[a]	2005 vs. 2002	2008 vs. 2006	2008 vs.2002[a]
Massachusetts	8.9	9.4	9.2	10.3▲	9.9	9.9	10.0	1.0▲	-0.3	1.1▲
Michigan	11.0	11.4	12.3	13.2▲	13.5	14.0▲	14.4▲	2.5▲	1.2▲	3.4▲
Minnesota	8.5	7.8	8.3	9.2▲	9.8▲	9.5	9.6	1.2▲	0.5▲	1.1▲
Mississippi	19.9	19.9	21.6▲	21.3	21.1	20.6	21.2	1.2▲	-0.1	1.3
Missouri	11.9	11.7	11.8	13.3▲	13.6	13.0▼	13.4	1.6▲	0.0	1.5▲
Montana	14.6	14.2	14.2	14.4	13.6	14.1	14.8	-1.0	0.4	0.2
Nebraska	11.0	10.8	11.0	10.9	11.5	11.2	10.8	0.5	-0.1	-0.1
Nevada	11.8	11.5	12.6	11.1	10.3	10.7	11.3	-1.5▼	0.2	-0.5
New Hampshire	6.4	7.7▲	7.6	7.5	8.0	7.1▼	7.6	1.6▲	0.1	1.2▲
New Jersey	7.5	8.4▲	8.5	8.7	8.7	8.6	8.7	1.2▲	0.0	1.2▲
New Mexico	18.9	18.6	19.3	18.5	18.5	18.1	17.1	-0.4	-1.4▼	-1.8▼
New York	13.1	13.5	14.2▲	13.8	14.2▲	13.7▼	13.6	1.1▲	-0.2	0.5
North Carolina	14.2	14.0	15.2	15.1	14.7	14.3	14.6	0.4	-0.5	0.3
North Dakota	12.5	11.7	12.1	11.2	11.4	12.1	12.0	-1.1	0.7	-0.6
Ohio	11.9	12.1	12.5	13.0	13.3	13.1	13.4	1.5▲	0.3	1.5▲
Oklahoma	15.0	16.1	15.3	16.5	17.0	15.9▼	15.9	2.0▲	-0.6	0.9
Oregon	13.2	13.9	14.1	14.1	13.3▼	12.9	13.6▲	0.0	-0.5	0.4
Pennsylvania	10.5	10.9	11.7▲	11.9	12.1	11.6▼	12.1▲	1.5▲	0.2	1.6▲
Rhode Island	10.7	11.3	12.8▲	12.3	11.1	12.0	11.7	0.4	-0.6	1.0
South Carolina	14.2	14.1	15.7	15.6	15.7	15.0	15.7	1.4▲	0.1	1.4▲
South Dakota	11.4	11.1	11.0	13.6▲	13.6	13.1	12.5	2.2	-1.2	1.1
Tennessee	14.5	13.8	14.5	15.5	16.2	15.9	15.5	1.7▲	-0.1	1.0
Texas	15.6	16.3	16.6	17.6▲	16.9▼	16.3▼	15.8▼	1.3▲	-1.8▼	0.2
Utah	10.5	10.6	10.9	10.2	10.6	9.7▼	9.6	0.1	-0.6	-0.9

Table 1. (Continued)

	Estimated Poverty Rate and Statistically Significant Differences over Previous Year							Change in Poverty Rates over Selected Periods and Statistically Significant Differences		
	2002	2003	2004	2005	2006[a]	2007[a]	2008[a]	2005 vs. 2002	2008 vs. 2006	2008 vs.2002[a]
Vermont	8.5	9.7	9.0	11.5▲	10.3	10.1	10.6	1.8▲	-0.9	2.0▲
Virginia	9.9	9.0	9.5	10.0	9.6	9.9	10.2	-0.4	0.2	0.3
Washington	11.4	11.0	13.1▲	11.9▼	11.8	11.4	11.3	0.4	-0.6▼	0.0
West Virginia	17.2	18.5	17.9	18.0	17.3	16.9	17.0	0.1	-1.0	-0.2
Wisconsin	9.7	10.5	10.7	10.2	11.0▲	10.8	10.4	1.2▲	0.2	0.7
Wyoming	11.0	9.7	10.3	9.5	9.4	8.7	9.4	-1.6▼	-0.1	-1.6▼
Number of states with statistically significant change in poverty:		5	10	14	7	14	11	27	13	21
Increase in poverty		5 ▲	8▲	13 ▲	4 ▲	1 ▲	8▲	25 ▲	6 ▲	18 ▲
Decrease in poverty		0 ▼	2▼	1 ▼	3 ▼	13 ▼	3▼	2 ▼	7 ▼	3 ▼

Source: Congressional Research Service (CRS) estimates from U.S. Census Bureau American Community Survey (ACS) data, 2002 to 2008.

Notes: ▲Statistically significant increase in poverty rate at the 90% statistical confidence level.

▼ tatistically significant decrease in poverty rate at the 90% statistical confidence level.

a. Comparisons to 2002 through 2005 estimates are not strictly comparable, due to inclusion of persons living in some non-institutional group quarters beginning in 2006 and after.

Table 1 provides estimates of state and national poverty rates from 2002 through 2008 from the ACS. Statistically significant changes from one year to the next are indicated by an upward-pointing arrow (▲) if a state's poverty rate was statistically higher, and by a downward-pointing arrow (▼) if statistically lower, than in the immediately preceding year or for other selected periods (i.e., 2002 to 2005, 2006 to 2008, and 2002 to 2008).[23] It should be noted that ACS poverty estimates for 2006 and later are not strictly comparable to those of earlier years, due to a change in ACS methodology that began in 2006 to include some persons living in non-institutionalized group quarters who were not included in earlier years.[24]

Table 1 shows that poverty among states was generally increasing over the 2002 to 2005 period, as measured by the ACS. This is in spite of the fact that the nation had emerged out of economic recession in November 2001. From 2002 to 2003, five states experienced statistically significant increases in their poverty rate, whereas none experienced a significant decrease in poverty. From 2003 to 2004, eight states saw their poverty rates increase, whereas two saw decreases. From 2004 to 2005, 13 states saw their poverty rates increase, whereas only one saw its poverty rate decrease. Comparing 2005 to 2002, 25 states had higher poverty rates in 2005 than in 2002, and only two states had lower poverty rates.

By 2007, the effects of the 2001 recession on state poverty rates were beginning to fade, as 12 states and the District of Columbia experienced statistically significant decreases in their poverty rates from 2006, and only one state (Michigan) saw its poverty rate increase over the period. However, by 2008, the ACS data show eight states (California, Connecticut, Florida, Hawaii, Indiana, Michigan, Oregon, and Pennsylvania) as experiencing statistically significant increases in their poverty rates, whereas three states (Alabama, Louisiana, and Texas) experienced statistically significant decreases. As the current recession was not officially pegged as beginning until December 2007, the 2008 ACS data do not fully capture economic circumstances of 2008, as the data were collected over a 23-month period centered on December 2007, the point at which the economic downturn was marked as having just begun (see text box, above). The 2008 ACS poverty estimates show 18 states as having statistically higher poverty rates than in 2002, and three states as having statistically lower poverty rates; *however, as noted earlier, these estimates are not strictly comparable, due to the inclusion of some persons in non-institutional group quarters in 2008 who were not included in the survey in 2002.*

APPENDIX. U.S. POVERTY STATISTICS: 1959-2008

Table A-1. Poverty Rates (Percent Poor) for Selected Groups, 1959-2008

		Related Children under Age18[a]			Adults		Race/Ethnicity[b]—All Ages			
Year	All Persons	Total	In Female-Headed Families	In All Other Families	Ages 18-64	Age 65+	White[b]	White Non-Hispanic[b]	Black[b]	Hispanic
2008	13.2	18.5	43.5	10.7	11.7	9.7	11.2[b]	8.6[b]	24.7[b]	23.2
2007	12.5	17.6	43.0	9.5	10.9	9.7	10.5[b]	8.2[b]	24.5[b]	21.5
2006	12.3	16.9	42.1	9.0	10.8	9.4	10.3[b]	8.2[b]	24.3[b]	20.6

Table A-1. (Continued)

Year	All Persons	Related Children Under Age18[a]			Adults		Race/Ethnicity[b]—All Ages			
		Total	In Female-Headed Families	In All Other Families	Ages 18-64	Age 65+	White[b]	White Non-Hispanic[b]	Black[b]	Hispanic
2005	12.6	17.1	42.8	9.3	11.1	10.1	10.6[b]	8.3[b]	24.9[b]	21.8
2004r	12.7	17.3	41.9	9.7	11.3	9.8	10.8[b]	8.7[b]	24.7[b]	21.9
2003	12.5	17.2	41.8	9.6	10.8	10.2	10.5[b]	8.2[b]	24.4[b]	22.5
2002	12.1	16.3	39.6	9.2	10.6	10.4	10.2[b]	8.0[b]	24.1[b]	21.8
2001	11.7	15.8	39.3	8.8	10.1	10.1	9.9	7.8	22.7	21.4
2000r	11.3	15.6	40.1	8.6	9.6	9.9	9.5	7.4	22.5	21.5
1999	11.8	16.3	41.9	9.0	10.0	9.7	9.8	7.7	23.6	22.8
1998	12.7	18.3	46.1	9.7	10.5	10.5	10.5	8.2	26.1	25.6
1997	13.3	19.2	49.0	10.2	10.9	10.5	11.0	8.6	26.5	27.1
1996	13.7	19.8	49.3	10.9	11.3	10.8	11.2	8.6	28.4	29.4
1995	13.8	20.2	50.3	10.7	11.4	10.5	11.2	8.5	29.3	30.3
1994	14.5	21.2	52.9	11.7	11.9	11.7	11.7	9.4	30.6	30.7
1993	15.1	22.0	53.7	12.4	12.4	12.2	12.2	9.9	33.1	30.6
1992r	14.8	21.6	54.6	11.8	11.9	12.9	11.9	9.6	33.4	29.6
1991r	14.2	21.1	55.5	11.1	11.4	12.4	11.3	9.4	32.7	28.7
1990	13.5	19.9	53.4	10.7	10.7	12.2	10.7	8.8	31.9	28.1
1989	12.8	19.0	51.1	10.4	10.2	11.4	10.0	8.3	30.7	26.2
1988r	13.0	19.0	52.9	10.0	10.5	12.0	10.1	8.4	31.3	26.7
1987r	13.4	19.7	54.7	10.9	10.6	12.5	10.4	8.7	32.4	28.0
1986	13.6	19.8	54.4	10.8	10.8	12.4	11.0	9.4	31.1	27.3
1985	14.0	20.1	53.6	11.7	11.3	12.6	11.4	9.7	31.3	29.0
1984	14.4	21.0	54.0	12.5	11.7	12.4	11.5	10.0	33.8	28.4
1983	15.2	21.8	55.5	13.5	12.4	13.8	12.2	10.8	35.7	28.1
1982	15.0	21.3	56.0	13.0	12.0	14.6	12.0	10.6	35.6	29.9
1981	14.0	19.5	52.3	11.6	11.1	15.3	11.1	9.9	34.2	26.5
1980	13.0	17.9	50.8	10.4	10.1	15.7	10.2	9.1	32.5	25.7
1979	11.7	16.0	48.6	8.5	8.9	15.2	9.0	8.1	31.0	21.8
1978	11.4	15.7	50.6	7.9	8.7	14.0	8.7	7.9	30.6	21.6
1977	11.6	16.0	50.3	8.5	8.8	14.1	8.9	8.0	31.3	22.4
1976	11.8	15.8	52.0	8.5	9.0	15.0	9.1	8.1	31.1	24.7
1975	12.3	16.8	52.7	9.8	9.2	15.3	9.7	8.6	31.3	26.9
1974	11.2	15.1	51.5	8.3	8.3	14.6	8.6	7.7	30.3	23.0
1973	11.1	14.2	52.1	7.6	8.3	16.3	8.4	7.5	31.4	21.9
1972	11.9	14.9	53.1	8.6	8.8	18.6	9.0	n/a	33.3	n/a
1971	12.5	15.1	53.1	9.3	9.3	21.6	9.9	n/a	32.5	n/a
1970	12.6	14.9	53.0	9.2	9.0	24.6	9.9	n/a	33.5	n/a
1969	12.1	13.8	54.4	8.6	8.7	25.3	9.5	n/a	32.2	n/a
1968	12.8	15.3	55.2	10.2	9.0	25.0	10.0	n/a	34.7	n/a
1967	14.2	16.3	54.3	11.5	10.0	29.5	11.0	n/a	39.3	n/a
1966	14.7	17.4	58.2	12.6	10.5	28.5	11.3	n/a	41.8	n/a
1959	22.4	26.9	72.2	22.4	17.0	35.2	18.1	n/a	55.1	n/a

Source: Prepared by the Congressional Research Service using U.S. Bureau of the Census data.

Notes: r = revised estimates. n/a = not available.

a. Beginning in 1979, restricted to children in primary families only. Before 1979, includes children in unrelated subfamilies.

b. Beginning in 2002, CPS respondents could identify themselves as being of more than one race. Consequently, racial data for 2002 and after are not comparable to earlier years. Here, in 2002 and after, the term white means of white race alone and the term black means of black race alone. Hispanics, who may be of any race, are included among whites and blacks unless otherwise noted.

End Notes

[1] Supporting data are based on the following: U.S. Census Bureau, Income, Poverty, and Health Insurance Coverage in the United States: 2008; Current Population Report No. P60-235, September 2009; and unpublished Census Bureau tables, available on the Internet at http://www.census.gov/hhes/www/poverty/poverty08.html.

[2] See, for example, Emily Monea and Isabel Sawhill, *Simulating the Effect of the "Great Recession" on Poverty*, Brookings Institution, Washington, DC, September 10, 2009, http://www.brookings.edu/~/media papers/2009/0910_poverty_monea_sawhill/0910_poverty_monea_sawhill.pdf.

[3] See CRS Report RL30797, *Trends in Welfare, Work, and the Economic Well-Being of Female-Headed Families with Children: 1987-2008*, by Thomas Gabe.

[4] See CRS Report RS20807, *Short History of the 1996 Welfare Reform Law*, by Joe Richardson and Vee Burke.

[5] For a more complete discussion of the U.S. poverty measure, see CRS Report R41187, *Poverty Measurement in the United States: History, Current Practice, and Proposed Changes*, by Thomas Gabe.

[6] The Department of Health and Human Services (HHS) releases poverty income guidelines that are derived directly from Census poverty thresholds. These guidelines, a simplified approximation of the Census poverty thresholds, are used by HHS and other federal agencies for administering programs, particularly for determining program eligibility. For current guidelines and methods for their computation, see http://aspe.hhs.gov/poverty/index.shtml.

[7] See http://www.census.gov/hhes/www/poverty/threshld/thresh08.html.

[8] The poverty measure was adopted as the "official poverty measure" by a directive issued in 1969 by the Bureau of the Budget, now the Office of Management and Budget (OMB). The directive was revised in 1978 to include revisions to poverty thresholds and procedures for updating thresholds for inflation using the Consumer Price Index (CPI). See OMB Statistical Policy Directive 14, available on the internet at http://www.ce nsus.gov/hhes/www/povmeas/ombdir14.html.

[9] Based on U.S. Department of Labor Bureau of Labor Statistics Consumer Expenditure Survey data, in 2005 the average family spent about 12.8% of pre-tax income on food (including food consumed at home and away from home), or about one-eighth of total income, as opposed to one-third in the mid-1950s. This implies that the multiplier for updating poverty thresholds based on food consumption would be 7.8 (i.e., 1/.128), or 2.6 times the multiplier of 3 subsumed under poverty thresholds developed in the 1960s.

[10] Alternative poverty estimates for 2008 will not be available until the late fall of 2009. The alternative poverty estimate shown here is Income Definition 14a, from U.S. Census Bureau, *Table 2. Percent of Persons in Poverty, By Definition of Income and Selected Characteristics: 2008*, available on the internet at http://www.census.gov/hhes/ www/cpstables/032009/rdcall/2_001.htm.

[11] See Panel on Poverty and Family Assistance: Concepts, Information Needs, and Measurement Methods, *Measuring Poverty: A New Approach*, ed. Constance F. Citro and Robert T. Michael (Washington, DC: National Academy Press, 1995). For estimates of the effects of the NAS panel recommendations, see U.S. Bureau of the Census. *Experimental Poverty Measures: 1999*. Current Population Report No. P60-216, October 2001. Also, for a discussion of NAS-based poverty measurement, see the 2008 edition of "Background Material and Data on the Programs within the Jurisdiction of the Committee on Ways and Means," informally known as the Green Book, Appendix E, Poverty, Income Distribution and Antipoverty Effectiveness, pp. 77-102, available on the internet at http://waysandmeans.house.gov/ media/p df/110/appE.pdf.

[12] For the full bill, see the Legislative Information System link to H.R. 2909.

[13] For the full bill, see the Legislative Information System link to S. 1625.

[14] See http://www.esa.doc.gov/.

[15] The working group includes representatives from the Census Bureau, BLS, the Council of Economic Advisors, the Department of Commerce, the Department of Health and Human Services, and OMB.

[16] See http://www.census.gov/hhes/www/poverty/SPM_TWGObservations.pdf.

[17] Beginning with the March 2003 CPS, the Census Bureau allows survey respondents to identify themselves as belonging to one or more racial groups. In prior years, respondents could select only one racial category. Consequently, poverty statistics for different racial groups for 2002 and after are not directly comparable to earlier years' data. The terms blacks and whites, above, refers to persons who identified with only a single racial group. The term Hispanic refers to individuals' ethnic, as opposed to racial, identification. Hispanics may be of any race.

[18] See U.S. Census Bureau detailed table, http://www.census.gov/hhes/www/cpstables/032009/pov/ new29_100_01.htm.

[19] Related children in families. For an in-depth discussion of child poverty, see CRS Report RL32682, *Children in Poverty: Profile, Trends, and Issues*, by Vee Burke, Thomas Gabe, and Gene Falk.

[20] The CPS asks several questions to determine whether individuals are considered to have a work disability. Persons are identified as having a work disability if they (1) reported having a health problem or disability that prevents them from working or that limits the kind or amount of work they can do; (2) ever retired or left a job

for health reasons; (3) did not work in the survey week because of long-term physical or mental illness or disability which prevents the performance of any kind of work; (4) did not work at all in the previous year because they were ill or disabled; (5) are under 65 years of age and covered by Medicare; (6) are under age 65 years of age and a recipient of Supplemental Security Income (SSI); or (7) received veteran's disability compensation. Persons are considered to have a severe work disability if they meet any of the criteria in (3) through (6), above. See http://www.census.gov/hhes/www/disability/ disabcps.html.

[21] See http://www.census.gov/hhes/www/macro/032009/pov/new26_002_01.htm.

[22] Two states' poverty rates are statistically different at the 90% statistical confidence interval if the confidence intervals bounding their respective poverty rates do not overlap with one another. However, some states with overlapping confidence intervals may also statistically differ at the 90% statistical confidence interval. In order to precisely determine whether two states' poverty rates differ from one another, a statistical test of differences must be performed. The standard error for the difference between two estimates may be calculated as: $SE_{StateA} - SE_{StateB} = \sqrt{SE^2_{StateA} + SE^2_{StateB}}$. Two estimates are considered statistically different if at the 90% statistical confidence interval the absolute value of the difference is greater than 1.645 times the standard error of the difference (i.e., $|Povrate_{StateA} - Povrate_{StateB}| > 1.645x(SE_{StateA} - SE_{StateB})$
Note that the standard error for a state's poverty estimate may be obtained by dividing the margin of error depicted in **Figure 3** by 1.645.

[23] Statistically significant differences are based on a 90% statistical confidence interval.

[24] Beginning in 2006, a portion of the population living in non-institutional group quarters has been included in the ACS in estimating poverty. The population living in institutional group quarters, military barracks, and college dormitories has been excluded in the ACS poverty estimates for all years. The part of the non-institutional group quarters population that has been included in the poverty universe since 2006 (e.g., people living in group homes or those living in agriculture workers' dormitories) is considerably more likely to be in poverty than people living in households. Consequently, estimates of poverty in 2006 and after are somewhat higher than would be the case if all group quarters residents were excluded—thus, comparisons with earlier year estimates are not strictly comparable.

In: Economic Policies in a Time of Financial Crisis
Editor: Heather D. Perkins
ISBN: 978-1-61122-686-7

Chapter 11

THE NATIONAL DEBT: WHO BEARS ITS BURDEN?

Marc Labonte

SUMMARY

The United States has been free of a national debt for only two years, 1834 and 1835. In its first year, 1790, the country faced a debt of $75 million. From FY1998 to FY2001, the federal government ran budget surpluses. Since then, the budget has returned to deficit, and the debt had risen to $7.5 trillion by 2009. It rose to a high of 108.6% of gross domestic product (GDP) at the end of World War II; declined to a post-World War II low of 23.8% of GDP in 1974; and, then, rose to another high of 49.5% of GDP in 1993.

The national debt results from borrowing to finance budget deficits. Historically, the major cause of debt accumulation has been war. The United States has financed the extraordinary expenditures associated with war by borrowing rather than by raising taxes or printing money. This pattern was broken by the large budget deficits of the 1980s, the first half of the 1990s, and the period subsequent to 2001, which caused the national debt to rise substantially as a fraction of GDP.

Although economists have long recognized that a national debt imposes an inescapable burden on a nation, they have debated whether the burden is borne by the generation who contracts the debt or is shifted forward to future generations. There has also been some controversy over the nature of the burden.

The current consensus among economists is that the burden of the national debt is largely shifted forward to future generations. However, the burden imposed by the national debt does not arise from debt per se, but from budget deficits that gives rise to a national debt. If an economy is fully employed and the government increases its expenditures, for example, the resultant increase in aggregate demand will cause interest rates to rise and this will reduce or "crowd out" interest-sensitive spending by the private sector. This type of spending is likely to be for capital purposes (e.g., business spending for plant and equipment and household spending for housing and durable goods including automobiles). As a result, the private capital stock inherited by future generations is likely to be smaller and their real income or output will likely be lower. It is the reduction in future output that constitutes the burden of the national debt and it is a burden borne largely by future generations. It is a burden that cannot be decreased by borrowing abroad even though foreign borrowing could leave unchanged the size of the private capital stock.

Crucial to the consensus view (and other views) is the assumption that the economy is fully employed. And the burden discussed must be regarded as a gross burden in the sense that certain intangible gains must be set against it such as freedom from tyranny and domination by a foreign power that might have occurred had the United States lost such a contest as World War II.

BACKGROUND

The United States, from its beginning in 1790 to the present, has been free of a national debt for only two years, 1834 and 1835.[1] The national debt has grown from $75.5 million in 1790 to $5.8 trillion in 2008. The history of the U.S. national debt as a percent of gross domestic product (GDP) since 1940 is shown in **Figure 1**.[2] The national debt reached a high of 108.6% of GDP in 1946. It then began a long decline, reaching a low of 32.5% in 1981. The large budget deficits of the 1980s and 1990s reversed this trend and pushed the percentage to another high of 49.5% in 1993. The federal budget surpluses from FY1998 to FY2001 were used to retire a portion of the publicly held national debt. Between FY1997 and FY2001, the publicly held portion of the debt declined by more than $400 billion. Since FY2002, a return to budget deficits has caused the debt to grow again.

When evaluating the burden of the national debt, the gross debt must first be divided into two parts: debt held by the public (including the Federal Reserve), shown in Figure 1, and the amount held in accounts called federal trust funds, the principal one being for social security.[3] Because trust fund debt is owed to one part of the government to another, it has no effect on the economy, and does not impose any burden.[4] Thus, it will be neglected in the discussion below. The publicly held debt is often subdivided into that portion that is domestically owned and that portion owned by foreigners. U.S. Treasury securities have become increasingly popular among foreigners. At the end of FY2009, more than half of the privately held federal debt (which excludes debt held in government trust funds and by the Federal Reserve) was owned by foreigners.

The need to finance wars has been the major reason for the growth of a national debt. In common with other major countries, the United States has rarely financed the surge in wartime expenditures exclusively by raising taxes. A large part of wartime expenditures have been bond financed. During the Civil War, from mid-1861 to mid-1865, the national debt grew from about $65 million to $2.7 billion. Between mid-1916 and mid-1919, the increased debt associated with World War I, grew from $1.2 billion to $25.5 billion. And from mid-1941 to mid-1946, the debt associated with World War II, rose from $49 billion to $269 billion. Thus, it has been a common practice of American public finance to increase the national debt during wartime and then reduce the debt, at least as a percentage of GDP, during times of peace. This pattern was broken during the 1980s and early 1990s when the national debt grew both absolutely and relative to GDP. Recently debt has again grown in wartime; however, the recent increase in the debt has greatly exceeded the cost of the war. Growth of the national debt has also occurred during periods of economic contraction.

THE TRADITIONAL VIEW OF THE BURDEN OF A NATIONAL DEBT

Is a national debt a burden on a country? If it is, what is the nature of the burden? Who bears this burden? Questions such as these have perplexed economists at least since the days of Adam Smith. Great Britain in his day had accumulated a large national debt fighting the Seven Years War (the French and Indian War) and was about to add a further considerable sum suppressing the rebellion in its American colonies.

Interestingly, mainstream macroeconomics views the burden of a national debt, not in terms of the debt per se, but in terms of government budget deficits that are the cause of the debt and its growth. Thus, the burden that a national debt imposes on a country is due to the government's budget deficits.[5]

To see clearly the nature of this burden and who bears it, assume that the country's resources are fully employed and that capital (or saving) cannot flow internationally between countries. Also assume that this country now engages in a war with a neighbor and that the increased expenditures associated with the war lead to a budget deficit that is financed by issuing bonds.

The increase in government expenditures increases aggregate demand. In a fully employed economy, in addition to raising prices, the increase in demand will lead to a rise in interest rates.[6] The increase in interest rates is the means by which the government obtains the additional resources to fight the war for the increase will discourage interest-sensitive spending by the private sector. This is primarily business spending for capital goods such as plant, equipment, and structures and spending by households for homes, automobiles, appliances and the like. Thus, the budget deficit "crowds out" private capital and the burden of the growing national debt represented by the bonds issued to finance the war, is the decrease in the private capital stock of the country. The level of output is determined by the capital stock, labor force, and productivity levels. Since the private capital stock inherited by future generations will be smaller, it implies that the level of output enjoyed by them will be lower.[7] The lower level of output is thus the ultimate burden of the debt and it is a burden that is largely shifted forwarded to future generations.[8]

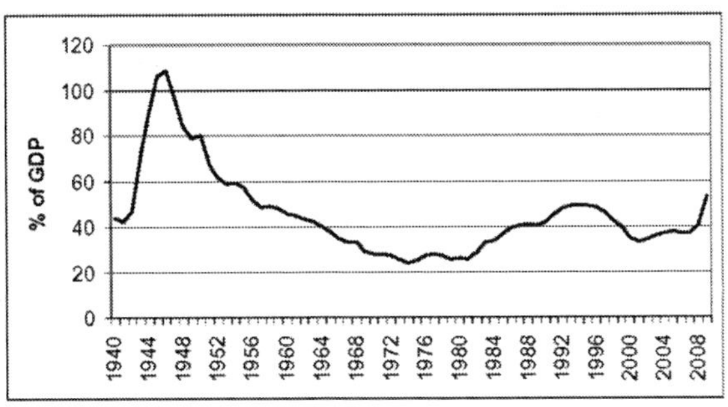

Source: Office of Management and Budget.

Figure 1. Federal Debt as a % of GDP, 1940-2009

Suppose Capital Can Flow Internationally

It might be thought that a high degree of international capital mobility could moderate the burden of the debt because foreign saving could supplement domestic resources such that the private capital stock need not diminish. Suppose, for example, that as interest rates tended to rise in response to the increased expenditures, foreign capital (or foreign saving) was attracted in sufficient volume to keep domestic interest rates from rising.[9] This would keep the domestic capital stock unchanged. Would this mean that there was no burden from a national debt? Unfortunately, this is not the case. Although it is true that the private capital stock inherited by future generations will remain unchanged, a portion of it will now be owned by foreigners. And the rewards from that capital will not flow to Americans, but will have to be transferred abroad.

Thus, having foreigners supply some or all of the resources for the war effort, as in this example, does not avoid the burden of the debt. Future generations will still have a lower level of income available to them.

Would Financing the Deficit by Issuing Money Eliminate the Burden?

In the preceding discussion, the budget deficit was financed by issuing interest-bearing debt or bonds. The government, however, has available another means for financing its budget deficit. Rather than borrowing the wherewithal it could simply print money (currency) and pay its bills.[10] Might not this method of finance reduce or eliminate the burden the national debt places on future generations? Although the simple answer is basically yes, the explanation is more complicated.

Financing a budget deficit in a fully employed economy by issuing money is inflationary. And inflation is a form of taxation. It is tax on the existing stock of money held by the public in the sense that it reduces the purchasing power of that money. It is by reducing the wealth and purchasing power of the private sector that inflation enables the government to obtain the additional resources to finance the war. Inflation (taxation) thus crowds out private spending, some of which may be spending on capital goods. The majority of that spending, however, is likely to be on current consumption. Because it is, the burden of these additional government expenditures, used in the example above, are almost exclusively borne by the current generation. The private capital stock inherited by future generations is unlikely to be diminished and, hence, they will not suffer much of a decrease in their standard of living. Thus, financing a budget deficit by substituting non-interest-bearing debt (money) for interest-bearing debt (bonds) does not eliminate the burden of the debt; it largely shifts the main burden from future generations to the present generation.[11]

Do All Budget Deficits That Increase the National Debt Impose a Burden?

The preceding analysis is framed in terms of a fully employed economy that experiences an increase in aggregate demand due to an increase in government expenditures. This increase in demand requires an increase in real interest rates to decrease or crowd out private sector spending. Yet there are circumstances under which a government budget deficit can arise or increase with little or no crowding out.

Suppose, for example, that the United States economy is, as it is now, in a recession and either expenditures are increased or taxes cut in an effort to "jump start" an expansion. It is possible in these circumstances for a budget deficit to grow without increasing interest rates. The reason being that the increase in income generated by the increase in demand generates additional saving for financing the deficit. The additional resources represented by the saving make it possible to maintain an undiminished private capital stock in the face of a rising budget deficit.[12] Thus, debt issued during a recession imposes a smaller burden than an equivalent amount issued during an economic expansion; if the recession is serious enough the burden is negligible.[13]

The Role of Interest Payments in the Traditional View

The accumulation of a national debt means that the government budget will contain as an expenditure item the interest payable on that debt. Does this impose a burden on future generations whose taxes will be used for debt service? In the traditional view, the answer depends on whether the debt is internally or externally held. For an internally held debt, the payment of interest is an income transfer from taxpayer to bond holder. In the simple case, if they are the same person, they are left neither poorer nor richer. If they are not the same person, then while the taxpayer is left with less income, the bond owner has a larger income. As a group, however, they are neither richer nor poorer by the payment of interest. The payment of interest is not an additional burden of an internally held debt. That burden, as noted above, is the lower level of output (income) enjoyed by future generations who inherit a reduced private capital stock.

When the national debt is externally held, the payment of interest abroad is a transfer of income from Americans to foreigners. This is not a separate burden from the national debt, however. As noted above, when a national debt is sold abroad, the private capital stock passed on to future generations need not be diminished. But a portion of that capital stock will be foreign owned and a portion of the income generated by that capital will accrue to foreigners. This is the interest or, more properly, debt service paid to them, and it reduces the level of income that accrues to Americans. Thus, the payment of interest to foreigners is how the burden of an externally held national debt is shifted forward to future generations of Americans.

A National Debt and National Interest Rates

It might be thought that a large national debt would have an effect on market interest rates since if the debt is short term, the government must be in financial markets more or less continuously as the debt rolls over frequently. Such is not the case. The rate of interest that prevails in a country over time is determined by saving and investment and these are what economists call flows. The national debt is what they call a stock. And it is the flows that govern the real rate of interest. The refinancing of the national debt when the budget is balanced should not alter the flows. Essentially, refinancing involves replacing maturing securities with ones that come due in the future. Since this makes no new net claim on the nation's saving, it should have no effect on interest rates. If this were not the case, we should observe real national interest rates fluctuating with the size of a nation's national debt. This pattern is not to be found consistently in the data.

There are historical examples in which countries have had difficulties in rolling over their maturing interest-bearing debts. Often these episodes have been attributed to a lack of confidence in the governments in question. When these episodes have occurred, they have often resulted in the monetization of the maturing debt with the result being serious inflation and rising market interest rates as the market rates come to embody expectations of inflation. Thus, a very large debt could increase interest rates by threatening the government's solvency. The U.S. debt is not near this point.

The Retirement of the National Debt

The budget surpluses from FY1998 through FY2001 were used to retire the national debt. By the end of 2001, debt held by the public was some $400 billion below its 1997 peak. What are the effects of debt retirement on the U.S. economy?

In the traditional model, the effect on the economy from retiring an internally held debt is just the reverse of what would happen if the national debt were increased. The budget surpluses augment the national pool of saving, a pool contributed to by the business and household sectors. An increase in the fraction of GDP that is saved leads to lower interest rates. This encourages (or "crowds in") interest-sensitive spending. From the previous discussion, this is business and household spending on capital goods. Thus, the budget surpluses increase the capital stock of the country and, over time, this raises the level of real income and the material well-being of Americans. This, then, is the benefit that comes from reducing the national debt. It is a benefit that comes from budget surpluses and it largely benefits future generations.

In a broader framework in which the U.S. economy is linked to foreign economies through trade and capital flows, the interaction of budget surpluses, retirement of the national debt, and its effect on the U.S. economy, is more complex. Retiring debt that is foreign owned relieves the United States from having to pay interest to foreigners. This raises the fraction of U.S. GDP that is available to Americans and this benefits the current generation as well as those alive in the future. In addition, since the higher saving rate leads to lower interest rates in the United States, some of that additional saving is likely to flow abroad augmenting the capital stock of foreign countries. This, in turn, increases the claims of Americans on foreign output (or decreases the net claim foreigners have on U.S. output) thereby enhancing their material well-being about the same as would have occurred if those resources had been used to augment the domestic capital stock.[14]

Does Implicit Debt Impose the Same Burden?

So far, this chapter has focused on *explicit* national debt, the issuance of U.S. Treasuries to the public. But the recent work of economists in the area of generational accounting has resulted in a better appreciation of the equivalence between explicit and *implicit* national debt. These economists argue that categories of government activity such as "expenditures," "revenues," and "deficits" are economically arbitrary. Instead, the focus should be on the economic incidence of any government policy over time, regardless of its label. They argue that today's explicit budget deficit is paltry compared with the large budget deficits that will accrue in the distant future as implied by current policy. And these implicit deficits currently impose the same burden on future generations as if they were made explicit today through the issuance of U.S. Treasuries.

This can be illustrated by examining the Social Security system. The retirement of the baby boomers means that the current "pay as you go" system will become insolvent in the future under current policy—benefits promised will greatly exceed payroll tax revenues. If it is assumed that all legally promised benefits will be met in the future, then large payroll tax increases will be necessary. Thus, future generations would be forced to consume fewer goods and services because a larger part of their income would be taxed and transferred to Social Security recipients.[15]

Taxing working generations in the future to pay unfunded retirement benefits is not the only way to deal with this problem. There is an alternative that imposes the same burden on future working generations. Imagine that the present discounted value of those future unfunded social security benefits were included as an outlay in this year's budget. Each baby boomer would be given a one-time payment today in lieu of their future unfunded benefits. This added expenditure would increase the size of the present budget deficit, reduce the national saving rate, and would be financed by issuing additional Treasury securities. This would increase interest rates, lower private capital spending, and reduce the size of the economy in the future. As a result, the pre-tax income of future generations would be smaller, but because they would not have to pay higher taxes to fund the additional social security benefits, their after tax income at that time would be the same as it would be in the situation above where the future unfunded benefits were paid for with higher taxes. Thus, an implicit debt imposes the same burden on future generations as an explicit debt because the two concepts are economically equivalent.

Conclusion

The current consensus view among economists is that the source of the burden associated with a national debt is the government budget deficit that gives rise to the debt. In a fully employed economy, the deficit "crowds out" private sector spending, especially spending on capital goods. Thus, a smaller private capital stock and a lower level of output are passed along to future generations and it is this lower level of output that is the ultimate burden of the national debt. And, it is a burden that is largely shifted forwarded to future generations. Thus, according to the consensus view, the burden of a national debt is borne by future generations.

Should the debt be sold abroad, there is still a burden since a portion of the output from the unchanged size of the private capital stock will accrue to foreigners.

When the national debt is retired through budget surpluses, the effect on the economy is the reverse of debt increases. Future generations acquire a larger capital stock (or a larger American owned capital stock) and a higher level of output (or increased material well-being).

APPENDIX A. STATISTICAL DATA

Table A-1. Federal Outlays, Receipts and Deficits/Surpluses FY1982-FY2009

Fiscal Year	Outlays		Receipts		Deficit or Surplus	
	$ Billions	% of GDP	$ Billions	% of GDP	$ Billions	% of GDP
2009	3,517.7	24.7	2,105.0	14.8	-1412.7	-9.9
2008	2,982.6	20.7	2,524.0	17.5	-458.6	-3.2
2007	2,728.7	19.6	2,568.0	18.5	-160.7	-1.2
2006	2,655.1	20.1	2,406.9	18.2	-248.2	-1.9
2005	2,472.0	19.9	2,153.6	17.3	-318.3	-2.6
2004	2,292.9	19.6	1,880.1	16.1	-412.7	-3.5
2003	2,159.9	19.7	1,782.3	16.2	-377.6	-3.4
2002	2,010.9	19.1	1,853.1	17.6	-157.8	-1.5
2001	1,862.9	18.2	1,991.1	19.5	128.2	1.3
2000	1,789.0	18.2	2,025.2	20.6	236.2	2.4
1999	1,701.8	18.5	1,827.5	19.8	125.6	1.4
1998	1,652.5	19.1	1,721.7	19.9	69.3	0.8
1997	1,601.1	19.5	1,579.2	19.2	-21.9	-0.3
1996	1,560.5	20.2	1,453.1	18.8	-107.4	-1.4
1995	1,515.8	20.6	1,351.8	18.4	-164.0	-2.2
1994	1,461.8	21.0	1,258.6	18.0	-203.2	-2.9
1993	1,409.4	21.4	1,154.3	17.5	-255.1	-3.9
1992	1,381.5	22.1	1,091.2	17.5	-290.3	-4.7
1991	1,324.2	22.3	1,055.0	17.8	-269.2	-4.5
1990	1,253.0	21.9	1,032.0	18.0	-221.0	-3.9
1989	1,143.7	21.2	991.1	18.4	-152.6	-2.8
1988	1,064.4	21.3	909.2	18.2	-155.2	-3.1
1987	1,004.0	21.6	854.3	18.4	-149.7	-3.2
1986	990.4	22.5	769.2	17.5	-221.2	-5.0
1985	946.3	22.8	734.0	17.7	-212.3	-5.1
1984	851.8	22.2	666.4	17.3	-185.4	-4.8
1983	808.4	23.5	600.6	17.5	-207.8	-6.0
1982	745.7	23.1	617.8	19.2	-128.0	-4.0

Sources: Office of Management and Budget, *Historical Tables. Fiscal Year 2011*, Washington, February 2010, table 1.3.

Table A-2. Federal Debt and Interest Outlays FY1982-FY2009

	Debt Held by the Public		Interest Outlays		
Year	$ Bil lions	% of GDP	$ Billions	% of Budget Outlays	% of GDP
2009	7,544.7	53.0	186.9	5.3	1.3
2008	5,803.0	40.2	252.8	8.5	1.7
2007	5,035.0	36.2	237.1	8.7	1.7
2006	4,829.0	36.5	226.6	8.5	1.7
2005	4,592.3	36.9	184.0	7.4	1.5
2004	4,295.5	36.8	160.2	7.9	1.4
2003	3,913.4	35.6	153.1	7.1	1.4
2002	3,540.4	33.6	170.9	8.5	1.6
2001	3,319.6	32.5	206.2	11.1	2.0
2000	3,409.8	34.7	223.0	12.5	2.3
1999	3,632.4	39.4	229.8	13.5	2.5
1998	3,721.1	43.0	241.1	14.6	2.8
1997	3,772.3	45.9	244.0	15.2	3.0
1996	3,734.1	48.4	241.1	15.4	3.1
1995	3,604.4	49.1	232.1	15.3	3.2
1994	3,433.1	49.2	202.9	13.9	2.9
1993	3,248.4	49.3	198.7	14.1	3.0
1992	2,999.7	48.1	199.3	14.4	3.2
1991	2,689.0	45.3	194.4	14.7	3.3
1990	2,411.6	42.1	184.3	14.7	3.2
1989	2,190.7	40.6	169.0	14.8	3.1
1988	2,051.6	41.0	151.8	14.3	3.0
1987	1,889.8	40.6	138.6	13.8	3.0
1986	1,740.6	39.5	136.0	13.7	3.1
1985	1,507.3	36.4	129.5	13.7	3.1
1984	1,307.0	34.0	111.1	13.0	2.9
1983	1,137.3	33.1	89.8	11.1	2.6
1982	924.6	28.7	85.0	11.4	2.6

Sources: Office of Management and Budget, *Historical Tables, Fiscal Year 2011*, Washington, February 2010, table 7.1 and table 3.1.

APPENDIX B. SELECTIVE VIEWS ON THE BURDEN OF A NATIONAL DEBT

Although economists have long recognized that a national debt imposes an inescapable burden on a nation, they have argued about who bears this burden.[16] In particular, whether the burden is borne by the generation that incurred the debt or whether it is shifted forward to a future generation or, in the language of the time, whether it is a "burden or mortgage on our children." This issue acquired new urgency when the view (since discarded) took hold in the economics profession that mature market economies might be incapable of generating sustained periods of more or less full employment without a continuous government budget deficit. If this were the case, the national debt could be expected to grow continuously. And if that debt were a burden on future generations, it would mean that the present generation would enjoy employment only by shifting a burden to future generations.

This appendix provides a flavor of the various arguments advanced by economists about the burden of the public debt, the nature of that burden, and who bears that burden. The arguments summarized in this appendix are all concerned with an internally held debt. It is recognized that an externally held debt must be treated differently.

The "We Owe It to Ourselves" View

As a result of the concern over whether the enjoyment of full employment by the current generation would shift a burden to the future, it became an accepted view during the 1930s, 40s, and 50s, that an *internally held* national debt would impose a burden only on the generation present when it was contracted and would impose no burden on future generations because we "owe the debt to ourselves." The words of Paul Samuelson best express the view that the current generation bears the burden of deficit finance. Drawing on wartime experience, he wrote: "*To fight a war now, we must hurl present-day munitions at the enemy; not dollar bills, and not future goods and services*." Thus, the alternative use of these resources in the private sector constituted the burden of the national debt and it was a burden borne by the generation that, in this case, fought the war.

That subsequent debt service imposed no burden on future generations can be clearly seen in the simple case where the owners of government bonds, the evidence of the national debt, were also taxpayers. Servicing the government debt would mean taking money from one pocket and putting it into the other. In other words, this is a mere income transfer. It is not a burden. Since future generations would inherit both the bonds and the tax liabilities needed to service the bonds, no burden would be shifted to the future. In a more complex case in which the bond owners and taxpayers were not the same people, the existence of a national debt would imply some income redistribution from the latter to the former. However, this would not be a burden for the society as a whole because there would be no loss of resources for the group as a whole to use.[17] Thus, the burden of an internally held debt, according to this view, is borne by the generation alive when the debt is contracted. And the burden consists of the alternative private sector uses of the resources that are withdrawn for use by the public sector.[18]

Should the national debt be owned by foreigners, this view argued that it would constitute a burden primarily on future generations. The current generation, by borrowing resources from abroad, would have more goods and services to consume than it produced. It thereby gains by incurring a foreign debt. To service this debt a portion of future national output would have to be transferred abroad thereby reducing the income of future generations who, the argument states, would have fewer goods and services to use than it produced. Thus, in the case of an external debt, we would not "owe it to ourselves" but to foreigners. And this was the important distinction as far as who bears the burden was concerned.

The Buchanan View

Prof. James Buchanan, a Nobel Prize winner in the 1980s, attacked the then orthodox view of burden of the debt in his popular text book on public finance first published in 1958.[19] Buchanan's argument is that the burden of an internally held national debt is shifted forwarded to future generations. It is not borne by the generation who contracted the debt. His argument is that when individuals buy government interest-bearing debt, they are making a voluntary decision to give up the current use of resources for a larger future income (larger by the amount of interest they receive on their now larger asset holdings). Since this is a voluntary decision, no burden is imposed on the purchaser (i.e., the generation present when the debt is contracted). In fact, since the purchase would not have been made had a superior alternative been available, the purchaser is actually better off than had an alternative use been made of that income. However, subsequent generations of taxpayers must surrender to the bond holders the wherewithal for debt service. And this necessity is forced on them. In this sense, it is the future generations who will bear the burden of an internally held debt and the burden is the taxes they must pay for debt service. This is not a voluntary decision, but one forced on them by the decisions of an earlier generation. Although Buchanan's view was subject to criticism by some economists, he was soon to get major support from others.[20]

The Bowen, Davis, and Kopf View

Acknowledging that Buchanan's view had stimulated their collective thinking, Professors Bowen, Davis, and Kopf (hereafter BDK) came up with an argument for why an internally held debt imposes a burden on future generations.[21] BDK define burden in terms of the lifetime consumption of a generation (as opposed to the resources that must be given up now to, let us say, fight a war). The generation whose lifetime consumption is reduced is, according to BDK, the generation burdened by a national debt. With this in mind, they argue that the generation that contracts the national debt need not be burdened by it so long as it does not pay the debt off. This is so, because while that generation must decrease its consumption to buy the debt (even if they are forced to do so), it can always sell it to the next generation before its members die and enjoy the added consumption it had to forego when it purchased the debt. This process can go on indefinitely until the debt is retired.[22] The generation that retires the debt, however, has no additional consumption to offset the consumption it gave up when it purchased the debt from the generation before it. Thus, BDK share in common with Buchanan a belief that the national debt is a "burden on our children." It is they who must ultimately retire the debt and, with retirement, undergo a permanent reduction in their consumption.[23]

The Barro View

The most recent, innovative, and serious challenge to the conventional view of the burden of a national debt comes from Prof. Robert Barro.[24] As noted in the body of this chapter, crowding out would not occur and the burden would not be shifted forward to future generations if the current generation would only save an additional amount of resources to match the increased demand for resources represented by the additional government expenditures that are financed by issuing interest-bearing debt. Barro has an ingenious argument for why such behavior could be forthcoming. Suppose, he says, that individuals live forever and that they have as a goal the maximization of consumption over time. To attain this goal, they have to be concerned about the private capital stock for it is an important determinate of income and income governs consumption. As in the standard macroeconomic model, the saving behavior of the public governs the resources available for capital goods purposes. How much of their income they save, and, hence, private investment, will depend on how they value current as opposed to future consumption.

If individuals live forever, Barro argues, they will be indifferent between the government using taxes or the sale of bonds to finance, let us say, additional expenditures related to war. If the additional expenditures are financed through an additional tax, the public, in an effort to keep the private capital stock (the key to its goal of maximizing consumption) unchanged, will reduce current consumption by the amount of the tax. As a result, the burden of the war-related expenditures will be felt when they are incurred.[25]

Alternatively, the government could have chosen to finance the additional expenditures through the sale of bonds or interest-bearing debt. Had this option been chosen, the public would have behaved in the same way. In order to keep the private capital stock at the optimum level over time, it would have to reduce its consumption and save a higher fraction of its income. This additional saving would then be used to buy the bonds and provide the resources to the government for the war.

It might be thought that the necessity to pay interest on the bonds over time (and, perhaps, provide for their redemption) would, by requiring additional taxes, shift a burden forward. This is not the case, for the taxpayer and the bondholder are the same people. Money is simply taken from one pocket as taxes and put back into the other pocket as interest. This is no additional burden. To the extent that the taxpayer and bondholder are different people, some income redistribution could be expected. Thus, if individuals live forever, they would be indifferent between financing these added expenditures through a tax increase or the sale of bonds.[26] And, the burden of the debt is felt in terms of reduced consumption. It is a burden borne at the time the additional expenditures are made.

Barro must deal with the fact that individuals do not live forever. To address this problem, he asks: are there circumstances under which they would behave as if they had eternal life? He argues that this behavior would be forthcoming if individuals treat the well being of their children on a par with their own. Since their children would behave similarly, and so on, individuals in the current generation would behave as if they lived forever. If individuals behaved in the way Barro argues, the conventional argument about the burden of a national debt, is likely to be wrong. Debt financed government expenditures will not crowd out the private capital stock because it will be offset by an equal amount of private sector saving.[27] This behavior is designed to ensure that future generations do not inherit a smaller private capital stock and, hence, a lower level of output and suboptimal consumption. Thus, the burden of the national debt is not shifted to them as the convention view argues.[28]

The attack on Barro's view has been both theoretical and empirical. On the theoretical side, it is argued that individuals for a number of reasons may be reluctant to equate the well-being of their children on a par with their own (this presumes that the individuals under scrutiny have children).[29] On the empirical side, the saving behavior of the private sector does not correlated well with the saving/dis-saving behavior of the public sector. The Barro view implies that this behavior should be highly correlated: on a one-to-one basis. Only in this way is the private capital stock passed on to future generations rendered immune to the public finances of government.

Appendix B. Conclusion

This appendix has provided a flavor of the various arguments advanced by economists about the burden of the public debt, the nature of the burden, and who bears that burden. It has basically been a debate about who bears the burden. According to the various views, the burden, depending on how it is defined, can be borne by the generation that contracted the debt or shifted forward to future generations. The arguments summarized in this appendix are all concerned with an internally held debt. It is recognized that an externally held debt must be treated differently.

End Notes

[1] In 1834 the national debt was $37,733 and in 1835 it was $37,513. It is generally believed that the bonds represented by these sums were lost, misplaced, or destroyed and, thus, would never be presented for payment.

[2] Official data on U.S. GDP are available subsequent to 1929. Finding a consistent series on the national debt prior to 1940 is difficult because the treatment of U.S. Agency debt is not consistent across time. When a somewhat comparable series for gross debt for the period 1929-1939 is used, it is shown to rise from 16.6% of GDP in 1930 to 44.3% in 1934. It then remains in the low 40% range until 1938, rising to 45.5% in 1939. However, the rise from 1930 to 1934 is due mainly to the decline in GDP during the Great Depression. During the period 1934-1938, the national debt grew at about the same rate as GDP.

[3] Traditionally, the national debt of a country has consisted only of its interest-bearing debt. Non-interest-bearing debt or currency, even though a *technical* liability of the government, has been excluded from national debt calculations.

[4] Because of various accounting conventions and practices used by the federal government, it is possible for the gross debt of the United States to rise even as the publicly held portion declines. And, indeed, this occurred from FY1998 to FY2001.

[5] The literature on the burden of a national debt is extensive. It is selectively reviewed in **Appendix B**.

[6] The mechanism by which this occurs is presented in the literature in several ways. Often is it said that the increase in government expenditures and the resultant rise in the budget deficit reduces national saving. The reduction in national saving then causes interest rates to rise to allocate the reduced flow of saving over private investment. Alternatively, the rise in real (or inflation adjusted) interest rates occurs because the government must float additional bonds to cover the deficit. And it is this increased demand for funds in financial markets which raises interest rates. Finally, the increase in real interest rates is said to come from an increased demand for money as income increases in response to the rise in aggregate demand. This increase in money demand, in the presence of a fixed money supply, causes interest rates, the price of money, to rise to restore equilibrium between demand and supply.

[7] If additional resources were made available through additional saving by the public, the increase in government expenditures would not raise real interest rates and crowd out private investment. (This is identified as the Barro view in **Appendix B**.) This would not, however, eliminate the burden of the debt. It would merely shift it forward to the present generation. The consumption of this generation would be reduced by the additional saving.

[8] Some of the burden will be borne by the current generation (or generation present when the debt is contracted) for they will share part of the lower output over their remaining life as well. Of course, this burden must be regarded as a gross burden. Some budget deficits are incurred to increase the stock of social capital such as highways, power grids, water supplies, etc. This capital may perform a very useful and complementary role relative to private capital in increasing output. In addition, offset against the burden of other types of spending may be a large immeasurable gain enjoyed by future generations such as freedom from tyranny and domination by another country.

[9] It should be recalled that foreign capital or saving comes to a country in the form of a trade deficit. It is the trade deficit or excess of imports over exports, that allows a country to use more goods and services than it

produces. It is this excess that makes it possible, in this example, to use resources for war and, at the same time, keep the capital stock from falling.

[10] This was the principal means used by the Continental Congress to finance the American Revolution. The Confederacy used this means heavily in the American Civil War. It was used to a lesser degree by the Union government.

[11] Another way of expressing what is occurring is to say that as inflation erodes the real value of the public's money holdings, it must refrain from using income for consumption in an effort to restore it's real money balances. This reduced level of consumption is then the burden of the debt and it is a burden borne by the current generation.

[12] Similarly, a budget deficit that rises as an economy goes into a downturn is unlikely to "crowd out" private investment since it will not force up interest rates. The most that can be said is that the deficit may keep interest rates from falling as much as they would otherwise. In that sense, the deficit reduces the hypothetical capital stock available to future generations.

[13] This part of the traditional view on debt burden seems to be incomplete or based on the implicit assumption that a national debt accumulated in periods when the economy is operating at less than full employment is retired during periods when the economy is operating at full employment. If this is not the case, and the country faces a budget deficit even at full employment, the prospect arises of an ever-growing national debt. A case can be made that should the debt continue to rise relative to GDP the fiscal regime may be unsustainable over the longer run.

[14] It was noted above that in the traditional view, the interest paid on an internally held debt is regarded as an income transfer and not as a burden. When an internally held debt is retired, the interest expenses of the government fall. If the taxes used to pay these expanses are not reduced through a tax cut, but are used instead to purchase goods and services, it increases the size of the government. Thus, a case can be made that some of the decline in the interest expenses in the federal budget from debt retirement should be matched by a tax cut. This argument does not apply to the portion of the interest expenses that are used to service the foreign held component of the national debt.

[15] Returning Social Security to solvency through benefit cuts would create an equivalent burden. Since retirees would receive lower benefits, they would be able to purchase fewer goods and services. Assuming taxes were raised or benefits were cut at the same date, the generational incidence of this burden would be slightly different, however. The burden of higher taxes would be felt by workers from that date forward, while the burden of lower benefits would be felt by retirees from that date forward. Thus, an older generation (retirees at that date) would share in the burden of a benefit cut.

[16] For a more comprehensive review of the burden of a national debt, see *Public Debt & Future Generations*, edited by James M. Ferguson (Chapel Hill: The University of North Carolina Press, 1964) and Randall Holcombe, John D. Jackson, and Asghar Zardkoohi, "The National Debt Controversy," *Kyklos*, 34 (1981), pp. 186-202.

[17] Notice that this argument neglects the fact that the budget deficit that gave rise to the debt could have crowded out private investment thereby reducing the capital stock inherited by future generations and the lower level of income that this reduction implies. It may well be that this view was substantially influenced by economic conditions during the depressed 1930s when budget deficits were unlikely to have crowded out private investment. It should also be noted that this and other arguments about the burden of a national debt abstracted from the possibility that the taxes to service the debt may have far reaching consequences for the incentives to work, save, invest, and take risks, all of which are important in market economies and that affect the long run level of output.

[18] This view of burden seems to imply that the resources withdrawn for use by the government comes at the expense of private sector consumption. For if private sector investment were curtailed, then some of the burden will be shifted to the future as suggested by the crowding out view discussed above. This view may also have been influenced by U.S. experience during World War II when a large part of crowding out did take the form of a decrease in private consumption. It should be noted that the above view of burden was formulated before economists had developed growth models. Once growth models were developed, they forced economists to think differently about debt burden.

[19] *Public Principles of Public Debt* (Homewood, IL: Richard D. Irwin, 1958).

[20] Prof. James Tobin was an important critic of Buchanan. He was concerned with Buchanan's view of burden. If a person voluntarily does something, it is no burden to that person, according to Buchanan. This suggests to Tobin that a person who voluntarily purchases a good on which an excise tax is levied incurs no tax burden. Yet, there is a whole literature in public finance on the "incidence and effects" of taxes that Buchanan's notion of burden seems to throws away. Perhaps, in reference to the national debt, it would be more appropriate and less troublesome to ask "who bears the incidence of the debt" rather than the burden of the debt.

[21] "The Public Debt: A Burden on Future Generations?" *American Economic Review*, 50 (September 1960), pp. 701-706 and "The Distribution of the Debt Burden: A Reply," *American Economic Review* 51 (March 1961), pp. 141-143.

[22] There is, however, the question of the time distribution of that consumption. Consumption is given up early in the life of the current generation to be recouped at a later period when the debt is sold to the next generation. But

consumption at a later date is unlikely to be of equal value to the consumption given up when the bonds are purchased. Because it is not, individuals must be rewarded for postponing consumption until later. And this is the role of interest in the BDK model. It is the reward paid to bond holders for postponing current consumption until later. The present discounted value of those interest payments and the principal, should be equal in value to the consumption that could be enjoyed today if the bonds were not purchased. From that perspective, the lifetime consumption of the current generation is not reduced. However, paying interest involves having to pay taxes, and taxes reduce the lifetime ability of any generations to consume. Thus, on balance, debt financing reduces the net lifetime consumption of every generation which means that part of the burden of debt is spread across all generations including the generation present when the debt was contracted.

[23] BDK were careful to remind the reader that there is nothing inherently undesirable with debt financing of government. For example, if such government spending was for capital goods that benefitted future generations, a case could be made that they should be burdened by their cost (or a sort of pay-as-you-use system).

[24] "Are Government Bonds Net Wealth?" *Journal of Political Economy*, 82 (November-December 1974), pp. 405-14.

[25] If individuals do not live forever, and it will be shown later that this isn't crucial to Barro's argument, it could be said that the burden of the war expenditures were felt by the generation alive when they were incurred.

[26] This taxpayer indifference between bond or tax financed government expenditures has been attributed to a founder of modern political economy, David Ricardo. It has been shown that this so-called Ricardian Equivalence is not the true view of Ricardo. On the contrary, Ricardo argued that the taxpayers would not be indifferent, but would generally prefer to finance such expenditures by selling bonds rather than paying additional taxes.

[27] Technically speaking, the current generation need not save a precisely offsetting sum from current income. This is because the current generation can always leave a bequest to the next generation.

[28] Barro further argues that if the current generation wanted to ensure that their children inherited a smaller private capital stock, they have a simple means to do so: they could save a smaller portion of their disposable income. They don't need a government budget deficit for that purpose. Thus, in the presence of a budget deficit, they are, according to Barro, likely to offset it with a higher saving rate. The opposite is supposed to occur when it is faced with a budget surplus.

[29] For a more complete theoretical critique of Barro, see James Tobin, *Asset Accumulation and Economic Activity* Chapter III, (Chicago: University of Chicago Press, 1980), pp. 49-96.

In: Economic Policies in a Time of Financial Crisis
Editor: Heather D. Perkins
ISBN: 978-1-61122-686-7

Chapter 12

INTEREST PAYMENTS ON THE FEDERAL DEBT: A PRIMER

Thomas Hungerford

SUMMARY

Of the three broad categories of federal spending, the only category that cannot be reduced by legislative action is net interest payments. Net interest payments accounted for about 7% of federal spending between 1962 and the late 1970s. With the high interest rates in the late 1970s and the large budget deficits in the 1980s, net interest payments eventually rose to 15% of federal spending. The low interest rates combined with budget discipline in the 1990s reduced net interest payments back down to 7% of federal outlays by 2003. Low interest rates kept net interest payments low to 2009. However, net interest payments are projected to increase dramatically over the next 10 years.

Federal spending is divided into three broad categories. First, discretionary spending is provided and controlled by the annual appropriations acts and includes such things as Fdefense and education spending.[1] Discretionary spending currently accounts for about 35% of federal outlays. Second, direct or mandatory spending is provided and controlled by laws other than appropriation acts and includes spending for such programs as Social Security and Medicare.[2] Mandatory spending accounts for over half of federal outlays. Lastly, net interest payments are interest payments on federal debt held by the public and currently account for almost 5% of federal outlays. The Congressional Budget Office (CBO) in their baseline projection has net interest payments growing to almost 14% of federal outlays by FY2020.

In February 2010, President Obama created the bipartisan National Commission on Fiscal Responsibility and Reform. The Commission's task is to identify policies that will improve the fiscal situation in the medium term and achieve fiscal sustainability in the long term. The policies could involve changes to the growth of entitlement spending, increases in revenues, and decreases in other spending. The recommendations of the Commission could serve as a basis for legislation to reduce federal deficits by increasing taxes and reducing spending. The only category of federal spending that cannot be reduced by legislative action (barring default on the public debt) is net interest payments.

While Congress cannot affect current net interest payments, congressional actions on the budget will affect future interest payments. This chapter examines net interest payments and the mechanisms through which Congress can affect net interest payments.

FEDERAL DEBT

Federal debt is composed of debt issued by the Treasury (Treasury securities) and debt securities issued by other federal agencies (agency securities). At the end of 2009, total federal securities amounted to more than $12 trillion, of which only $23.5 billion (less than 0.2%) were agency securities. Federal debt is held either by the public (that is, private investors) or in government accounts. Currently, about 36% of federal debt is held in various government accounts. For example, the two Social Security trust funds currently hold about $2.5 trillion in Treasury securities. The rest of the federal debt is held by the public (foreign and domestic), including individuals, pension funds, banks, and other investors.

Figure 1 shows the level of total federal debt and debt held by the public since 1962 as a percentage of gross domestic product (GDP). Both measures of debt fell as a proportion of GDP between 1962 and the mid-1970s. Beginning in 1981, total federal debt began to climb as tax cuts, increases in defense spending, and a recession increased budget deficits. Total debt continued growing relative to GDP until the mid-1990s. As budget deficits gave way to budget surpluses after 1997, and as the economy expanded, federal debt fell as a percentage of GDP. The mild recession and the tax cuts in 2001 moved the federal budget back into deficit and federal debt consequently increased.

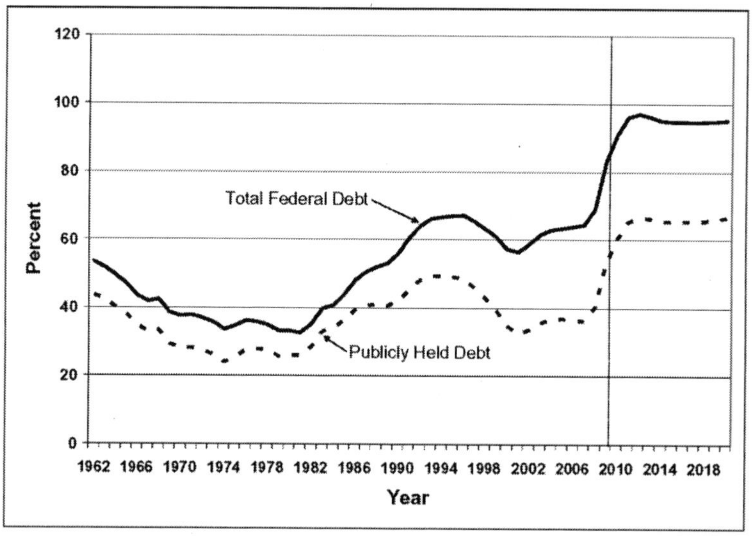

Source: OMB and CBO.

Figure 1. Total U.S. Federal Debt and Debt Held by the Public, FY1962-FY2020 (as a percentage of GDP)

Between 1962 and 1982, total federal debt and debt held by the public followed roughly parallel trends. After the mid-1980s, however, trends in total federal debt and debt held by the public began to diverge. This was mainly due to changes in the Social Security program enacted in 1983 which increased revenues and reduced the growth in benefit payments. As a result, the Social Security program began to run surpluses (surplus monies are invested in Treasury securities), increasing the share of federal debt held in government accounts. CBO's baseline projection indicates that total federal debt and debt held by the public will continue to diverge over the next 10 years.[3]

INTEREST PAYMENTS ON THE FEDERAL DEBT

In FY2009, total or gross interest on Treasury debt securities amounted to about $383 billion—about 11% of federal outlays. However, not all of this flowed from the Treasury to the public—about $200 billion was credited to government accounts such as the Social Security trust funds. The interest payments on the Treasury securities held in government accounts do not represent funds or real resources available for spending. Rather these interest payments are merely a bookkeeping entry transferring funds from one government account to another.[4]

The upper line in **Figure 2** shows the evolution of gross interest payments since 1962. Gross interest payments remained at about 7% to 8% of outlays until the late 1970s. After 1978, interest payments rapidly increased to reach almost 18% of outlays by 1997. After 1997, gross interest payments fell as a percentage of outlays as interest rates fell and the federal budget moved from deficit to surplus. When federal budget deficits reappeared in 2002, gross interest payments began rising.

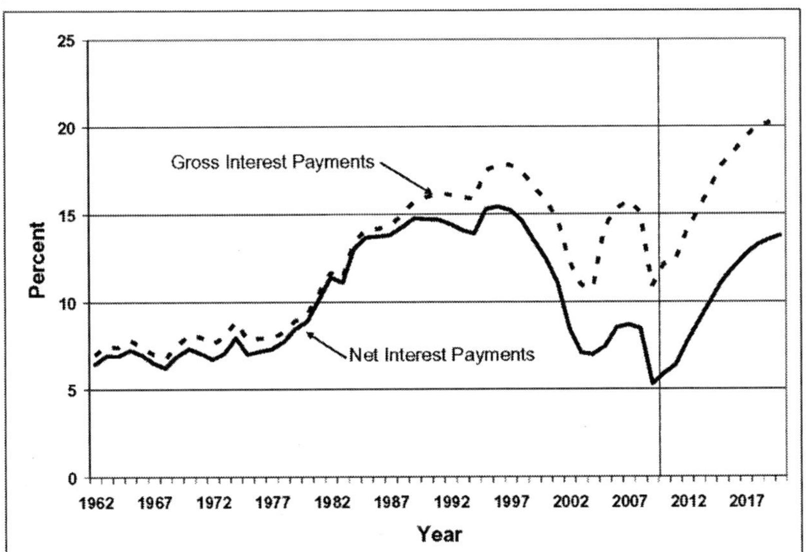

Source: OMB and CBO.

Figure 2. Gross and Net Interest on Treasury Debt Securities, FY1962-FY2020 (as a percentage of federal outlays)

Net interest payments are the component of gross interest payments that involves a transfer of funds or real resources from the government to the public. The lower line in Figure 2 shows the evolution of net interest payments since 1962. For the most part, net interest payments followed the same basic trend as gross interest payments. However, the gap between gross and net interest payments widened after the mid-1980s.[5] As with gross interest payments, net interest payments fell as a percentage of federal outlays when federal debt declined in the late-1990s. Net interest payments began to increase in 2004 but leveled out because of falling interest rates. Additionally, net interest payments fell dramatically in 2009 due to very low interest rates. Large budget deficits in 2009 and 2010, however, will lead to rising net interest payments for the next five to six years.[6] CBO projects that, under plausible scenarios, net interest payments could continue rising indefinitely.[7]

DETERMINANTS OF NET INTEREST PAYMENTS

The primary determinants of net interest payments are (1) the interest rate or yield on U.S. Treasury securities, and (2) the level of debt held by the public. Figure 3 shows the evolution of net interest payments, debt held by the public, and the interest rate since 1967. The interest rate is the yield on five-year constant maturity U.S. Treasury bonds. Both net interest payments and debt held by the public are expressed as a percentage of GDP, and are indexed so that the value in 1967 is equal to one.[8]

Net interest payments increased rapidly beginning in 1977 at about the same time that interest rates increased dramatically (see **Figure 3**). Net interest payments continued to increase after interest rates fell in the early 1980s because of the increase in debt held by the public. The increase in debt held by the public was due to the large budget deficits in the first years of the Reagan Administration and counteracted the effect of falling interest rates on net interest payments. As both interest rates and debt held by the public fell after 1997, net interest payments fell as a percentage of GDP and as a proportion of federal outlays.

The government can, to some extent, control the effective interest rate paid on its debt by varying the maturity of its securities. The federal government issues both short-term and long-term debt. The yield on Treasury securities varies with the maturity of the securities. Typically, short-term securities have a lower yield than longer-term securities, and the yield curve, therefore, is upward sloping.[9] Occasionally, the yield curve will invert with longer-term securities having a lower yield than short-term securities, but this happens neither often nor for extended periods.

A primary goal of debt management is to obtain the lowest borrowing cost over time.[10] Over the past 30 years, the mean maturity of marketable Treasury securities held by private investors has varied between about three years and six years. Since 2000, the range has narrowed to between five and six years. However, this apparent stability masks changes in the types of securities issued. In 2001, for example, the Treasury stopped issuing 30-year bonds.[11] Although shorter-term Treasury securities tend to have lower yields than longer-term securities, they also are more volatile. Consequently, the financing costs of short-term securities can change dramatically over fairly short periods. This volatility and uncertainty complicate efforts to obtain the lowest borrowing costs over time.

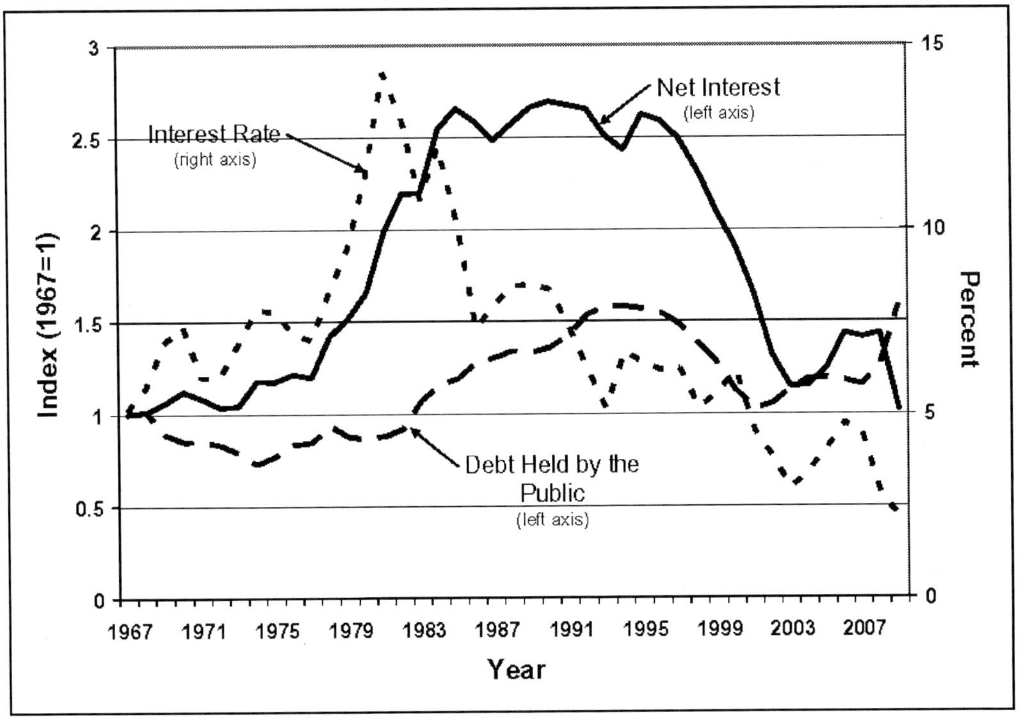

Source: OMB and Federal Reserve Board.

Figure 3. Interest Rate, Net Interest Payments, and Debt Held by the Public, FY1967-FY2009

Congressional actions affecting the budget deficit will affect federal debt, which, in turn, affects future net interest payments. Budget deficits and federal debt can also affect the interest rates on Treasury securities.[12] Increasing federal debt will increase the supply of Treasury securities. This will tend to push down the price and increase the yield of these securities.[13] Recent studies have estimated that increasing debt held by the public by one percent of GDP will increase future interest rates by two to six basis points (0.02 to 0.06 percentage points).[14] Thus budget deficits increase federal debt and future interest rates, which in turn increase future net interest payments.

End Notes

[1] For more information on discretionary spending see CRS Report RL34424, *Trends in Discretionary Spending*, by D. Andrew Austin and Mindy R. Levit.

[2] For more information on mandatory spending see CRS Report RL33074, *Mandatory Spending Since 1962*, by D. Andrew Austin and Mindy R. Levit.

[3] CBO's baseline projection starts with Congress's most recent budgetary decisions and then assumes that no policy changes will be made over the projection period. For entitlement programs CBO assumes that current laws will continue unchanged and by law assumes that discretionary spending will grow at the rate of inflation throughout the projection period. For revenues, CBO assumes that the provisions in the 2001 and 2003 tax cuts will expire on schedule, and that more individuals will be subject to the alternative minimum tax (AMT). Furthermore, the baseline projection does not include the budgetary effects of any new stimulus legislation. CBO's baseline is not intended to be a prediction of future budgetary outcomes. See CBO, *The Budget and Economic Outlook: Fiscal Years 2010 to 2020*, January 2010.

[4] In essence, the interest payments are used to purchase more Treasury securities. While not representing real resources available for current spending, the government will eventually have to find real resources (by raising taxes or reducing spending) for the redemption of these securities, under current law.

[5] The widening of this gap is due, in part, to the increases in the Social Security trust fund resulting from the 1983 amendments to the Social Security Act. These amendments led to increasing revenues to the Social Security program, and reduced the growth in benefits.

[6] CBO projects that the deficit will be more than $1,300 billion in 2010 and $980 billion in 2011. See CBO, *Budget and Economic Outlook*, January 2010.

[7] See CBO, *The Long-term Budget Outlook*, June 2010.

[8] The index is created by dividing the value in each year by the value in 1967. This is done so that both series fit on the same graph.

[9] The yield curve is the relationship of the yield on securities and the maturity of those securities.

[10] See CRS Report RL34682, *Federal Debt Management: Concepts, Options, and Policies (1945-2008)*, by James M. Bickley.

[11] Treasury began issuing 30-year bonds again in February 2006.

[12] The strength of the economy, inflation expectations, and the actions of the Federal Reserve Board also have an important effect on interest rates.

[13] There is an inverse relationship between the price of a bond and the yield of the bond.

[14] See Eric Engen and R. Glenn Hubbard, *Federal Government Debts and Interest Rates*, National Bureau of Economic Research, Working Paper no. 10681, August 2004; William G. Gale and Peter R. Orszag, "Budget Deficits, National Saving, and Interest Rates," *Brookings Papers on Economic Activity*, vol. 2004, no. 2 (2004), pp. 101-187; and Thomas Laubach, *New Evidence on the Interest Rate Effects of Budget Deficits and Debt*, Board of Governors of the Federal Reserve System, Finance and Economics Discussion paper no. 2003-13, May 2003.

In: Economic Policies in a Time of Financial Crisis
Editor: Heather D. Perkins
ISBN: 978-1-61122-686-7

Chapter 13

IS THE U.S. CURRENT ACCOUNT DEFICIT SUSTAINABLE?

Marc Labonte

SUMMARY

America's current account (CA) deficit (the trade deficit plus net income payments and net unilateral transfers) rose as a share of gross domestic product (GDP) from 1991 to a record high of about 6% of GDP in 2006. It began falling in 2007, and reached 3% of GDP in 2009. The CA deficit is financed by foreign capital inflows. Many observers have questioned whether such large inflows are sustainable. Even at 3% of GDP, the deficit is probably still too large to be permanently sustained, and many economists fear that the decline is temporary and caused by the recession. Further, a large share of the capital inflows have come from foreign central banks in recent years, and some are concerned about the economic and political implications of this reliance. Some fear that a rapid decline in capital inflows would trigger a sharp drop in the value of the dollar and an increase in interest rates that could lower asset values and disrupt economic activity. However, economic theory and empirical evidence suggest that the most plausible scenario is a slow decline in the CA deficit, which would not greatly disrupt economic activity because production in the traded goods sector would be stimulated.

The financial crisis that worsened in September 2008 would seem to be a good test case of the type of event that could lead to the feared "sudden stop" in foreigners' willingness to finance the CA deficit. While the recession deepened following the crisis, it has not been via a sudden decline in the dollar or a sudden broad spike in U.S. interest rates. On the contrary, the dollar appreciated in value in the months after the crisis and foreign demand for U.S. Treasury bonds has risen since the crisis worsened. On the other hand, there was a large decline in private foreign capital inflows beginning in 2008; had it not been for foreign government purchases of U.S. securities, the CA would have been in surplus in 2009, all else equal.

One long-term consequence of large and chronic CA deficits has been the growing foreign ownership of the U.S. capital stock. A large CA deficit is not sustainable in the long run because it increases U.S. net debt owed to foreigners, which cannot rise without limit. A larger debt can be serviced only through more borrowing or higher net exports. For net exports to rise, all else equal, the value of the dollar must fall. This explains why many economists believe that both the dollar and the CA deficit will fall further at some point in the future. To date, debt service has not been burdensome. Because U.S. holdings of foreign assets have earned a higher rate of return than U.S. debt owed to foreigners, U.S. net investment income has remained positive, even though the United States is a net debtor nation.

Since 1980, most episodes of a declining CA deficit in industrialized countries have been associated with slow economic growth. Only two episodes were associated with a severe disruption in economic activity. Because most of the episodes involved small countries, these cases may differ in important ways from any corresponding episode in the United States. Historically, a few other countries have had a higher net foreign debt-to-GDP ratio than the United States has at present; however, if CA deficits continue at current levels, the U.S. net foreign debt could eventually be the highest ever recorded.

This chapter also reviews studies on the CA deficit's sustainability. Some of the studies suggest that a large dollar depreciation could eventually be required to restore sustainability. But the inflation-adjusted 25% depreciation of the dollar from 2002-2008 had little effect on the CA deficit, which kept growing until 2007. The CA deficit did not decline rapidly until after the financial crisis of September 2008—a period with little trend movement in the dollar.

INTRODUCTION

America's current account (CA) (exports less imports plus net income payments and net unilateral transfers) has been in deficit every year but one since 1982. After a year in surplus in 1991, it steadily rose as a share of gross domestic product (GDP) to a record high of 6.1% of GDP in 2005 and 2006. It fell slightly in 2007 and 2008, and reached 3% of GDP in 2009 (see Figure 1). The 2009 CA relative to GDP still exceeded the share reached in most years before the 2000s. By accounting identity, the CA deficit is equal to net inflows of foreign capital to the United States and reflects the imbalance between domestic saving and investment.

If the CA deficit continued its decline since 2007, it would soon reach a sustainable level. The decline may be attributed to cyclical causes that are short-lived, however. As a result of the recession and financial crisis, domestic saving is higher, domestic private investment is lower, and so the need to borrow from abroad has diminished. As the economy returns to normal, domestic saving may fall and domestic investment is expected to rebound, either of which would increase the reliance on foreign borrowing. Further, the large increase in the federal budget deficit since 2007 requires financing—if maintained—from foreign or domestic sources. Without fundamental changes in underlying saving and investment patterns, the decline in the CA deficit will only be temporary.

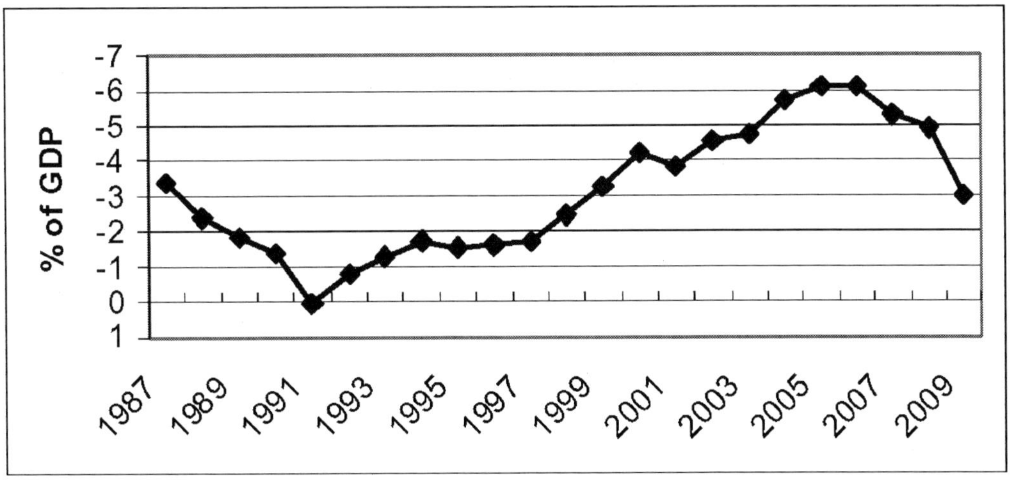

Source: Bureau of Economic Analysis.

Figure 1. Current Account Deficit as a Share of GDP, 1987-2009

Some observers have questioned whether the CA deficit is sustainable. It has not prevented the economy from generally attaining full employment—the United States has run large CA deficits since the mid-1990s, yet unemployment has remained low in most of those years. The CA deficit has both positive and negative effects on the economy. Production of exports and import-competing goods is arguably lower than it would be in the absence of a CA deficit, but interest rates are also lower than they would be in the absence of foreign capital inflows. As a result, interest-sensitive spending on capital investment, residential investment, and consumer durables (e.g., automobiles and appliances) is higher.[1]

Those expressing concern about the CA deficit typically define unsustainability to mean that the United States would have difficulty financing the CA deficit at some point in the near future, and the resulting adjustment process would harm the U.S. economy. Basically, the CA deficit is sustainable as long as foreigners are willing to continue buying American assets. It is not enough for foreigners to reduce their demand for U.S. assets, since this would cause yields on U.S. assets to automatically rise until the market once again cleared. But if the desirability of U.S. assets were to change rapidly (due to a loss in confidence in the U.S. economy, for example), foreign capital inflows and the value of the dollar could decline quickly; at a minimum, foreigners would require significantly higher interest rates than they do at present for inflows to continue. For the U.S. to literally be unable to continue financing its current account deficit, foreign demand would have to fall so much that asset yields could not rise enough for foreigners to be willing to hold U.S. assets again.[2]

But what would make foreign investors change their minds about U.S. assets? Federal Reserve Chairman Ben Bernanke has argued that foreigners will continue to increase their holdings of U.S. assets as long as a "global savings glut" remains that leaves them with few other desirable investment alternatives.[3] If both lender and borrower are rational, many economists believe that the CA deficit can be mutually beneficial—it allows the lender to enjoy a higher rate of return than could be enjoyed at home and allows the borrower to operate with a larger capital stock than could be financed from domestic saving. As long as those investments yield a high enough rate of return to service the debt, borrowing should not reduce future domestic income in absolute terms.

Some economists, however, doubt this interpretation and are concerned that the large CA deficit[4] is symptomatic of wider economic imbalance.[5] They argue that a country cannot persistently rely on foreign borrowing to finance its investment needs, so the United States must eventually raise its low saving rate. They maintain that by financing a large budget deficit and housing boom (until 2006), much of the foreign borrowing is being used in ways that do not expand the economy's productive capacity, and therefore such borrowing does not enhance our ability to service foreign debt. Because foreign borrowing is not sustainable, they argue, Americans will eventually be forced to significantly increase their saving (equivalently, to reduce their consumption) and reduce their investment rates, and the U.S. economy will slow.[6] As a long-term solution, these economists prescribe policy measures to raise saving and reduce overall spending as the appropriate response to an excessively large CA deficit. This could be done through microeconomic policies, such as policies to encourage higher private saving, and macroeconomic policies, such as a tightening of monetary and fiscal policy, although this response would risk inducing the same recession that they fear the CA deficit may eventually cause (particularly if the economy were weak already).

As a consequence of large CA deficits, a growing share of the U.S. capital stock is owned by foreigners and a rising fraction of U.S. income will need to be diverted overseas in the form of interest and dividends to foreigners. The process cannot continue indefinitely, or else foreigners would eventually hold a larger share of American assets in their portfolios than they desire. But though economists may feel confident that the CA deficit will decline in the long run, long run predictions do not offer much help in predicting short-term trends. Foreigners may wish to increase their holdings of American assets (in which case the CA deficit would persist) in the near term. One common assumption is that the CA deficit would, at most, continue until the share of American assets held in foreign portfolios equaled America's share of world output; by this measure, foreigners still hold too few American assets. For example, citizens of the euro area hold an estimated 53% of their wealth in euro-denominated assets and 19% in U.S. dollar-denominated assets, whereas the Japanese hold an estimated 63% of their wealth in yen-denominated assets and 4% in dollar-denominated assets.[7] This is referred to as a "home bias" in saving because all countries hold more of their own assets, and fewer foreign assets, than optimal portfolio diversification would suggest. This bias is considered unlikely to disappear entirely, in which case CA deficits will ease before this benchmark is met. In any case, the reason why home bias would decline for foreigners but not Americans, as continuing CA deficits would imply, remains unclear. On the other hand, if the U.S. economy grows faster than the rest of the world in the future, then (small) CA deficits would be needed for foreigners to maintain U.S. asset holdings equal to the U.S. share of world GDP.[8]

One reason that U.S. imports cannot exceed exports indefinitely (and the dollar could eventually fall) is that today's CA deficits have a consequence for future trade balances. The accumulation of net debt that Americans owe to foreigners will need to be serviced in the future, and debt service will take the form of a payment from the United States. To offset the payment, the United States must export more or borrow more. But, all else equal, foreigners will only be induced to buy more exports if the dollar depreciates.[9] Net investment income payments make up a small fraction of the CA deficit today, but economist Edwin Truman estimates that if CA deficits continued to equal 6% of GDP, net income payments would eventually reach 4.5% of GDP, leaving a trade deficit of only 1.5% of GDP.[10] In other words, a constant trade deficit would imply a growing CA deficit because of growing net investment income payments.

In 2008, the United States had a net foreign debt of $3.5 trillion, but received net investment income of $126 billion from the rest of the world. What is surprising about these data is that the United States still consistently has positive net investment income despite its large net debt, and shows no long-term downward trend as the foreign debt grows. That is because U.S. holdings of foreign assets have earned a higher rate of return than U.S. debt owed to foreigners. Between 1981 and 2008, the United States earned an average estimated real rate of return of 3.1% more on its foreign assets than its foreign liabilities.[11] This estimated rate of return differential has prevented foreign borrowing from becoming burdensome and suggest that the U.S. net foreign debt could become significantly larger before debt payments would become burdensome. Kouparitsas estimates that if these rate-of-return differentials were to continue, the United States could maintain a current account deficit of 0.9-1.3% of GDP indefinitely without any increase in its net foreign debt.[12] However, this favorable rate-of-return differential may not continue in the future if foreigners believe that the dollar will depreciate and demand a higher rate of return on U.S. borrowing as compensation. If U.S. interest rates rose, the debt could become burdensome quickly.

ECONOMIC IMPACT OF A DECLINING CURRENT ACCOUNT DEFICIT

Although some reduction in the CA deficit is inevitable (although not necessarily in the near future), it need not be sudden. It should be emphasized that economic theory suggests that a *slow decline* in the CA deficit and dollar would not be troublesome for the overall economy. In fact, a slow decline could have an expansionary effect on the economy, because the increase in net exports could have a more stimulative effect on aggregate demand in the short run than the decrease in investment and other interest-sensitive spending caused by lower capital inflows. More realistically, the trade deficit would not decline exogenously, but in response to a slowing of overall domestic demand. Therefore, a falling trade deficit may tend to coincide with slower economic growth in practice, but that does not indicate that a falling trade deficit has *caused* growth to slow.

Historical experience seems to support the idea that a slow decline in the trade deficit need not be harmful to the economy—the dollar declined by about 40% in real terms and the CA deficit declined continually in the late 1980s, from 2.8% of GDP in 1986 to nearly zero during the early 1990s. Yet economic growth was strong throughout the late 1980s. (More recent experience is considered in the next section.)

A potentially serious short-term problem would emerge if foreigners *suddenly* decided to reduce the fraction of their saving that goes to the United States in the form of a capital inflow, or if they suddenly decided to repatriate part of their liquid financial assets. The initial effect could be a sudden and large depreciation in the value of the dollar, as the supply of dollars on the foreign exchange market increased, and a sudden and large increase in U.S. interest rates, as an important funding source for investment and the budget deficit was withdrawn from the financial markets. Most likely, the *direct* trade effects of these shifts in lending patterns by foreigners would not cause a recession because the dollar depreciation would lead to a trade surplus (or smaller deficit), which expands aggregate demand.[13] (Empirical evidence suggests that the full effects of a change in the exchange rate on traded goods takes time, so the dollar may have to "overshoot" its eventual depreciation level in order to achieve a significant adjustment in trade flows in the short run.) However, the *indirect* interest rate effects, which typically only partially offset the direct effects, could cause a recession if the change is sudden. Large increases in interest rates could cause problems for the U.S. economy, as these increases reduce the market value of debt securities, cause prices on the stock market to fall, and jeopardize the solvency of various debtors and creditors. Resources may not be able to shift quickly enough from interest-sensitive sectors to export sectors to make this transition fluid.[14] The Federal Reserve could mitigate the interest rate spike by reducing short-term interest rates, although this reduction would influence long-term rates only indirectly and could increase inflation.

Is a scenario where the dollar crashes a likely one? Economic theory typically assumes that financial market participants act rationally. If the rationality assumption is a good one, then the potential for a sudden decline is slim. After all, foreigners would be demanding high rates of return to buy U.S. assets today if they could foresee that the foreign currency value of these assets is likely to fall sharply in the near future. Of course, financial markets do not always seem driven by rational behavior in practice, but as a result, theory has little predictive power of the timing or likelihood of a "sudden stop." Given the traditional role the United States has played as an investment safe haven, sudden capital outflows seem unlikely. On the contrary, investment might be attracted to U.S. assets in a liquidity crisis because the U.S. offers more liquid financial markets (e.g., U.S. Treasury bond markets) than do most foreign counterparts.

THE RECENT DECLINE IN THE CA DEFICIT AND THE FINANCIAL CRISIS

As discussed above, a destabilizing interruption in the financing of the CA deficit would likely be triggered by some sudden change in investor sentiment about U.S. assets. The financial crisis, beginning in August 2007 with the illiquidity of the U.S. subprime mortgage market and deepening in September 2008, would seem to be a good test case for how a large change in investor sentiment would affect the CA deficit. Overall, the CA to GDP ratio declined by about half between 2007 and 2009, but this did not lead to sharp changes or negative effects for the dollar or interest rates that could be harmful to the economy. The dollar continued its long and gradual downward trend until April 2008, before it started rising—through the worst of the crisis—until March 2009. Interest rates on U.S. Treasuries fell to extremely low levels during the crisis despite the large increase in the budget deficit, as U.S. Treasuries continued to be seen as a desirable destination during the "flight to quality." Other interest rates generally fell along with U.S. Treasury yields, although risk premiums on private assets rose and some private borrowers were shut out of credit markets entirely because of the crisis. Problems recently experienced in U.S. financial markets have been widely viewed as "once in a lifetime" events. If these events failed to cause a sudden flight from U.S. assets and an inability to finance the CA deficit, it is hard to imagine what would.

While the overall data provides little evidence to support fears of a "sudden stop" in financing the CA deficit, a closer look at the data is less reassuring. The crisis led to a large decline in private capital flows in 2008—both foreign purchases of U.S. assets and U.S. purchases of foreign assets that had countervailing effects on the CA balance. (Private foreign demand for Treasuries was high in 2008 and 2009, but foreigners sold private U.S. securities on net.) In 2009, private U.S. net purchases of foreign assets returned to half of their pre-crisis level, but private foreigners continued to sell U.S. assets on net. Were the U.S. reliant on private purchases alone, the CA would have seen a large swing from deficit in 2008 to surplus in 2009, all else equal. Had such a large swing occurred, interest rates and the dollar may not have been as stable as they were.

Instead, the CA remained in deficit because of large purchases of U.S. assets from official sources (foreign governments or international institutions).[15] This trend was not new—the steady financing of the CA deficit has depended heavily on official capital inflows since 2002.[16] Official capital inflows have exceeded $200 billion per year since 2003, and $400 billion since 2006. Had these central banks decided not to increase their dollar-denominated foreign reserves, the CA deficit and the value of the dollar might have fallen precipitously. Further, the 25% fall in the dollar from 2002 to 2008 was larger than average against some trading partners who do not intervene in foreign exchange markets, and very small against trading partners who do intervene.

Going forward, some analysts fear that official capital inflows could prove unreliable or provide foreign governments with leverage that would undermine U.S. policy aims. Because official inflows are likely financed by considerations other than rate of return, it is difficult to predict how they will evolve in the future. (In the past few years, official inflows have proven much steadier than private.) But given the importance of the United States as a foreign export market, deliberately taking a step that could potentially precipitate a U.S. economic crisis could be against a foreign country's economic self-interest, and reduce the value of the U.S. assets already owned by the country. The financial crisis has demonstrated that foreign governments, desiring to maintain the status quo, have been willing to increase their purchases of U.S. securities while others are reducing their U.S. holdings.

The story told in this section is based on capital flow data, but these data should be viewed with caution during the financial crisis. Private capital flows are hard to track. Individual entries in the capital accounts have shown large swings from quarter to quarter during the crisis that raise issues of reliability, and the statistical discrepancy in 2008 and 2009 was about half the size of the current account deficit. Furthermore, there is a problem of causality in interpreting these results. The instability in the economy and international capital flows are generally viewed as being caused by the financial crisis, but causality could also run in the other direction, making it hard to distinguish to what extent the financial crisis should be attributed to movements in international capital flows.

HISTORICAL PARALLELS

Problems with financing large budget and CA deficits in Greece from 2009 to 2010 are a reminder that problems around the world with CA sustainability are not unusual. But the usefulness of most comparisons to historical experience abroad is limited by the fact that the

United States economy and financial system are so much larger than those of other countries. As a result, an economic occurrence in the United States has ramifications for the world economy that could have feedback effects for the U.S. economy, whereas changes in the CA balance of most small countries will most likely not affect the world economy. It also means that the amount of borrowing required to finance the U.S. CA deficit is a much larger share of world saving. Another difference is the role that the dollar plays as the world's "reserve currency." Because the dollar is the world's preferred currency for a store of value, medium of exchange, and unit of account, holders may be less willing to abandon it than they would any other currency. If so, the United States may be able to run higher sustainable CA deficits than other countries.

In the developing world, a large CA deficit has often been a leading indicator of financial and currency crisis. This was the case in many recent crises, including Mexico, East Asia, Turkey, Brazil, and Argentina. The applicability of these experiences to the United States may be limited, however, because of three key differences between the United States and these countries. First, the United States has a flexible exchange rate regime. Countries with fixed exchange rates can be forced into crisis when their foreign exchange reserves are exhausted by "speculators" betting against the currency; similar bets are harder to make against flexible exchange rates. Second, the United States has traditionally been seen as a "safe haven" for investment. Third, unlike developing countries, the United States is able to borrow in its own currency, so that depreciation reduces rather than increases the burden of servicing its debt.[17] Therefore, historical comparisons have tended to focus on the experience of other industrialized countries.

Economist Sebastian Edwards found that since 1970, only two other industrialized countries, Ireland and New Zealand, had high CA deficits that were long-lasting (seven and five years, respectively). He found that large countries that experienced sharp declines in their CA also saw per capita GDP growth decline by 3.6% to 5.0%.[18]

Economists at Goldman Sachs, a financial firm, analyzed all episodes in industrialized countries since 1980 where the CA improved by more than 2% of GDP. It found 31 cases where the adjustment occurred under circumstances of economic disruption and 13 where there was no comparable disruption. In the disruption episodes, the economy typically started from a position of overheating and the output gap (the difference between actual and potential output) worsened by an average of 3.6% of GDP, whereas in the benign episodes, the economy started from a position of excess capacity and the output gap improved by 1.9%. The fact that the economy was initially overheating in the disruption episodes suggests that causality may run in the opposite direction—the CA shift may be a symptom rather than a cause of economic slowdown. In the disruption cases, there was little real exchange rate depreciation; in the benign cases, it averaged 5.1%. In most cases, the adjustment took several years. In all cases, consumption growth was negative on average and (surprisingly) interest rates on average fell. In only two cases (Portugal in the early 1980s and Finland in the early 1990s) was the CA decline associated with a severe recession. (The recession and CA decline in Finland were widely attributed to the collapse of the Soviet Union, among other factors.) Some of these cases may not be applicable to the U.S. experience, however, because the sample includes countries that had a small CA deficit or CA surplus. Only eight of these episodes involved a larger CA deficit as a share of GDP than the U.S. deficit today, and all eight episodes involved small countries.[19]

The International Monetary Fund conducted a similar study.[20] It found 42 cases where an advanced economy had an initial CA deficit of at least 2.5% of GDP, and the CA deficit subsequently declined by at least 50%. It found, on average, that the real exchange rate declined by a cumulative 12.2%, causing a shift in the CA of 5.7% of GDP over the next 4.6 years, moving the CA from deficit to surplus (on average). GDP growth fell by an annual average of 1.4% during the reversal, causing the output gap to deteriorate by an average of 3% of GDP, from peak to trough of the business cycle. In 11 of these cases, the slowdown in economic growth was large, but, unlike the United States, 9 of these 11 did not have a floating exchange rate. In 10 other cases, there was no slowdown in growth following the CA reversal.

However, not all cases of large CA deficits end in a reversal. Besides the United States, the IMF identified five other advanced economies that have had large CA deficits that have persisted to date: Australia (which has run a CA deficit of more than 2% since 1980), Greece (since 1996), New Zealand (1989), Portugal (1996), and Spain (1999). All except Australia have had CA deficits that were considerably larger than the U.S. in recent years. Greece, Portugal, and Spain have fared badly in the recent economic downturn, but Australia and New Zealand have fared relatively well.

In a similar study, economists Debelle and Galati found little evidence that CA adjustments historically lead to significant disruption in financial markets. They found little change in the composition of capital flows before adjustment, which they argue is evidence that current account adjustment is caused by, rather than the cause of, broader macroeconomic imbalances.[21]

Economists Hung and Kim use statistical regressions to estimate the probability of an exchange rate crash based on several macroeconomic variables across many industrialized countries over time, and estimate that the United States had a 9% probability of a dollar crash in 2006. They find that the current account balance (and the regression overall) has relatively little predictive power for a currency crash.[22]

The size of the CA deficit in any given year may be less important in determining sustainability than how persistent CA deficits increase a country's net foreign debt over time. Economists Maurice Obstfeld and Kenneth Rogoff found that in 2003 the net debt owed to foreigners was about 23% of GDP for the United States, near an all-time high. (It was about 24% of GDP in 2008.) Were CA deficits to continue at more than 5% of GDP per year, U.S. net debt to foreigners would reach 70% of GDP within 30 years. Although this implies a relatively small yearly debt service burden, many countries that have experienced CA reversals in the postwar period had smaller net foreign debt-to-GDP ratios, between 20% and 80% of GDP. Obstfeld and Rogoff identify only one country (Ireland) with a net foreign debt-to-GDP ratio that has exceeded 80%. Thus, the authors conclude that large U.S. CA deficits cannot be sustained indefinitely.[23]

Similarly, simulations by Federal Reserve economists Bertaut et al. suggest that the net foreign debt could increase to 60% of GDP by 2020, but this would result in annual net investment income payments of only 0.5% of GDP. They found net foreign debt of 20% of GDP to be fairly typical by international standards, found 16 countries where net investment income payments exceeded 1% of GDP, and found five other countries with net debt around 60% of GDP. The authors found econometric evidence that countries with high net foreign debt had modestly higher interest rates and mixed effects on the exchange rate.[24]

A Review of Five Estimates

Five recent academic papers address the sustainability issue. In the papers, the models used to estimate changes in the dollar and CA are not empirically derived; they are simulations based on theoretical assumptions meant to be consistent with reality.[25]

Obstfeld and Rogoff have estimated how much the dollar would need to depreciate in order to make the CA deficit disappear.[26] In their model, shocks to aggregate demand or shifts in the demand or supply of tradeable goods could cause the CA deficit to decline; their model does not allow for exogenous changes in the demand for U.S. assets to affect the CA deficit. They estimate that the real exchange rate would depreciate between 14.7% and 33.6% if a CA deficit equal to 5% of GDP were eliminated by a change in aggregate demand, and between 9.8% and 25.5% if eliminated by a change in the supply of tradeable goods. They estimate that depreciation would be accompanied by a 3.9% to 7.1% decline in the terms of trade. The predicted dollar depreciation is so large because about three-quarters of U.S. output is nontradeable, production cannot be quickly shifted into tradeable goods to take advantage of the depreciation, and import and export prices change much more slowly than the exchange rate. This model does not predict how much larger the CA deficit could get or how quickly it will eventually fall.[27]

Economists Blanchard, Giavazzi, and Sa explicitly allow asset demand to influence the exchange rate, and they assume that assets from different countries are not perfect substitutes. In their model, a CA deficit would eventually decline because demand for U.S. assets is finite. Although an increase in the demand for U.S. assets would initially cause the dollar to appreciate, they argue, it would later depreciate to finance debt service (though it would remain above its pre-appreciation value). They estimate that a 15% decline in the dollar would be associated with a decline in the CA deficit equal to 1.4% of GDP. About one-third of the decline in the CA deficit results from U.S. debt being denominated in U.S. dollars, because a depreciation reduces its value. Blanchard et al. estimate that stabilizing the net-debt-to-GDP ratio at 2003 levels would require the dollar to immediately depreciate by 56% and the CA deficit to decline to 0.75% of GDP. However, assuming foreigners desire to maintain holdings of U.S. assets at their current share, their model predicts that the depreciation would be stretched over a few decades, depreciating by 2.7% a year, at most. If foreigners decided to reduce their holding of U.S. assets, the model predicts a larger, but still gradual, depreciation.[28]

Edwards uses a similar model to simulate how much the dollar would depreciate from its 2004 level depending on different assumptions about the foreign demand for U.S. assets. Unlike Blanchard et al., he projects fairly rapid declines in the CA deficit and dollar in the future. Under his optimistic scenario, in which he assumes that the U.S. net debt will rise to 60% of GDP by 2010 and then remain constant, the CA deficit would peak at 7.3% of GDP in four years, before eventually declining to 3.2% of GDP (with most of the decline occurring in the first four years after the peak). The real value of the dollar would appreciate while the deficit was increasing, but it would decline 21% in the first three years after the deficit began falling. If net debt were to decline to 50% of GDP after 2010 instead of remaining at 60% of GDP, which would still be about double its current level, the decline in the CA deficit and dollar would be greater. Edwards calculates that the deficit would fall by 5.3% of GDP and the dollar would depreciate by 28% after three years, which would bring both measures close to their long-term projected levels.[29]

Economists Roubini and Setser simulate what would happen to the net foreign debt over the next 10 years under three scenarios.[30] In the first scenario, imports and exports continue to grow at historical rates. The CA deficit would exceed 12.8% of GDP and the net foreign debt would exceed 80% of GDP by 2012. In this scenario, the authors do not believe it is plausible to assume that foreigners would be willing to finance borrowing of this magnitude, and use this scenario to argue that the current path is unsustainable. In the second scenario, the trade deficit stabilizes at 5% of GDP. The CA deficit would still increase to 8.8% of GDP in 2012 (because of higher net investment income payments), at which point the net foreign debt would exceed 70% of GDP. Servicing a debt of this size, they estimate, would cost 3% of GDP in 2012. To reduce the trade deficit to 5% of GDP, they estimate that the dollar would need to depreciate by about 10% from its 2004 level. This scenario (and the first scenario) is not sustainable in the long run because the net foreign debt would grow continuously. In the third scenario, the trade deficit declines by the end of the projection to the point where the net foreign debt stabilizes as a share of GDP. They estimate that the net foreign debt would stabilize with a trade deficit of 0.8% and a CA deficit of 1.3% of GDP. If the CA deficit gradually declined to this level in 2012, the net foreign debt would stabilize at nearly 60% of GDP, which would cost an estimated 1.75% of GDP to service in 2012. To achieve a reduction in the CA deficit of this magnitude, they estimate that the dollar would need to depreciate substantially and the federal budget would need to be balanced. All of these scenarios assume that relative interest rates remain similar to past values as the net foreign debt rises; if foreigners demanded higher interest rates, then this would feed through to a much larger CA deficit and debt path than simulated.

Economist Paul Krugman estimates that the dollar would need to depreciate by at least 35% from its 2005 value in real terms in the long run for the trade deficit to be reduced to zero.[31] He looks for evidence of whether this depreciation will happen gradually or abruptly. For the depreciation to be smooth, Krugman argues that it must be anticipated by rational investors, in which case they would currently require a rate of return premium to hold U.S. assets (to offset the loss suffered from the future dollar depreciation). To determine how large the premium would have to be, he considers two hypothetical paths for the dollar. In one path, the dollar declines by 1.75% annually, and net foreign debt peaks at 118% of GDP, or at least one-third of the total U.S. capital stock. If foreigners are unwilling to hold that much U.S. debt, the dollar would have to depreciate more rapidly. In the other path, the dollar declines by 3.5% annually, and net foreign debt peaks at 58% of GDP. Yet he finds no evidence of a rate of return premium anywhere near the magnitude of either 1.75% or 3.5%—after adjusting for inflation, U.S. interest rates are very close to foreign rates. This implies that foreigners do not foresee any significant dollar depreciation in the future. Therefore, he argues that when investors eventually realize how much the dollar will depreciate, they will likely sharply reduce their demand for U.S. assets, causing the dollar to plummet.

Recent experience suggests that the dollar depreciation required to put the CA deficit on a sustainable path may indeed be large. From 2002 to 2006, the dollar depreciated by 16% in inflation-adjusted terms. Despite the depreciation, the CA deficit continued to rise, both in dollar terms and as a share of GDP, from 4.5% of GDP in 2002 to 6.1% of GDP in 2006. In response to the weaker dollar, exports rose rapidly from 2004 onward, but this did not lead to a lower current account deficit because imports also continued to rise rapidly. This experience points to the fact that external factors, which can be held constant in the models discussed in this section, also influence the CA and the dollar in reality.[32] The CA deficit began declining in 2007, along with the continued decline in the dollar through 2008. Paradoxically, the largest decline in the CA deficit has occurred in 2009, although the real value at the end of 2009 was nearly the same as the value at the end of 2007.

The wide dispersion of estimates on the dollar depreciation associated with a decline in the CA deficit points to the complex and imperfectly understood factors that determine the dollar's value, the lack of a consensus exchange rate model that performs well empirically, and the sensitivity of theoretical models to changes in uncertain empirical parameters. Further complicating model-based projections, the path of CA adjustment is also subject to non-market forces, such as the accumulation of foreign reserves by central banks. Furthermore, no model reliably answers the underlying question of how much and how quickly the CA deficit will potentially decline.

CONCLUSION

In the long run, running a CA deficit at current trend levels (i.e., growing faster than GDP) would result in net foreign debt continually growing relative to GDP. This is unsustainable if foreigners have a limited appetite for U.S. assets. Thus, in the long run, the CA deficit will most likely decline, although it need not decline to zero to stabilize the net foreign debt relative to GDP. Relative to GDP, the CA deficit declined by about half between 2007 and 2009. It is too soon to say whether this decline is being caused by temporary cyclical factors or represents the beginning of a long-term adjustment process. To date, the net foreign debt has placed no burden on the U.S. economy because U.S.-owned foreign assets have earned more than foreign-owned U.S. assets.

Whether policymakers should be concerned about a future decline in the CA deficit depends on whether the decline were to happen in an orderly or disruptive way. There is little reason to think that a gradual decline would have a deleterious effect on the overall economy. But a sudden decline, brought on by a sudden reduction in foreign capital inflows, could be disruptive to U.S. financial markets, causing negative spillover effects for the broader economy. While a sudden reduction in foreign capital inflows cannot be ruled out—it has happened to foreign countries—it seems highly unlikely. The United States is different in a number of ways from the countries that have experienced CA crises—it is much larger, its financial markets and economy are highly developed, it has a floating exchange rate, and it is seen as a safe haven in times of financial turmoil. Nonetheless, even if the risk of a sudden CA reversal is small, it is arguably worth policy consideration since it could be highly costly to the U.S. economy.

The recent financial crisis in the United States bears resemblance to the sort of scenario envisioned by economists concerned about a sudden, destabilizing outflow of capital. Yet when the crisis worsened in September 2008, the dollar began appreciating and heightened demand for certain U.S. assets, such as U.S. Treasuries, drove their prices up to unusually high levels. A large and potentially destabilizing net withdrawal of private foreign capital in 2008 and 2009 was offset by official capital net inflows (primarily purchase of U.S. assets by foreign governments), however.

End Notes

[1] For an overview, see CRS Report RL31032, *The U.S. Trade Deficit: Causes, Consequences, and Cures*, by Craig K. Elwell.

[2] It is widely assumed that a rapid change in the current account would be caused by changes in financial markets, not goods markets. Although theoretically a rapid decline in imports could also cause the CA deficit to shrink, little empirical evidence exists that broad trade patterns change that quickly.

[3] Ben Bernanke, "The Global Saving Glut and the U.S. Current Account Deficit," the Sandridge Lecture, Virginia Association of Economics, March 10, 2005, available on the Federal Reserve Board of Governors website. For an analysis, see CRS Report RL33140, *Is the U.S. Trade Deficit Caused by a Global Saving Glut?*, by Marc Labonte.

[4] For the purposes of this chapter, a CA deficit is considered large if it exceeds the trend growth rate of the economy.

[5] See, for example, Edwin Truman, "Postponing Global Adjustment," Institute of International Economics, Working Paper no. 05-6, July 2005.

[6] As discussed in the section "The Recent Decline in the CA Deficit and the Financial Crisis," saving has risen and investment and economic growth has fallen since 2008, but not necessarily because foreigners were unwilling to finance the CA deficit.

[7] Olivier Blanchard, Francesco Giavazzi, Filipa Sa, "The U.S. Current Account and the Dollar," Massachusetts Institute of Technology, Working Paper no. 05-02, May 2005.

[8] Engel and Rogers argue that the CA deficit can be fully explained by investors' anticipation that the U.S. share of industrialized countries' output will rise in the future. Their model omits developing countries, however, which have played a large role in world CA deficits and growth recently. Charles Engel and John Rogers, "The U.S. Current Account Deficit and the Expected Share of World Output," National Bureau of Economic Research, Working Paper no. 11921, January 2006.

[9] Another possibility for how the CA deficit could improve would be if the U.S. terms of trade improved in the future. There is no consensus on any policy tools that can directly improve the terms of trade.

[10] Edwin Truman, "Postponing Global Adjustment," Institute for International Economics, Working Paper no. 05-6, July 2005.

[11] Maurizio Habib, "Excess Returns on Net Foreign Assets: The Exorbitant Privilege from a Global Perspective," ECB Working Paper 1158, European Central Bank, February 2010.

[12] Michael Kouparitsas, "Is the U.S. Current Account Sustainable?" Federal Reserve Bank of Chicago, *Chicago Fed Letter*, no. 215, June 2005. Curcuru et al. cast doubt on whether the favorable rate of return differential can be expected to continue in the future. Stephanie Curcuru et al., "The Stability of Large External Imbalances," National Bureau of Economic Research, working paper 13074, May 2007.

[13] A sharp decline in the value of the dollar would also reduce living standards, all else equal, because it would raise the price of imports to households. This effect, which is referred to as a decline in the terms of trade, would not be recorded directly in GDP, however.

[14] For a more formal explanation, see J. Bradford DeLong, "Some Simple Analytics for a 'Hard Landing'," working paper, University of California at Berkeley, April 2005. Interestingly, one study found that countries with larger declines in the CA deficit experienced, on average, higher GDP growth. See Hilary Croke, Steven Kamin, and Sylvain Leduc, "Financial Market Developments and Economic Activity During Current Account Adjustments," *International Finance Discussion Papers*, Federal Reserve, no. 827, February 2005.

[15] In 2009, the withdrawal of foreign private capital from the U.S. was also offset by the reversal of more than $500 billion in Federal Reserve liquidity swaps.

[16] For more information, see CRS Report RS21951, *Financing the U.S. Trade Deficit: Role of Foreign Governments*, by Marc Labonte.

[17] In dollar terms, depreciation would not affect the value of dollar-denominated liabilities. However, in foreign currency terms or in terms of the purchasing power that it conveys to foreign lenders, depreciation reduces the value of U.S. liabilities.

[18] Sebastian Edwards, "Is the Current Account Deficit Sustainable?" National Bureau of Economic Research, Working Paper no. 11541, August 2005. Since his study, both Ireland and New Zealand have again run large CA deficits.

[19] Dominic Wilson and Roopa Purushothaman, "Do Current Account Adjustments Have to Be Painful?" *Global Economics Weekly*, Goldman Sachs, no. 05/04, February 2005. Similar results are found in Hilary Croke, Steven Kamin, and Sylvain Leduc, "Financial Market Developments and Economic Activity During Current Account Adjustments," *International Finance Discussion Papers*, Federal Reserve, no. 827, February 2005.

[20] International Monetary Fund, "Exchange Rates and the Adjustment of External Imbalances," *World Economic Outlook*, April 2007, ch. 3.

[21] Guy Debelle and Gabriele Galati, "Current Account Adjustments and Capital Flows," Bank of International Settlements, Working Paper no. 169, February 2005.

[22] Juann Hung and Young Kim, "Implications of Past Currency Crises for the U.S. Current Account Adjustment," Congressional Budget Office, Working Paper no. 2006-7, June 2006. The authors define a currency crash as a decline in value of at least 25% in one year that is accelerating.

[23] Maurice Obstfeld and Kenneth Rogoff, "The Unsustainable U.S. Current Account Position Revisited," National Bureau of Economic Research, Working Paper no. 10869, October 2004.

[24] Carol Bertaut, Steven Kamin, and Charles Thomas, "How Long Can the Unsustainable U.S. Current Account Deficit Be Sustained?" *IMF Staff Papers*, vol. 56, no. 3 (2009), p. 596.

[25] In addition to the papers reviewed, similar research includes, Hamid Faruqee et al., "Smooth Landing or Crash? Model Based Scenarios of Global Current Account Rebalancing," National Bureau of Economic Research, Working Paper no. 11583, August 2005; Richard Clarida, *G-7 Current Account Imbalances: Sustainability and Adjustment* (Chicago, IL: University of Chicago Press, 2006); Robert Dekle et al., "Global Rebalancing With Gravity," National Bureau of Economic Research, Working Paper no. 13846, March 2008.

[26] Maurice Obstfeld and Kenneth Rogoff, "The Unsustainable U.S. Current Account Position Revisited," National Bureau of Economic Research, Working Paper no. 10869, October 2004.

[27] Using a similar model and parameters, Cavallo and Tille suggest that the reduction in the current account balance and depreciation of the dollar could be smoother and more gradual (although ultimately by a similar magnitude) if one assumes that the net foreign debt is held constant and changes in asset valuations due to exchange rate effects are used to temporarily finance current account deficits. They estimate that the dollar would ultimately depreciate by 31%. Michele Cavallo and Cedric Tille, "Current Account Adjustment With High Financial Integration," Federal Reserve Bank of San Francisco, *Economic Review*, 2006, p. 31.Using a similar model and parameters, Engel and Rogers argue that if the U.S. grows faster than other industrialized countries in the future, then little dollar depreciation would be required to reduce the CA deficit. Charles Engel and John Rogers, "The U.S. Current Account Deficit and the Expected Share of World Output," National Bureau of Economic Research, Working Paper no. 11921, January 2006.

[28] Olivier Blanchard, Francesco Giavazzi, Filipa Sa, "The U.S. Current Account and the Dollar," Massachusetts Institute of Technology, Working Paper no. 05-02, May 2005.

[29] Sebastian Edwards, "Is the CA Deficit Sustainable?" National Bureau of Economic Research, Working Paper no. 11541, August 2005.

[30] Nouriel Roubini and Brad Setser, "The U.S. as a Net Debtor: The Sustainability of the U.S. External Imbalances," working paper, August 2004, http://pages.stern.nyu.edu/~nroubini/papers/Roubini-Setser-US-External-Imbalances.pdf.

[31] Paul Krugman, "Will There Be a Dollar Crisis?" *Economic Policy*, July 2007, p. 436.

[32] Explanations for why the CA deficit did not fall when the dollar fell are discussed in Gian Maria Milesi-Ferretti, "Fundamentals at Odds? The U.S. Current Account Deficit and the Dollar," International Monetary Fund, working paper 08/260, November 2008.

In: Economic Policies in a Time of Financial Crisis
Editor: Heather D. Perkins
ISBN: 978-1-61122-686-7

Chapter 14

U.S. TRADE DEFICIT AND THE IMPACT OF CHANGING OIL PRICES

James K. Jackson

SUMMARY

Petroleum prices rose sharply in the first half of 2008, at one time reaching more than $140 per barrel of crude oil. After July 2008, however, petroleum prices and import volumes fell at a historically rapid pace; in January 2009, prices of crude oil fell below $40 per barrel. Since then, crude oil prices have nearly doubled, while the average monthly volume of imports of energy-related petroleum products has fallen nearly 10% year over year. Despite the drop in the volume of crude oil imports, the rise in the cost of energy imports through 2009 and early 2010 could add more than $100 billion to the nation's trade deficit in 2010 over that experienced in 2009. The strength of the U.S. economic recovery in the second half of 2010 could increase both the volume of energy imports and the price of those imports. This chapter provides an estimate of the initial impact of the changing oil prices on the nation's merchandise trade deficit.

BACKGROUND

According to data published by the Census Bureau of the Department of Commerce,[1] the prices of petroleum products over the first half of 2008 rose sharply, generally rising considerably faster than the change in demand for those products, before falling at a historic rate. After falling each month between August 2008 and February 2009, average petroleum prices reversed course and rose by 85% between February and December 2009, climbing to nearly $80 per barrel at times. Through the first three months of 2010, petroleum prices have hovered around $74 per barrel, but futures contracts indicate that prices could reach about $85 per barrel by the fall of 2010. As a result of changing petroleum prices, the price changes in imported energy-related petroleum products worsened the U.S. trade deficit in 2006, 2007,

2008, and likely will again in 2010. Energy-related petroleum products is a term used by the Census Bureau that includes crude oil, petroleum preparations, and liquefied propane and butane gas. Crude oil comprises the largest share by far within this broad category of energy-related imports. In 2009, the slowdown in the rate of growth in the U.S. economy reduced the amount of energy the country imported and helped to push down world energy prices. As economic growth improves, energy imports will increase and energy prices are expected to rise. In isolation from other events, lower energy prices tend to aid the U.S. economy, which makes it a more attractive destination for foreign investment. Such capital inflows place upward pressure on the dollar against a broad range of other currencies. To the extent that the additions to the merchandise trade deficit are returned to the U.S. economy as payment for additional U.S. exports or to acquire such assets as securities or U.S. businesses, the U.S. trade deficit could be mitigated further.

Table 1. Summary Data of U.S. Imports of Energy-Related Petroleum Products, Including Oil (Not Seasonally Adjusted)

	January through March					
	2009		2010			
	Quantity (thousands of barrels)	Value ($ thousands)	Quantity (thousands of barrels)	% change 2008 to 2009	Value ($ thousands)	% change 2008 to 2009
Total energy-related Petroleum Products	1,118,040	$46,007,956	1,012,011	-9.5%	$75,532,056	64.2%
Crude oil	844,703	$33,926,909	788,051	-6.7%	$58,122,816	71.3%
	January through December					
	2009		**2010**			
	(Actual values)		**(Estimated values)**			
	Quantity (thousands of barrels)	**Value ($ thousands)**	**Quantity (thousands of barrels)**	**% change 2008 to 2009**	**Value ($ thousands)**	**% change 2008 to 2009**
Total energy-related Petroleum products	4,263,292	$245,482,572	3,858,984	-9.5%	$403,012,978	64.2%
Crude oil	3,311,883	$188,498,323	3,089,764	-6.7%	$322,912,044	71.3%

Source: Census Bureau, Department of Commerce. Report FT900, *U.S. International Trade in Goods and Services,* May 12, 2010. Table 17.

Note: Estimates for January through December 2009 were developed by CRS from data through March 2010 and data through 2009 published by the Census Bureau using a straight line extrapolation.

Summary data from the Census Bureau for the change in the volume, or quantity, of energy-related petroleum imports and the change in the price, or the value, of those imports for 2009 and for 2010 are presented in **Table 1**. The data indicate that during the first three months of 2010, the United States imported 1,012 million barrels of energy-related petroleum products, valued at $76 billion. Energy-related imports for this three-month period were down 9.5% in volume terms from the same period in 2009 and cost nearly twice as much as such imports during the same period in 2009.

The data also indicate that the United States imported 4.3 billion barrels of total energy-related petroleum products in 2009, valued at $245 billion, compared with a total value of $439 billion in 2008. Also, in 2009, the quantity of energy-related petroleum imports fell by 4.0% compared with the comparable period in 2008; crude oil imports also fell by 2.7% from the same period in 2008. Year-over-year, the average value of energy-related petroleum products imports fell by 44%, while the average value of crude oil imports fell by 45%. As **Figure 1** shows, imports of energy-related petroleum products can vary sharply on a monthly basis. In 2009, imports of energy-related petroleum products averaged about 355 million barrels a month. Through the first three months of 2010, such imports have averaged 337 million barrels a month, primarily due to low imports in February.

In value terms, energy-related imports fell from $439 billion in 2008 to $245 billion in 2009, or a decrease of 44%, to account for about 16% of the value of total U.S. merchandise imports. Energy prices rose sharply in 2007 and continued from January through July 2008, not following previous trends of falling during the winter months. As Figure 2 shows, the cost of U.S. imports of energy-related petroleum products rose from about $17 billion per month in early 2007 to $53 billion a month in July 2008, but fell to $13.6 billion in February 2009, reflecting a drop in the price and in the volume of imported oil. The average price of imported oil in March 2010 was up 80% from the average price in March 2009. Energy imports accounted for $27 billion a month in March 2010, up from $16 billion a month in 2009, as indicated in Table 2.

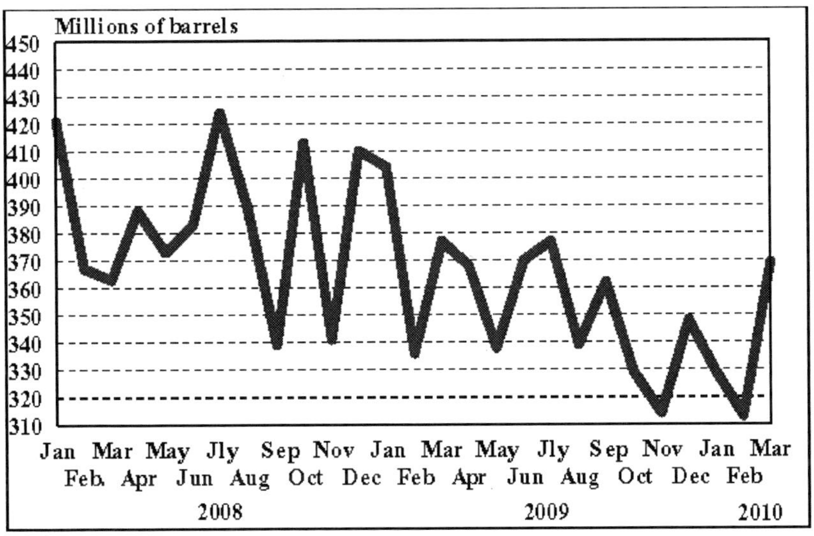

Source: Department of Commerce

Figure 1. Quantity of U.S. Imports of Energy-Related Petroleum Products

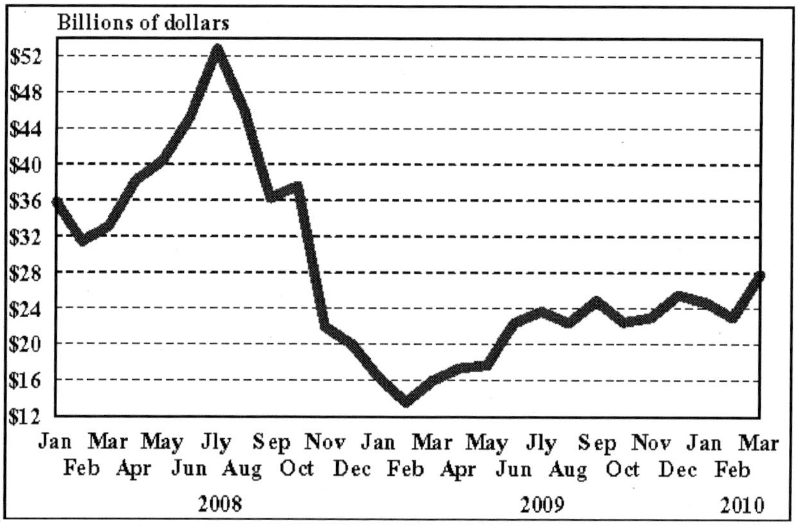

Source: Department of Commerce

Figure 2. Value of U.S. Imports of Energy-Related Petroleum Products

Table 2. U.S. Imports of Energy-Related Petroleum Products, Including Crude Oil (Not Seasonally Adjusted)

Period	Total energy-related petroleum products		Crude oil			
	Quantity (thousands of barrels)	Value ($ thousands)	Quantity (thousands of barrels)	Thousands of barrels per day (average)	Value ($ thousands)	Unit price (dollars)
2009						
Jan.-Dec.	4,263,292	$245,482,572	3,311,883	9,074	$188,498,323	$56.92
Jan.-Mar.	1,118,040	46,007,956	844,703	9,386	33,928,909	40.17
January	404,658	16,342,408	300,137	9,682	11,949,605	39.81
February	335,912	13,618,145	254,874	9,103	9,996,300	39.22
March	377,470	16,047,403	289,693	9,345	11,983,004	41.36
April	367,943	17,403,719	292,601	9,753	13,633,848	46.60
May	338,081	17,703,718	261,888	8,448	13,410,641	51.21
June	369,963	22,415,123	280,424	9,347	16,592,370	59.17
July	377,218	23,720,887	296,274	9,557	18,510,434	62.48
August	338,539	22,389,783	268,429	8,659	17,381,693	64.75
September	361,956	24,872,287	286,217	9,541	19,511,645	68.17
October	329,245	22,450,143	258,829	8,349	17,441,313	67.39
November	314,238	22,969,832	245,448	8,182	17,805,957	72.54
December	348,069	25,549,123	277,069	8,938	20,281,513	73

Table 2. (Continued)

Period	Total energy-related petroleum products		Crude oil			
	Quantity (thousands of barrels)	Value ($ thousands)	Quantity (thousands of barrels)	Thousands of barrels per day (average)	Value ($ thousands)	Unit price (dollars)
2010						
Jan.-Mar.	1,012,011	75,532,056	788,051	8,756	58,122,816	73.76
January	329,246	24,681,956	245,273	7,912	18,122,185	73.89
February	313,293	23,040,666	243,305	8,689	17,742,303	72.92
March	369,473	27,809,434	299,473	9,660	22,258,328	74.32

Source: Census Bureau, Department of Commerce. Report FT900, *U.S. International Transactions in Goods and Services.* May 12, 2010. Table 17.

a. Energy-related petroleum products is a term used by the Census Bureau and includes crude oil, petroleum preparations, and liquefied propane and butane gas.

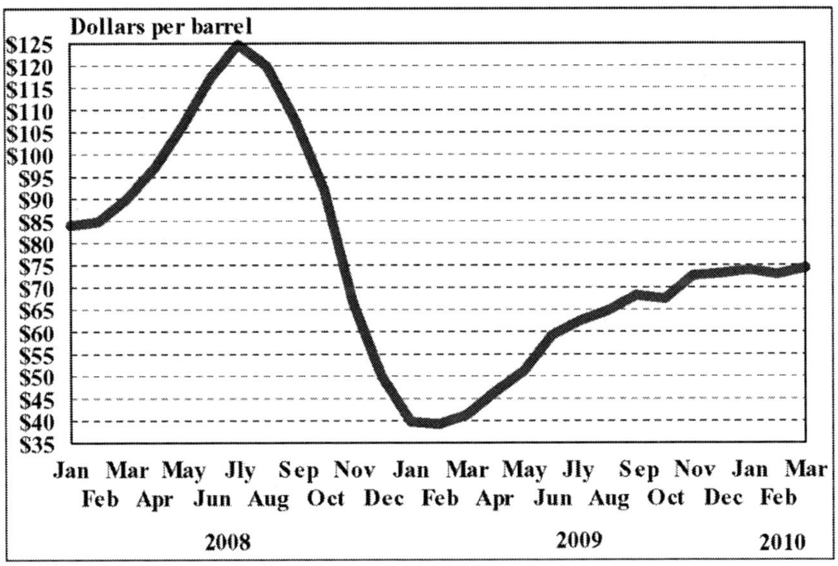

Source: Department of Commerce

Figure 3. U.S. Import Price of Crude Oil

As a result of the overall drop in the overall value of energy-related imports in 2009, the trade deficit in energy-related imports amounted to $204 billion, down by nearly half from the $386 billion recorded in 2008, and accounted for 40% of the total U.S. trade deficit of $517 billion for the year. In the three-month period of January-March 2010, the rise in oil prices, year over year, combined with an increased demand for energy imports, pushed up the overall value of energy imports, which accounted for 46% of the total merchandise trade deficit. This share is up from the 34% share of the trade deficit experienced during the same period in 2009.

Crude oil comprises the largest share of energy-related petroleum products imports. According to Census Bureau data[2], imports of crude oil fell from an average of 9.8 million barrels of crude oil imports per day in 2008 to an average of 9.1 million barrels per day in 2009, or a decrease of 7%. In March 2010, such imports averaged 9.7 million barrels per day, or an increase of 3.4% over the volume of such imports recorded in March 2009. From January 2008 to June 2008, the average price of crude oil increased from $84 per barrel to $117 per barrel, or an increase of 39%, as shown in **Figure 3**. As a result, the value of U.S. crude oil imports rose from about $27 billion a month in January 2008 to $35 billion a month in June 2008.

Data for 2009 indicate that a number of factors, primarily the economic recession, had a large impact on pushing down oil prices in the first three months. As economic growth picked up, the higher demand tended to raise pressure on oil prices, which rose through the end of the year. The rise in oil prices combined with an increase in the volumes of oil imports experienced during the period combined to raise the overall cost of imported energy. At times, crude oil traded for nearly $148 per barrel in July 2008, indicating that the cost of energy imports would have a significant impact on the overall costs of U.S. imports and on the value of the U.S. trade deficit. Since those record prices, the price per barrel of imported crude oil fell to under $40 per barrel at times in January and February 2009. For the year 2009, the imported volume of energy-related petroleum products fell by 44%, due in large part to a slowdown in economic activity. At an average price of $56 per barrel in 2009, compared with an average price of $95 per barrel in 2008, energy-related import fell by nearly $130 billion as a factor in the overall U.S. trade deficit. For 2010, the total cost of energy imports could rise to more than $300 billion at an average price of $75 per barrel and could rise to nearly $330 billion at an average price of $85 per barrel and account for nearly half of the annual trade deficit.

Issues for Congress

The rise in the prices of energy imports experienced since early 2000 through March 2010 could have a significant impact on the annual U.S. trade deficit in 2010, should those price increase stick, or run even higher. The rise in energy prices may well affect the U.S. rate of inflation and could have a slightly negative impact on the rate of economic growth in 2010. Various factors, dominated by the rate of economic growth in the United States and Western Europe, could combine to push up the cost of energy imports, which will have a slightly negative impact on the pace of the economic recovery. Typically, energy import prices have followed a cyclical pattern that has caused energy prices to rise in the summer and decline in the winter. The slowdown in the rate of economic growth in the United States and elsewhere in 2009 sharply reduced the demand for energy imports and caused oil prices to tumble from the heights they reached in July 2008. An important factor that often affects crude oil prices is the impact Atlantic hurricanes have on the production of crude oil in the Gulf of Mexico The oil spill in the Gulf of Mexico and concerns over the safety of oil wells in the region could dampen somewhat oil production and further strain supplies as summer demand increases.

The return to a positive rate of economic growth will continue to place upward pressure on the prices of energy imports and contribute to the nation's merchandise trade deficit. Some of the impact of this deficit could be offset if some of the dollars that accrue abroad are returned to the U.S. economy through increased purchases of U.S. goods and services or through purchases of such other assets as corporate securities or acquisitions of U.S. businesses. Some of the return in dollars likely will come through sovereign wealth funds (SWFs), or funds controlled and managed by foreign governments, as foreign exchange reserves boost the dollar holdings of such funds. Such investments likely will add to concerns about the national security implications of foreign acquisitions of U.S. firms, especially by foreign governments, and to concerns about the growing share of outstanding U.S. Treasury securities that are owned by foreigners.

It is likely that the economy will again face high and rising prices for imported energy products as national economies recover to a more robust rate of economic growth. It is possible for the economy to adjust to the higher prices of energy imports by improving its energy efficiency, finding alternative sources of energy, or searching out additional supplies of energy. There may well be increased pressure applied to Congress to assist in this process. For Congress, the increase in the nation's merchandise trade deficit could add to existing inflationary pressures and complicate efforts to stimulate the economy should the rate of economic growth flatten out. In particular, Congress, through its direct role in making economic policy and its oversight role over the Federal Reserve, could face the dilemma of rising inflation, which generally is treated by raising interest rates to tighten credit, and a slow rate of economic growth, which is usually addressed by lowering interest rates to stimulate investment. A sharp rise in the trade deficit may also add to pressures for Congress to examine the causes of the deficit and to address the underlying factors that are generating that deficit. In addition, the rise in prices of energy imports could add to concerns about the nation's reliance on foreign supplies for energy imports and add impetus to examining the nation's energy strategy.

End Notes

[1] Census Bureau, Department of Commerce. Report FT900, *U.S. International Trade in Goods and Services,* May 12, 2010. Table 17. The report and supporting tables are available at http://www.census.gov/foreign-trade/Press-Release/ current_press_release/ftdpress.pdf.

[2] Report FT900, U.S. International Trade in Goods and Services, May 12, 2010. Table 17.

In: Economic Policies in a Time of Financial Crisis
Editor: Heather D. Perkins
ISBN: 978-1-61122-686-7

Chapter 15

TRENDS IN DISCRETIONARY SPENDING

D. Andrew Austin and Mindy R. Levit

SUMMARY

Discretionary spending is provided and controlled through appropriations acts, which fund many of the activities commonly associated with such federal government functions as running executive branch agencies, congressional offices and agencies, and international operations of the government. Essentially all spending on federal wages and salaries is discretionary.

Federal spending in 2009 accounted for just under a quarter (24.7%) of the U.S. economy, as measured by gross domestic product (GDP). Federal spending since 1962 has averaged about a fifth of GDP. (Years denote federal fiscal years unless noted otherwise.) Discretionary spending accounted for 35.2% of total outlays in 2009, as extraordinary federal responses to financial turmoil sharply increased mandatory spending (59.5% of outlays in 2009), reducing discretionary spending's share of total spending.

In 1962, discretionary spending accounted for 47.2% of total outlays and was the largest component of federal spending until the mid-1970s. Since then, discretionary spending as a share of federal outlays and as a percentage of GDP has fallen. The long-term fall in the share of discretionary spending as a portion of total federal spending is largely due to rapid growth of entitlement outlays and slower growth in defense spending relative to other federal spending in past decades.

Discretionary spending is often divided into defense, domestic discretionary, and international outlays. Trends in those categories may indicate broad national priorities as reflected in federal spending decisions. Defense and domestic discretionary spending compose nearly all of discretionary spending. In 1962, discretionary spending equaled 12.3% of GDP, with defense spending making up 9.0% of GDP. In 2010, total discretionary spending is estimated to fall to 9.6% of GDP with defense spending totaling 4.9% of GDP. Military spending has increased sharply over the last decade. On average, from 2000 to 2010, defense outlays grew 6.8% per year in real terms, whereas non-defense discretionary outlays grew 5.6% per year in real terms.

The G. W. Bush and Obama Administrations each created their own division of security and non-security spending. Dividing spending into security and non-security components, however, presents many conceptual and practical difficulties. Some federal activities, such as Coast Guard patrols, advance non-security and security interests. Furthermore, federal programs tasked with non-security aims in normal times may respond to specific homeland security challenges. Non-defense security discretionary budget authority increased sharply after Hurricane Katrina, although changes in outlays were less dramatic. Non-defense non-security outlays, which have ranged between 3% and 3.5% of GDP since the mid-1980s, are estimated to reach about 4% of GDP in 2010, largely due to economic stimulus measures and other recession-related spending.

The Obama Administration in its recent budget submission called for a three-year freeze on non-security discretionary spending. Weak economic conditions have depressed federal revenues and may continue to increase government social safety-net expenditures. Some contend that additional stimulus measures are needed to reduce high unemployment levels, while others have called for imposing greater budgetary stringency. Over the long term, projected future growth in entitlement program outlays may put severe pressure on discretionary spending unless policy changes are enacted or federal revenues are increased.

WHAT DOES DISCRETIONARY SPENDING INCLUDE?[1]

Discretionary spending is provided in, and controlled by, annual appropriations acts, which fund many of the routine activities commonly associated with such federal government functions as running executive branch agencies, congressional offices and agencies, and international operations of the government.[2] Essentially all spending on federal wages and salaries is discretionary.[3]

Discretionary spending is often contrasted with mandatory, or direct, spending. Mandatory spending includes federal spending on entitlement programs, the Supplemental Nutrition Assistance Program (formerly known as the Food Stamps program), and other spending controlled by laws other than appropriation acts.[4] Spending levels for mandatory programs are generally controlled by eligibility criteria and size of the eligible population.

Budget Authority and Outlays

The distinction between outlays and budget authority is important to understanding the federal budget and, particularly, discretionary spending. Appropriations legislation, which controls discretionary spending, grants budget authority to accomplish specific ends. Budget authority is what federal agencies can legally spend. Budget authority has been compared to funds deposited into a checking account, which then can be used for specified federal purposes. Outlays are disbursed federal funds. Therefore, an outlay is not recorded until the federal government disburses appropriated funds to purchase goods and services.

Table 1. Categories of Federal Spending

Entitlement	Budget Authority Provided by Law Other than Appropriation Acts Medicare Social Security	Budget Authority Provided by Appropriation Acts Appropriated Entitlements (e.g., veterans' compensation, Medicaid, TANF[a]) SNAP[b] (with caveats)
Not an Entitlement	Salaries for Members of Congress Mandatory non-entitlements (e.g., Forest Service payments to states)	Discretionary Spending[c] (defense, non-defense domestic discretionary, and international)

Source: Compiled by CRS.

a. Temporary Assistance for Needy Families.

b. The Supplemental Nutrition Assistance Program (SNAP) was formerly known as the Food Stamps program.

c. Discretionary spending programs. See discussion in text.

Table 1 illustrates the different categories of federal spending (i.e., mandatory and discretionary spending) by contrasting the type of budget authority needed for specific purposes.

Outlay data are used to assess the macroeconomic effects of the federal budgets, whereas budget analysis of specific federal programs is typically based on budget authority, because that is what Congress controls directly. Congressional appropriations, which grant budget authority for specific purposes, are not always tightly linked to changes in outlays in the following year. While budget authority can be granted for a single year, some appropriations (such as for many military construction projects) provide budget authority for multiple years, or indefinitely. Thus outlays that flow from an appropriated sum might be spread over several fiscal years, implying that budget authority totals will differ from outlay totals for a single fiscal year.[5]

TRENDS IN DISCRETIONARY SPENDING

The composition of the federal budget has changed dramatically since the early 1960s. Over time, the share of total discretionary spending in federal spending has fallen, whereas the share of mandatory spending has increased. Discretionary spending accounted for 67.5% of total outlays in 1962, but only 35.2% of total outlays in 2009.[6] Mandatory spending, by contrast, rose from 26.1% of total outlays in 1962 to 59.5% in 2009.

In contrast to the longer term trends, between 2000 and 2010, discretionary spending grew more quickly than mandatory spending. After falling for three decades between the late 1960s and the late 1990s as a share of the economy, discretionary spending increased 6.2% a year in real terms on average from 2000 to 2010.[7] Over the same period, the share of discretionary spending as a proportion of federal outlays grew from 34.4% in 2000 to 35.2% in 2009.

The economic recession that began in late 2007 reduced incomes and increased unemployment, which in turn increased the number of people eligible for income support programs and outlays on some discretionary programs. Extraordinary federal responses to financial turmoil in 2008 and 2009, however, increased mandatory spending even more sharply, which reduced the share of discretionary spending in federal outlays. More normal financial conditions and renewed economic growth in the second half of calendar year 2009 may help decrease spending on some mandatory programs and stem decreases in Medicare and Social Security payroll tax revenues.

How Has the Composition of Discretionary Spending Changed?

In 1962, discretionary spending comprised 67.5% of total outlays, with mandatory spending and net interest accounting for 26.1% and 6.5%, respectively. Discretionary spending as a share of total outlays reached its peak in 1963. By 2009, discretionary spending fell to 35.2% of total outlays. Mandatory spending accounted for 57.7% of total outlays, with net interest at 4.5% in 2009.[8] Figure 1 shows discretionary and mandatory spending, and net interest payments—categories defined in the Budget Enforcement Act (P.L. 101-508)—since 1962 as a share of total outlays.

The peak estimated in mandatory spending in 2009 is largely attributable to the state of the economy and enacted federal financial interventions, leading to an analogous spike in overall spending. This also led to a decline in discretionary spending's share of total outlays (from 38.0% in 2008 to 35.2% in 2009), though discretionary spending is estimated to rise in nominal terms. Over the longer term, discretionary spending's share of total outlays is projected to decline further. By 2020, according to CBO baseline projections, that assume projected discretionary outlays hold steady in real terms, discretionary spending will fall to a historical low of 28.9% of total outlays.

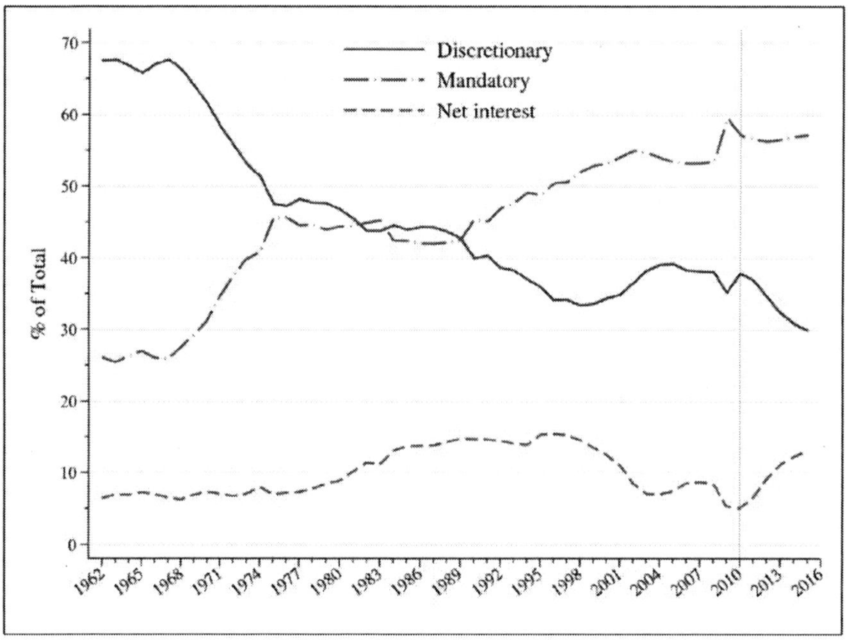

Source: OMB.

Notes: FY2010 values estimated; FY2011-FY2015 are President's proposed levels.

Figure 1. Discretionary Outlays by BEA Category As a Percentage of Total

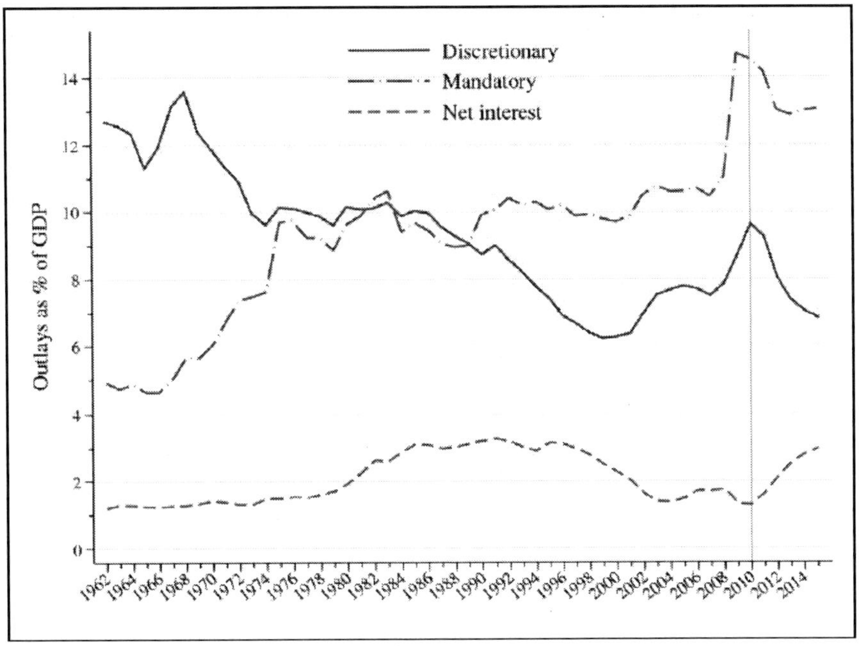

Source: OMB (February 2010 budget submission) and CRS calculations.
Notes: FY2010 values estimated; FY2011-FY2015 are President's proposed levels.

Figure 2. Components of Federal Spending As a percentage of GDP, FY1962-FY2015

Trends in discretionary spending as a share of gross domestic product (GDP) provides another perspective on how the composition of federal outlays has changed. Measuring budget components as a share of GDP compares their size to the economy as a whole, and implicitly incorporates inflation and population growth. **Figure 2** shows components of federal spending as a percentage of GDP since 1962.

While discretionary spending was the largest component of federal spending until the mid-1970s, mandatory spending in 2009 accounted for nearly three-fifths of total federal spending. In 2009, mandatory spending accounted for about 6% more of GDP than discretionary spending, although that gap is expected to narrow to 3.9% in 2010.

Medicare and Medicaid have continued to grow faster than overall federal spending, contributing to the majority of the increase in mandatory spending over this period. Social Security spending, the other large component of mandatory spending, has been relatively stable in the last decade when measured as a share of GDP.

Total federal spending as a share of GDP is estimated to have peaked in 2009 as a result of the current economic situation and enacted federal financial interventions. While discretionary spending declined as a percentage of total outlays in 2009, it rose as a percentage of GDP because the economy shrank in 2008 and early 2009. Over the longer term, discretionary spending's share of GDP is projected to decline further. By 2020, discretionary spending is projected to fall to 6.7% of GDP, similar to the levels it reached in the late 1990s and early 2000s.

Because of the decline in discretionary spending as a percentage of total outlays and as a percentage of GDP and the resulting increase in the share of mandatory spending over time, controlling the federal budget may have become more difficult for Congress. In other words, because net interest payments and mandatory spending are set automatically, less money is available to allocate to other government agencies and programs unless revenues rise or Congress modifies eligibility requirements and benefits of mandatory spending programs.

Discretionary Spending and National Priorities

Discretionary spending can be subdivided into defense, domestic, and international categories. Such divisions may provide a rough indicator of national priorities as reflected in federal spending decisions. **Figure 3** shows these categories of discretionary spending as a share of GDP over the period 1969-2009. Discretionary defense spending as a percentage of GDP fell from 8.7% in 1969 to 3.0% in 2000, and then rose to an estimated 4.9% of GDP in 2010. Over the same period, domestic and international discretionary spending have changed less dramatically as a percentage of GDP. Domestic discretionary spending increased in the late 1970s but fell in subsequent decades as a share of the economy, remaining closer to its post-1969 average.

Although discretionary spending has increased rapidly in the past half decade, spending in some government departments and agencies has grown very slowly or has been cut, while spending in other areas has expanded rapidly. Funding for defense and emergency and disaster management increased after the events of September 11, 2001, and even more sharply in the wake of Hurricane Katrina. In recent years, disaster funding has receded, allowing non-defense discretionary spending as a share of GDP to fall until federal responses to the economic recession pushed spending back up.

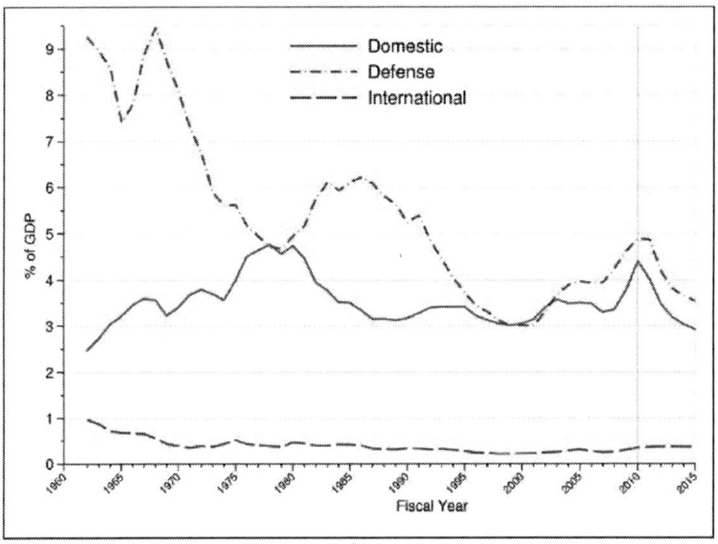

Source: OMB and BEA.

Notes: Defense is budget function 050, International is function 150, and Domestic is the remainder. FY2010 values estimated; FY2011-FY2015 levels are proposed by the President. FY2010 includes the Administration's request for a $33 billion supplemental for the Afghan surge. FY2010 reflects DOD's request for its base budget and an additional $159 billion for war costs.

Figure 3. Discretionary Outlays By Broad Category As a percentage of GDP

Discretionary Defense Spending

Defense spending increased sharply in the mid-1960s as the United States' involvement in Vietnam deepened. After large-scale withdrawals of American troops from Vietnam began in 1969, defense spending as a share of GDP fell for the next decade. The Soviet invasion of Afghanistan prompted the Carter Administration, and then the Reagan Administration, to boost military expenditures resulting in an increase in defense spending during the early 1980s. After the Berlin Wall was opened in November 1989 and communist governments in central and eastern Europe collapsed, defense spending as a share of GDP dropped to historically low levels, providing what some called a "peace dividend." Defense spending again rose after the attacks of September 11, 2001, and wars in Afghanistan and Iraq began.

Increased defense spending accounted for 53% of the increase in discretionary spending in real terms over the past decade. Discretionary defense spending increased 6.8% per year on average in real terms between 2000 and 2010.[9] Discretionary defense spending, which had fallen to 3.0% of GDP by the late 1990s, rose sharply to 4.0% of GDP in 2005, and is estimated to reach 4.9% of GDP in 2010 and 2011. General Mike Mullen, Chairman of the Joint Chiefs of Staff, has said that he considered 4% of GDP "an absolute floor" for future defense spending.[10] The trajectory of defense discretionary spending depends in large part on the scale of future operations in Iraq and Afghanistan, as well as on decisions about major procurement programs. Some analysts have expressed some doubts about the sustainability of current defense budget plans.[11] However, others contend that defense expenditures as a proportion of GDP should be expected to fall over the long term because the cost of defending the nation depends on factors that are largely independent of economic growth.

Discretionary Domestic Spending

Trends in domestic discretionary spending are less dramatic. Domestic spending supports the largest number of federal agencies and programs, including science and technology research, natural resources, energy, education, and numerous others. None of the individual programs within the domestic discretionary category have approached 1% of GDP since 1962. Most of these programs spent less than 0.5% of GDP during that period.

Domestic discretionary spending, 3.2% of GDP in 1969, rose to a peak of 4.8% in 1978. Domestic non-defense discretionary spending's share of GDP fell during the Reagan Administration, reaching 3.1% of GDP in 1987.[12] Since then it has fluctuated between 3.0% and 3.6% of GDP. Domestic discretionary spending in 2009 accounted for 4.1% of GDP.

Discretionary International Spending

Discretionary spending for international programs since 1969 has averaged 0.3% of GDP, reaching its peak of 0.5% of GDP in 1975. Since that time, international spending has generally trended downward. Between 2001 and 2010, spending on international programs rose from 0.2% of GDP to 0.3% of GDP. The majority of the funding in this category in recent times has been devoted to diplomatic missions, foreign aid, and international finance.

Discretionary Security and Non-Security Spending

The G. W. Bush and Obama Administrations have each created their own division of security and non-security discretionary spending as a way of communicating their budgetary priorities. The Obama and Bush Administration budgets have presented summaries of discretionary funding that split out security spending from non-security spending.[13] Unlike the division of discretionary spending into the categories of domestic, international, and defense, which has become routine in budget analyses, no standard method of dividing security spending from non-security spending has been universally accepted. In particular, the G. W. Bush and Obama Administration definitions vary in significant ways.

What is "Homeland Security" or "Security" Spending?

Any division of spending into security and non-security components would likely present conceptual and practical difficulties.[14] Moreover, the widely used term "homeland security," which comprises some but not all non-defense security spending, does not already readily translate in budgetary categories.

The Obama Administration defines security spending as funding for:

- Department of Defense-Military;
- Department of Energy's National Nuclear Security Administration;
- International Affairs (function 150; includes State Department and some other agencies);
- Department of Homeland Security; and
- Department of Veterans Affairs.[15]

Activities within budget subfunction 053 (Atomic Energy Defense Activities) outside of the National Nuclear Security Administration by this definition are classed as non-security. While the G. W. Bush Administration defined certain parts of the Department of Homeland Security within its "security" classification, the Obama Administration includes all of that department's funding.

The G. W. Bush Administration defined security funding as spending on the "Department of Defense, Homeland Security activities Government-wide; and International Affairs."[16]

The Obama Administration includes funding for the Department of Veterans Affairs and excludes Justice Department agencies such as the Federal Bureau of Investigation (FBI) under its security rubric, while the Bush Administration's definition included the FBI and other law enforcement bureaus and excluded the Department of Veterans Affairs.

Most homeland security spending, by either definition, takes place in the Department of Defense, the Department of Homeland Security, and the Department of Energy. Many other federal agencies spend at least some portion of their budget on what are arguably homeland security tasks, so that a significant amount of homeland security spending takes place in agencies and programs whose primary focus is not security oriented. Some federal activities, such as Coast Guard patrols and research at the Centers for Disease Control and Prevention, advance interests clearly linked to security objectives as well as those which are not. Moreover, some federal programs tasked with non-security aims in normal times may respond to specific homeland security challenges. These issues complicate budgetary analyses of homeland security spending.

The President's budget submission must report homeland security spending.[17] This definition, drawn more narrowly than "security," can exclude some activities not closely tied to security concerns, such as military bands. OMB's security spending estimates are based on reports from 32 agencies with homeland security responsibilities. Those agencies provide OMB with budget reports that provide a level of detail unavailable in publicly available data.

Trends in "Security" and "Non-Security" Discretionary Spending

Figure 4 shows trends in discretionary spending, divided into defense, non-defense security, and non-security categories in terms of budget authority, while **Figure 5** shows the same categories in terms of outlays. Because budget authority can translate into outlays that stretch over several years, changes in outlays tend to be more gradual.

Non-security discretionary spending (according to an approximation of the Bush Administration security spending definition), which had been about 6% of GDP in the late 1970s, dropped sharply in the early 1980s before stabilizing around 3% of GDP after 1986.[18] Changes in non-defense security discretionary spending have been less dramatic. **Table 2** shows average real growth rates for security and non-security components of discretionary spending.

The Obama Administration in its first budget submission contended that many domestic priorities had been underfunded and proposed several cuts in defense spending, many of which Congress adopted.[19] The Obama Administration in its FY2011 submission, however, called for a three-year freeze on discretionary non-security spending.[20] Previously, the Bush Administration had said that holding down growth in "non-security" discretionary spending was a major fiscal priority.[21] Non-security discretionary outlays (using the Bush Administration definition) rose from 3.1% of GDP in 2007 to 4.2% of GDP in 2010, after having increased earlier in the decade. Non-defense security discretionary budget authority increased sharply after Hurricane Katrina hit in 2005, while changes in outlays, shown in Figure 5, were less dramatic, in large part because the Gulf Coast recovery lasted longer than expected.[22]

FISCAL STIMULUS AND THE BUDGET

Congress in early 2009 responded to weak economic conditions and dramatic job losses that sharply increased unemployment rates by passing a major fiscal stimulus package.[23] The resulting measure, the American Recovery and Reinvestment Act of 2009 (ARRA; H.R. 1, P.L. 111-5), enacted on February 17, 2009, included stimulus spending and tax cuts estimated at the time to total $787.2 billion. ARRA includes funds for discretionary spending on education initiatives, support for state governments, public housing, infrastructure, and health care. CBO more recently estimated the total budgetary effect of ARRA at $862 billion between 2009 and 2019.[24]

Table 2. Average Real Growth in Discretionary Spending Using approximation of G. W. Bush Administration Definition of "Security")

Time Period	Total	Non-Security	Defense	Non-Defense Security	GDP
FY2005-FY2010	5.45%	5.94%	5.34%	2.70%	3.28%
FY2000-FY2010	6.20%	5.40%	6.79%	7.86%	4.06%
FY1990-FY2010	3.04%	4.04%	2.18%	4.73%	4.79%

Source: OMB, CRS calculations.

Notes: Defense is Defense-Military function (050). See **Appendix** for definition of security spending. FY2010 outlays include proposed $41.1 billion supplemental appropriation.

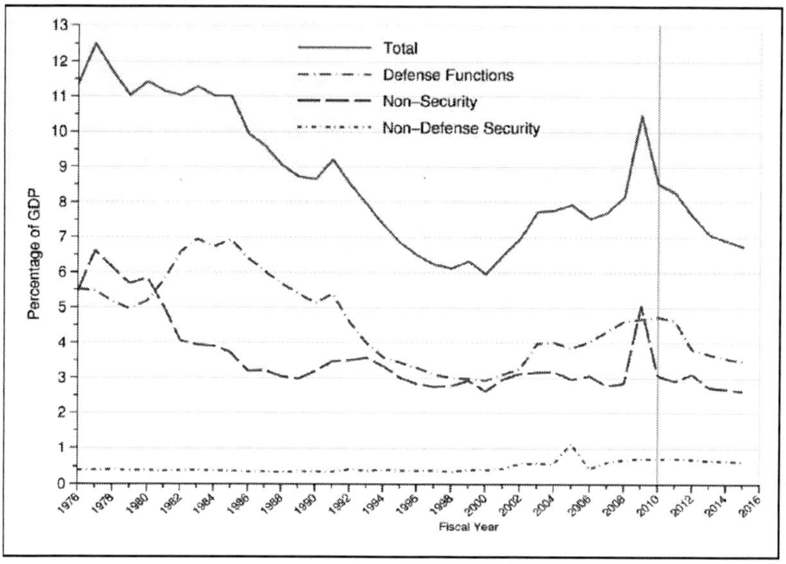

Source: Source: OMB and BEA.

Notes: The security category here replicates totals presented in the FY2011 Budget submission (Summary Table S-11). Defense here includes Dept. of Defense-Military spending. Non-defense security includes Dept. of Energy's National Nuclear Security Admin., International Affairs (function 150), Dept. of Homeland Security and Dept. of Veterans Affairs. FY2010 values estimated; FY2011-FY2015 levels are proposed by the President. Some supplemental appropriations passed in 2010 may not be included. Graph by Andrew Austin, CRS.

Figure 4. Discretionary Budget Authority by Type Using FY2011 Definition of "Security"

THE FY2011 BUDGET AND BEYOND

Budgetary priorities may change as the Obama Administration and Congress confront ongoing financial and economic challenges. In response to economic downturn, federal spending has automatically increased as more people have become eligible for income support programs and revenues have decreased as incomes of households and profits of many firms have fallen. These "automatic stabilizers" have a countercyclical effect, although most macroeconomists doubt that they would be themselves sufficient to stave off slow growth for the next few years.

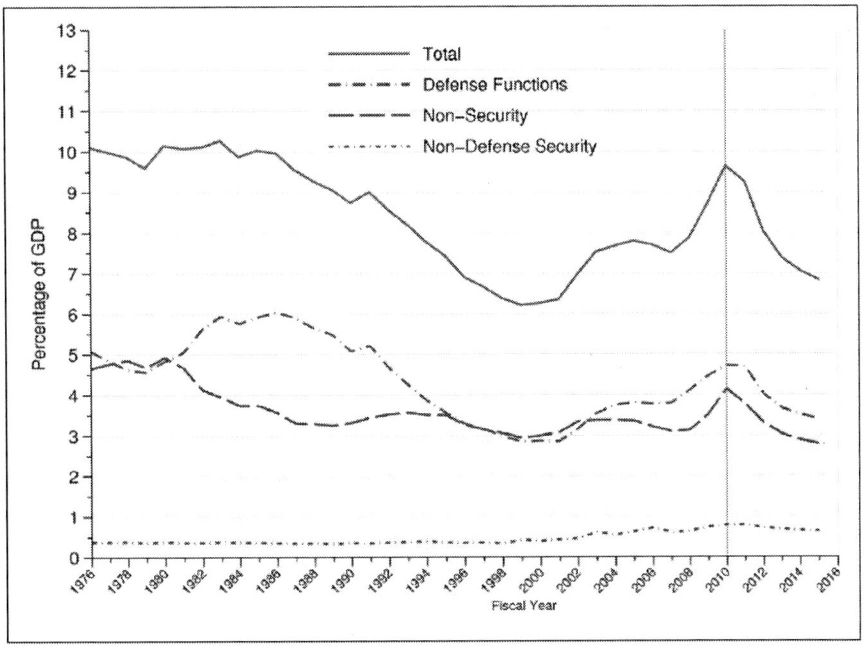

Source: OMB and BEA.

Notes: The security category here replicates totals presented in the FY2011 Budget submission (Summary Table S-11). Defense here includes Dept. of Defense-Military spending. Non-defense security includes Dept. of Energy's National Nuclear Security Admin., International Affairs (function 150), Dept. of Homeland Security and Dept. of Veterans Affairs. FY2010 values estimated; FY2011-FY2015 levels are proposed by the President. Some supplemental appropriations passed in 2010 may not be included. Graph by Andrew Austin, CRS.

Figure 5. Discretionary Outlays by Type Using FY2011 Definition of "Security"

In addition to "automatic stabilizers," the federal government has responded to this financial turmoil with an extraordinary set of measures aimed at housing and credit markets. In February 2008, Congress enacted a $152 billion package (P.L. 110-185, Economic Stimulus Act of 2008) to stimulate consumption that sent refunds to taxpayers and let firms depreciate their capital more quickly. Later in the year, the Federal Reserve created a panoply of lending facilities to provide financial institutions with loans in exchange for various types of collateral. On October 3, Congress passed the Emergency Economic Stabilization Act of 2008 (EESA; P.L. 110-343), which authorized the Treasury Secretary to use $700 billion (subject to certain Congressional restrictions and notifications) to intervene in financial markets or to inject capital into key financial institutions as part of a Troubled Asset Relief Program (TARP).

The ultimate costs of these responses and their budgetary impact will depend on how the economy performs, how well firms with federal credit guarantees weather future financial shocks, and whether the government receives positive returns on its asset purchases. Several major financial institutions have repaid TARP funds to Treasury.

New shocks to the financial system and the economy could present Congress with new demands for federal responses. Many state governments continue to face significant budget challenges, residential and commercial real estate markets remain depressed in many parts of the country, and many households are struggling with high debt levels and an uncertain labor market. Mandatory spending tied to means-tested social programs has been increasing due to persistent unemployment, while federal revenues will likely fall as individuals' incomes drop and corporate profits sink. Funding requests for military operations in Iraq and Afghanistan will likely continue. New policies and requests, if implemented, could affect discretionary spending levels in FY2011 and beyond.

DISCRETIONARY SPENDING IN THE LONG TERM

Congress can change, continue, or reverse trends in discretionary spending directly through annual appropriations decisions, or indirectly by modifying certain federal budget procedures, such as reinstating statutory limits on discretionary spending. If discretionary spending were held constant in real terms, as the CBO baseline presumes, then discretionary spending per capita would decrease as population grows and it would shrink as a share of GDP as the economy grows. On average the U.S. population grew 1% a year and per capita GDP grew 2.25% per year from 1962 to 2005.[25] If those trends were to persist, then holding discretionary spending constant in real terms implies per capita discretionary spending would shrink by 1% a year and discretionary spending as a share of the economy would shrink by 3.25% per year.

Over the long run, growth in entitlement spending will present severe fiscal challenges. Recent research on long-term fiscal challenges has focused on continued increases in the per beneficiary cost of health care, as well as the more predictable demographic changes that will occur as the baby boom generation retires. Projections from a variety of sources predict that spending on Medicare and Social Security will increase sharply as a share of GDP in coming decades.[26] CBO projects that Medicare will expand from 4.0% of GDP in 2020 to 9.0% in 2050 and to 13.5% in 2080. Social Security outlays are projected to grow from 5.3% of GDP in 2020 to 6.0% of GDP by 2035. Federal Medicaid outlays, 1.8% of GDP in 2008, are projected to reach 3.2% of GDP in 2050.[27]

Social Security, Medicare, and Medicaid outlays as a proportion of GDP are projected to equal or exceed the present share of federal revenues as a proportion of GDP (17.7% in 2008) sometime before the middle of the 21st century. Maintaining current levels of discretionary spending would then require either substantial tax increases or major changes in those entitlement programs.

APPENDIX. APPROXIMATING THE DEFINITION OF "SECURITY" SPENDING USED IN THE G. W. BUSH ADMINISTRATION

Table A-1 lists parts of the federal government whose funding is used to approximate the G..W. Bush Administration's definition of security spending. This approximation of security spending categories is defined using federal subfunction- and account-level data from the OMB Public Budget Database. **Table A-1** specifies which items are included in this definition of security spending. This definition of security spending has the advantage that it can be applied over a longer period of time, providing historical context for current spending decisions.[28]

This listing uses OMB function and subfunction codes along with specific account codes to identify agencies and programs that match, at least in large part, the definition of security spending put forth in the President's FY2009 budget submission.[29] As noted in the text, some activities such as U.S. Coast Guard harbor patrols may serve security and non-security ends. Some agencies, such as the Centers for Disease Control and Prevention, perform some tasks that are closely associated with security concerns as well as other tasks that are not. Finally, some grant programs designed to support non-security aims have been used to address security concerns such as recovery from the events of September 11, 2001.

Figure A-1 shows trends in discretionary spending in terms of budget authority, divided by security and non-security categories using the approach described above. **Figure A-2** presents those trends in terms of outlays.

Table A-1. Listing of Items Included in Security Category Used in CRS Analysis of Discretionary Spending

	Subfunction code	Within Departments	Bureau or Purpose (within Dept.)	Account	Description
51	Department of Defense-Military	All	All	All	
53	Atomic energy defense activities	All	All	All	
54	Defense-related activities	All	All	All	
152	International security assistance	All	All	All	
153	Conduct of foreign affairs	All	All	All	
401	Ground transportation	Dept. of Transportation	Transportation Security Agency Fed. Motor Carrier Safety Admin.	8274	Border Enforcement Program
402	Air transportation	Dept. of Homeland Security Dept. of Homeland Security	Transportation Security Agency Security, Enforcement, & Investigations: Transportation Security	508	
403	Water transportation	Dept. of Homeland Security	U.S. Coast Guard	247	Port safety development
		Dept. of Transportation	Maritime Administration	1769	National Defense Tank Vessel Construction Program
451	Community development	Dept. of Homeland Security	All	All	
453	Disaster relief and insurance	Dept. of Homeland Security	All	All	
551	Health care services	Dept. of Homeland Security	All	All	

Table A-1. (Continued)

	Subfunction code	Within Departments	Bureau or Purpose (within Dept.)	Account	Description
552	Health research & training	Dept. of Health and Human Services	Centers for Disease Control and Prevention	943	Disease Control, Research, and Training
751	Federal law enforcement activities	All	All		
754	Criminal Justice assistance	Dept. of Homeland Security	All		
809	Deductions for Offsetting Receipts	Dept. of Homeland Security	All		
804	General property and records management	Dept. of Homeland Security	Federal Protective Service	542	
908	Other interest accounts	Dept. of Homeland Security	General Fund Proprietary Interest Receipts, nec	143500	

Source: Created by CRS, January 15, 2009.

Note: The Security Spending category defined here will differ from Security spending categories developed by OMB and CBO, which are based on more detailed budget data.

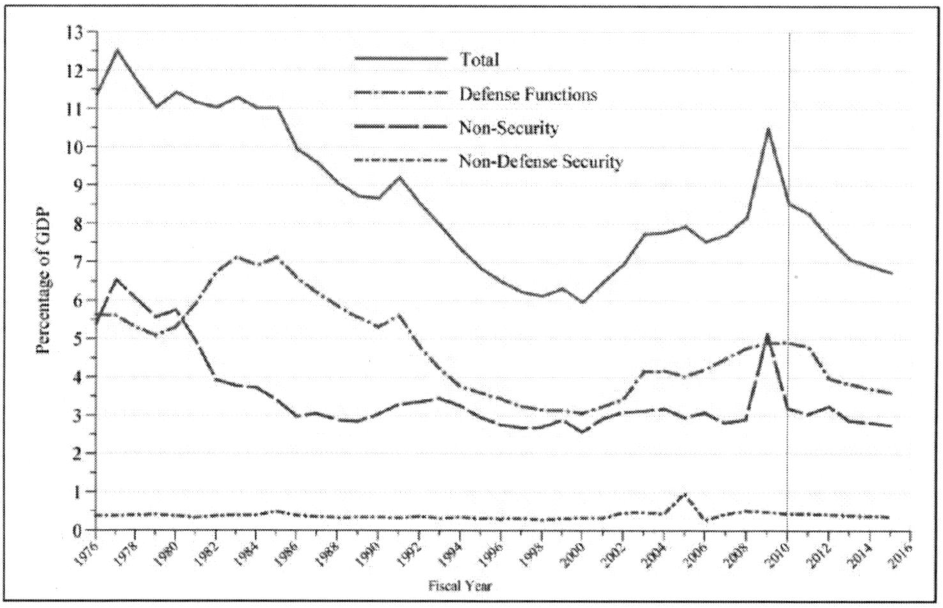

Source: OMB and BEA. See text for definition of security category. The Security spending category defined here differs from Security spending categories developed by OMB and CBO. Defense includes subfunctions 051DOD-Military, 053 Atomic energy defense, and 054 Defense-related activities.

Notes: FY2010 values estimated; FY2011-FY2015 levels are proposed by the President. Some supplemental appropriations passed in 2010 may not be included.

Figure A-1. Discretionary Budget Authority by Type Using approximation of G. W. Bush Administration definition of security spending As a percentage of GDP, FY1976-FY2015

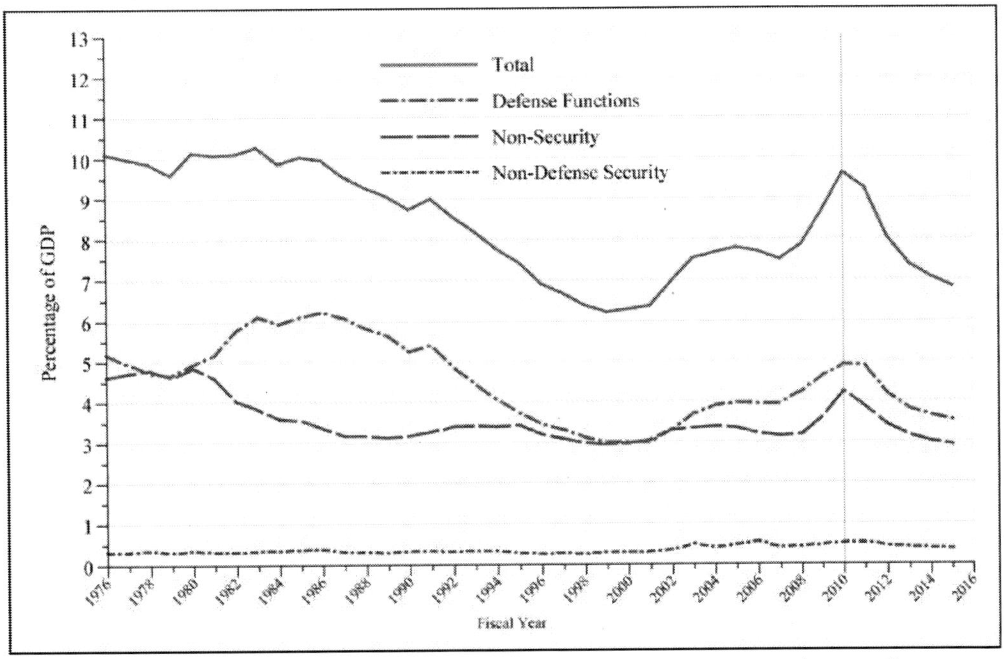

Source: OMB and BEA. See text for definition of security category. The Security spending category defined here differs from Security spending categories developed by OMB and CBO. Defense includes subfunctions 051DOD-Military, 053 Atomic energy defense, and 054 Defense-related activities.

Notes: FY2010 values estimated; FY2011-FY2015 levels are proposed by the President. Some supplemental appropriations passed in 2010 may not be included.

Figure A-2. Discretionary Outlays by Type Using approximation of G. W. Bush Administration definition of security spending As a percentage of GDP, FY1976-FY2015

End Notes

[1] This chapter was originally written by Philip Winters, who has retired from CRS.

[2] Annual appropriations acts fall within the jurisdiction of the House and Senate Appropriations Committees.

[3] Exceptions exist. For example, salaries for Members of Congress, the President, and federal judges are classified as mandatory spending, as are essentially all federal retirement and disability costs. Direct spending is controlled by committees with legislative jurisdiction.

[4] For details, see CRS Report RL33074, *Mandatory Spending Since 1962*, by D. Andrew Austin and Mindy R. Levit.

[5] While federal officials often have some discretion to choose how quickly appropriated funds are spent, they face constraints imposed by legislation designed to protect Congress's power of the purse. According to the Anti-Deficiency Act, a federal official cannot spend government money beyond what is available through appropriations or a fund by law. See Government Accountability Office, *Antideficiency Act Background*, available at http://www.gao.gov/ada/ antideficiency.htm for code citations and explanations. The Congressional Budget Act and Impoundment Control Act of 1974 (P.L. 93-344) limits the ability of federal officials to withhold or delay spending of appropriated funds without Congressional approval.

[6] Years in this chapter refer to federal fiscal years unless otherwise noted. Figures for FY1962-FY1968 from U.S. Office of Management and Budget, *Budget for FY2011*, *Historical Tables*, available at http:// www.whitehouse.gov/omb/ budget/Historicals/. Figures for FY1969 and beyond from the U.S. Congressional Budget Office, *Historical Tables*, available at https://www.cbo.gov/budget/historical.shtml.

[7] Estimated FY2010 outlays include a proposed $41.1 billion supplemental appropriation.

[8] Mandatory spending without offsetting receipts was 57.7% of total outlays in 2009. With offsetting receipts, the figure was 53.2%.

[9] Defense discretionary spending includes enacted supplemental requests. OMB, *Budget for Fiscal Year 2011, Historical Tables*, Table 8.2, available at http://www.whitehouse.gov/omb/budget/Historicals/. 2010 spending includes proposed $41.1 billion supplemental appropriation.

[10] *New York Times*, October 22, 2007. Transcript available at http://www.nytimes.com/2007/10/22/washington/22mullen-text.html.

[11] Testimony of CBO Assistant Director J. Michael Gilmore, in U.S. Congress, House Budget Committee, *The 2009 Future Years Defense Program: Implications and Alternatives*, hearings, 111th Cong., 1st sess., February 4, 2009; Testimony of CRS Specialist in Defense Policy and Budgets Stephen Daggett, in U.S. Congress, House Budget Committee, *Sustainability of Current Defense Plans*, hearings, 111th Cong., 1st sess., February 4, 2009.

[12] For a summary of Reagan-era spending changes, see David Stockman, *The Triumph of Politics* (New York: Harper&Row, 1986), pp. 401-411.

[13] For details, see U.S. Office of Management and Budget, *Budget of the U.S. Government, FY2009*, Tables S-2 and S-4, and the "Homeland Security Funding Analysis" chapter in the *Analytic Perspectives* volume. In circular A-11, OMB defines federal homeland security activities as those that "focus on combating and protecting against terrorism, and that occur within the United States and its territories, or outside of the United States and its territories if they support domestically-based systems or activities. Such activities include efforts to detect, deter, protect against, and, if needed, respond to terrorist attacks."

[14] For a discussion of defining security or homeland security, see U.S. Congressional Budget Office, "Federal Funding for Homeland Security: An Update," Economic and Budget Issue Brief, July 20, 2005.

[15] See notes to U.S. Office of Management and Budget, *Budget of the U.S. Government, FY2011*, Tables S-11.

[16] U.S. Office of Management and Budget, *Budget of the U.S. Government, FY2009*, Table S-2.

[17] The Homeland Security Act of 2002 (P.L. 107-296) requires this chapter, which supersedes a report on anti-terrorism activities mandated by the National Defense Authorization Act of 1998 (P.L. 105-85). An appendix (*Homeland Security Mission Funding by Agency and Budget Account*) was omitted from the printed FY2011 budget documents, but is available at http://www.whitehouse.gov/omb/budget/fy2011/assets/homeland_supp.pdf.

[18] See the Appendix for details on these calculations. [19] For example, the Administration states that "now is precisely the time for the country to make the long overdue investments that will fundamentally transform our economy so that we can compete and thrive in the decades ahead." U.S. Office of Management and Budget, *A New Era of Responsibility: Renewing America's Promise*," February, 2009.

[20] The proposed freeze in non-security discretionary spending is defined in terms of "budgetary resources," which incorporates transportation funding obligation limitations. See notes to U.S. Office of Management and Budget, *Budget of the U.S. Government, FY2011*, Tables S-11.

[21] U.S. Office of Management and Budget, *Budget of the U.S. Government, FY2009,* "The Budget Message of the President," p. 1.

[22] More details on Homeland Security funding can be found in CRS Report RL34482, *Homeland Security Department: FY2009 Appropriations*, coordinated by Jennifer E. Lake.

[23] For more information on budget issues, see CRS Report R41097, *The FY2011 Federal Budget*, by Mindy R. Levit.

[24] U.S. Congressional Budget Office, *Budget and Economic Outlook: Fiscal Years 2010 to 2010*, January 2010, Appendix A, available at http://www.cbo.gov/ftpdocs/108xx/doc10871/BudgetOutlook2010_Jan.cfm.

[25] These figures based on CRS calculations derived from CBO and Census Bureau data.

[26] See U.S. Congressional Budget Office, *Budget and Economic Outlook: Fiscal Years 2010 to 2010*, January 2010, pp. 20-21.

[27] U.S. Congressional Budget Office, *The Long-Term Budget Outlook*, June 2009, available at http://www.cbo.gov/doc.cfm?index=10297.

[28] OMB historical data from different years are not necessarily fully comparable due to changes in accounting treatment, redefinition of activity areas, changes in the structure of federal agencies, and for other technical reasons.

[29] Office of Management and Budget, *Budget of the U.S. Government FY2009, Analytic Perspectives*, ch. 23, "Homeland Security Funding Analysis."

In: Economic Policies in a Time of Financial Crisis
Editor: Heather D. Perkins
ISBN: 978-1-61122-686-7

Chapter 16

OUTSOURCING AND INSOURCING JOBS IN THE U.S. ECONOMY: AN OVERVIEW OF EVIDENCE BASED ON FOREIGN INVESTMENT DATA

James K. Jackson

SUMMARY

Foreign direct investment is sparking a national debate. Local communities compete for investment projects, while many of the residents of those communities fear losing their jobs to foreign outsourcing. Some opponents argue that such job losses have a disproportionately negative impact on local communities. Economists generally argue that free and unimpeded international capital flows have a positive impact on both domestic and foreign economies. This issue is complicated by the fact that broad, comprehensive data on U.S. multinational companies was not developed to address the issue of jobs outsourcing. This chapter provides an overview of CRS Report RL32461, *Outsourcing and Insourcing Jobs in the U.S. Economy: Evidence Based on Foreign Investment Data*, that analyzes the extent of direct investment into and out of the economy and the relationship between direct investment and the broader economic changes that are occurring in the U.S. economy.

The United States is the largest foreign direct investor in the world and the largest recipient of such investment funds.[1] On a historical cost basis, or book value basis, the Department Tof Commerce estimates that by the end of 2008 U.S. firms had accumulated $3.2 trillion worth of direct investment abroad, compared with the $2.3 trillion foreign investors had spent to acquire or establish businesses in the United States.[2] As **Figure 1** shows, direct foreign investment flows generally have increased since 2003, while U.S. direct investment abroad dropped sharply in 2005 as a result of one-time tax provisions, but then rebounded sharply in 2006.[3] Recent Department of Commerce data indicate that foreigners invested a record $325 billion in U.S. businesses and real estate in 2008, according to data published by the Department of Commerce and invested more than $200 billion in 2007.[4] New spending by U.S. firms on businesses and real estate abroad, or U.S. direct investment abroad,[5] rose sharply in 2006 to $235 billion up from the $8 billion net they brought home in 2005.

U.S. AND FOREIGN MULTINATIONAL COMPANIES

By the end of 2007, there were more than 2,300 U.S. parent companies with more than 26,000 affiliates operating abroad. In comparison, foreign firms had about 11,000 affiliates operating in the United States. U.S. parent companies employed over 22 million workers in the United States, compared with the 11.7 million workers employed abroad by U.S. firms and the 6 million persons employed in the United States by foreign firms. Although the U.S.-based affiliates of foreign firms employ fewer workers than do the foreign affiliates of U.S. firms, they paid almost as much in aggregate employee compensation in the United States as did the U.S. affiliates operating abroad. The data also suggest that U.S. parent companies are more efficient than either the U.S. affiliates of U.S. firms or foreign firms operating in the United States with higher output per employee. Foreign firms operating in the United States are more capital intensive relative to employment than U.S. parent firms or U.S. affiliates, likely reflecting the newer age of the capital stock of the foreign firms. The foreign affiliates of U.S. parent companies, however, had a third higher value of gross product than did the affiliates of foreign firms operating in the United States. In addition, the foreign affiliates of U.S. firms had total sales that were a third higher than that of the U.S. affiliates of foreign firms. The foreign affiliates of U.S. firms, however, paid more than three times more in taxes to foreign governments than did the affiliates of foreign firms operating in the United States. The overseas affiliates of U.S. parent companies also paid nearly twice as much in taxes relative to their sales as did U.S. parent companies and as did foreign-owned affiliates operating in the United States.

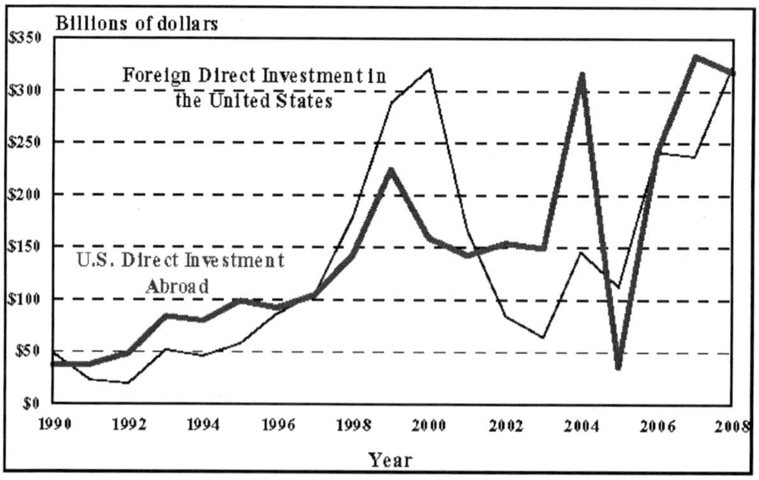

Source: CRS from U.S. Department of Commerce data.

Figure 1. Foreign Direct Investment in the United States and U.S. Direct Investment Abroad, Annual Flows 1990-2008 (in Billions of Dollars)

Table 1. Select Data on U.S. Multinational Companies and on Foreign Firms Operating in the United States, 2007 (Dollar Amounts are in Millions of Dollars)

	U.S. Multinational Companies		U.S. Affiliates of Foreign Firms
	Parent Companies	Affiliates	
Number of firms	2,270	26,342	10,941
Employment (thousands)	22,003	11,738	6,016
Employee compensation	$1,392,180	$475,595	$433,065
Gross product	$2,588,811	$1,117,585	$657,558
Total assets	$19,964,935	$14,201,291	$12,732,967
Sales	$8,614,733	$5,517,143	$3,553,593
Taxes	$257,292	$179,922	$57,731
R&D Expenditures	NA	$35,019	$44,158

Source: U.S. Direct Investment Abroad: Operations of U.S. Parent Companies and Their Foreign Affiliates, Preliminary 2007 Estimates; and Foreign Direct Investment in the United States: Operations of U.S. Affiliates of Foreign Companies, Preliminary 2007 Estimates.

Within the U.S. economy, U.S. multinational corporations (MNCs) rank among the largest U.S. firms and play an important role in the U.S. economy. According to the total output of U.S. parent companies, or gross product, they produced $2.59 trillion in goods and services in 2007, up slightly from the $2.54 trillion dollars they produced in 2006. This amount comprised about 21% of total U.S. private industry gross product, a share of total gross product of U.S. parent companies that has remained fairly consistent since the early 1990s despite significant changes in the U.S. economy as a whole.

EMPLOYMENT

A major source of contention in the United States regarding foreign investment focuses on the impact such investment is having on U.S. employment.[6] Some observers argue that recent actions by U.S. parent companies are different from previous experiences with foreign investment because the parent companies are shifting jobs, capital, and technology offshore to their foreign affiliates in ways that are distinctly different from previous periods, and thereby are reducing employment in the United States. The Department of Commerce's Bureau of Economic Analysis provides the most comprehensive set of data on U.S. direct investment abroad and on foreign direct investment in the United States. These data, however, were not designed to link employment gains or losses in the United States, either for individual jobs, individual companies or in the aggregate, with the gains and losses of jobs abroad. The data indicate, though, that the employment trends of U.S. parent companies are sensitive to economic conditions in the U.S. economy, particularly during periods in which economic growth slows down, as it did in the early 1980s, 1990s, and in the early 2000s.

Foreign investment data seem to indicate that, despite, or perhaps because of, the growing international linkages between economies, an expansion or a contraction in the rate of growth in the U.S. economy affects employment among U.S. parent companies more than it affects employment among the overseas affiliates of these parent companies. Nevertheless, changes in jobs among U.S. parent companies that are related to the overall rate of growth of the economy also affect the rate of growth in other countries and, therefore, in employment among the foreign affiliates, though not necessarily by the same magnitude, as indicated in **Figure 2**.

International linkages between U.S. and foreign economies mean that economic conditions in the United States have an impact on economic conditions abroad, there appears to be no distinct pattern between the creation or loss of jobs within U.S. multinational companies and a commensurate loss or creation of jobs among the foreign affiliates of those companies. Indeed, within most of the major developed countries, those economic forces that spur direct investment inflows also boost direct investment outflows. As a result, foreign direct investment may create jobs in the foreign affiliate that substitute for jobs in the parent company, but foreign investment may also positively affect job creation in both the parent company and the foreign affiliates, which makes it difficult to identify any broad trend regarding outsourcing.

TRADE

Another aspect of foreign direct investment that causes concern is the impact foreign direct investment has on the amount of foreign trade associated with those investments. Some observers argue that U.S. direct investment abroad supplants U.S. exports, jobs, and research and development funds, thereby reducing employment and wages in the U.S. economy. Others are concerned that outward direct investment alters the industrial composition of domestic production and trade flows, which can affect the sectoral and regional distribution of employment and the relative demand for skilled and unskilled labor.[7] According to this scenario, as firms invest abroad, they shift production abroad and replace U.S.-based production with exports back to the United States, thereby eliminating jobs in the United States. As production shifts abroad, jobs are lost in the United States and goods that once were produced in the United States are now imported from abroad. Most studies indicate that, on balance, direct investment abroad increases U.S. exports and helps sustain employment and wages at home.[8]

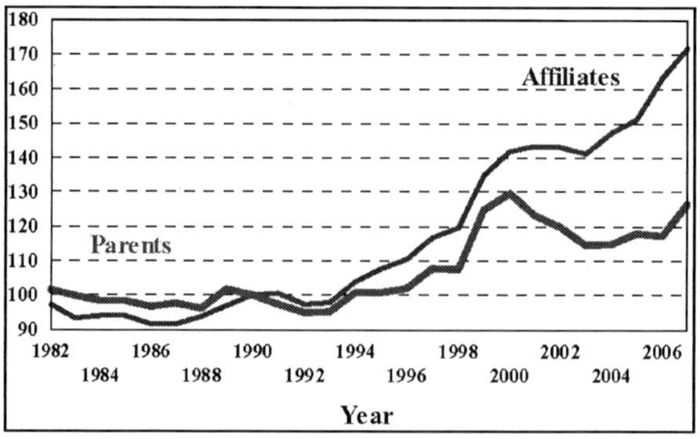

Source: Department of Commerce.

Figure 2. Index of Employment of U.S. Parent Companies and Their Foreign Affiliates, 1992-2007 (1990 = 100)

There is little doubt that some firms do indeed replace domestic production with production from abroad, which would shift trade patterns, but the share of U.S. trade represented by U.S. parent companies and their affiliates since the 1990s did not increase as would be expected. Instead, intra-firm exports and imports fell as a share of total U.S. exports and imports during the 1990s. From 2000 to 2003, intra-firm trade, both exports and imports, increased as a share of total U.S. exports and imports respectively, but since 2003, intrafirm trade in exports and imports has fallen as a share of total U.S. exports and imports.

For some observers, another concern is that U.S. parent firms have started moving service jobs offshore, or outsourcing, in sectors that once were thought to be immune to such activities.[9] U.S. foreign affiliates had $763 billion in services sales in 2007. Of this amount, 5.2% consisted of service sales back to the U.S. parent company. The largest share—73%—of sales of services were made in the local market. This share is substantially higher than the comparable share for sales of goods and services combined and is consistent with the general view that the distinguishing feature of services is that they are consumed where they are produced..

CONCLUSION

Data published by the Bureau of Economic Analysis offer no conclusive evidence that current investment trends are substantially different from those of previous periods. The data also show that U.S. direct investment abroad and foreign direct investment in the United States generally move in the same direction so that those forces which encourage U.S. firms to invest abroad also encourage foreign firms to invest in the United States. From the data examined, it is not apparent that U.S. parent companies are outsourcing jobs at a faster pace or in a manner that is fundamentally different or distinct from previous periods. There is an important caveat to these conclusions, however. The data published by the BEA were not developed to address the issue of jobs outsourcing and it is not possible with the BEA data to track job losses or gains in specific industries, specific companies, or specific plants with changes in jobs abroad. In addition, the BEA data lag behind current events by two years, which means that assessing these activities may seem to be out of sync with the more limited anecdotal examples that appear in the popular press.

The data do indicate, though, that an increase in economic growth in the U.S. parent companies relative to the rate of growth in the foreign affiliates likely increases pressure within the economy to complete structural changes and to shift capital and labor from declining sectors to expanding sectors. Such changes may also lead to a greater number of jobs being outsourced, but this effect likely would be muted by the overall strong demand for jobs within the economy and by new foreign investments in the economy.

On the other hand, an economic slowdown among U.S. parent companies relative to the rate of growth among foreign affiliates likely would lead to an overall decline in employment throughout the economy. U.S. parent companies may or may not respond to an economic slowdown by outsourcing jobs abroad because the dominating presence of the U.S. economy in the world economy means that an economic slowdown in the United States likely reduces economic growth abroad as well and that the foreign affiliates of those parent companies may not be a position to add more jobs. The uneven effect of an economic slowdown among U.S.

parent companies on their investment behavior abroad likely means that jobs outsourcing may appear to be more acute during periods in which the long-term structural changes in the economy coincide with the short-term economic adjustments that arise from a slowdown in the rate of growth of the U.S. economy.

For Congress, the data on direct investment seem to indicate that the number of jobs created by U.S. parent companies and by the foreign affiliates of those parent companies is tied closely to the overall performance of the U.S. economy. Such economic measures as employment, trade, and investment will rise and fall among U.S. parent companies and their foreign affiliates generally in tandem. Swings in the rate of growth in the economy that are associated with the business cycle tend to affect U.S. parent companies more than they affect their foreign affiliates and more than those U.S. firms that are purely domestic. Policies that ameliorate the business cycle, especially the downside of the cycle when the economy is experiencing a slow rate of economic growth, likely would do the most to help U.S. parent companies. Furthermore, Congress may choose to address the economic plight of those workers and communities that experience a disproportionate share of the adjustment costs that are associated with the business cycle by providing specialized assistance or other types of short-term support.

End Notes

[1] This is true on a historical cost, or *cumulative* position basis, but the sharp drop in foreign direct inflows after 2000 has meant that other countries have occasionally displaced the United States as the largest recipient of annual foreign direct inflows.

[2] Ibarra, Marilyn, and Jennifer Koncz, Direct Investment Positions for 2008, *Survey of Current Business*, July 2009, p 32. The position, or stock, is the net book value of U.S. parent company's equity in, and outstanding loans to, their affiliates abroad. A change in the position in a given year consists of three components: equity and intercompany inflows, reinvested earnings of incorporated affiliates, and valuation adjustments to account for changes in the value of financial assets. The Commerce Department also publishes data on the U.S. direct investment position valued on a current-cost and market value bases. These estimates indicate that U.S. direct investment abroad increased by $247 billion, but fell when measured by market value by $2.2 trillion in 2008 to reach $3.7 and $3.1 trillion, respectively. Nguyen, Elena L., The International Investment Position of the United States at Yearend 2008, *Survey of Current Business*, July 2009, p.10.

[3] The United States defines foreign direct investment as the ownership or control, directly or indirectly, by one foreign person (individual, branch, partnership, association, government, etc.) of 10% or more of the voting securities of an incorporated U.S. business enterprise or an equivalent interest in an unincorporated U.S. business enterprise. 15 CFR § 806.15 (a)(1). Similarly, the United States defines direct investment abroad as the ownership or control, directly or indirectly, by one person (individual, branch, partnership, association, government, etc.) of 10% or more of the voting securities of an incorporated business enterprise or an equivalent interest in an unincorporated business enterprise. 15 CFR § 806.15 (a)(1).

[4] Weinberg, Douglas B., Erin M. Walker, and Gregory A. Tenentes., U.S. International Transactions: Fourth Quarter and Year 2008. *Survey of Current Business*, April 2009. p. 28. Direct investment data reported in the balance of payments differ from capital flow data reported elsewhere, because the balance of payments data have not been adjusted for current cost adjustments to earnings.

[5] The United States defines direct investment abroad as the ownership or control, directly or indirectly, by one person (individual, branch, partnership, association, government, etc.) of 10% or more of the voting securities of an incorporated business enterprise or an equivalent interest in an unincorporated business enterprise. 15 CFR § 806.15 (a)(1).

[6] For a comprehensive look at how offshore outsourcing has affected U.S. workers, see CRS Report RL32292, *Offshoring (a.k.a. Offshore Outsourcing) and Job Insecurity Among U.S. Workers*, by Linda Levine. Also, see Drezner, Daniel W., The Outsourcing Bogeyman, *Foreign Affairs,* May/June, 2004; and Engardio, Pete, Aaron Berstein, and Manjeet Kripalani, Is Your Job Next? *Business Week,* February 3, 2003. P. 50-60.

[7] *International Investment Perspectives: 2006 Edition*, the Organization for Economic Cooperation and Development. p. 99.

[8] Ibid., p. 101; Brainard, S. Lael and David A. Riker, *Are U.S. Multinationals Exporting U.S. Jobs?* NBER Working Paper 5958, National Bureau of Economic Research, March 1997.

[9] Lohr, Steve. "High-End Technology Work Not Immune to Outsourcing." *The New York Times*, June 16, 2004, p. C1.

In: Economic Policies in a Time of Financial Crisis
Editor: Heather D. Perkins
ISBN: 978-1-61122-686-7

Chapter 17

JOB LOSS AND INFRASTRUCTURE JOB CREATION SPENDING DURING THE RECESSION

Linda Levine

SUMMARY

After the long economic expansion that characterized much of the current decade, the nation entered its 11th postwar recession in December 2007. The subsequent decrease in jobs and comparison of the latest recession to the Great Depression intensified congressional interest in passing legislation early in 2009 aimed at encouraging creation of new jobs and warding off further loss of jobs.

To mitigate all but one recession since the 1960s, Congress chose to increase federal spending on public works (infrastructure). (See CRS Report 92-93 9, *Countercyclical Job Creation Programs.*) Public works expenditures traditionally have gone to certain types of construction activities (e.g., building highways and bridges, dams and flood control structures) which indirectly increase demand in industries that supply their products to construction firms (e.g., manufacturing). Today, the definition of infrastructure has been expanded to include green economic activities (commonly referred to as green jobs), which include industries that utilize renewable resources (e.g., electricity generated by wind), produce energy-efficient goods and services (e.g., mass transit), and install energy-conserving products (e.g., retrofitting buildings with thermal-pane windows).

A question that typically arises during congressional consideration of economic stimulus legislation is which approach produces the most bang for the buck. In the instant case, this means how many jobs might be supported by federal expenditures on traditional and green infrastructure projects. Once stimulus legislation is signed into law, the focus of Congress customarily turns to estimates of the number of jobs that result as federal funds are allocated to specific activities. Therefore, after briefly examining the trend in employment since the recession's onset, the report turns to an in-depth look at estimates of job creation, including the limitations of the methodology often used to derive them and the difficulties associated with developing job estimates for green infrastructure in particular.

The report closes with a review of what is known to date about the number of jobs supported by infrastructure spending and other provisions in the American Recovery and Reinvestment Act (ARRA, P.L. 111-5). Section 1512 requires entities that receive ARRA appropriations from federal agencies, totaling approximately $271 billion, to include in quarterly reports to the agencies the number of direct jobs created or maintained as a result. Recipients of ARRA funds awarded by the Department of Transportation (DOT) must comply with the Section 1512 job reporting requirement; in addition, Section 1201 of P.L. 111-5 requires the DOT to estimate the direct, indirect, and total jobs associated with ARRA-funded transportation projects. Section 1513 of the act requires the Council of Economic Advisers (CEA) to report quarterly on the effect of ARRA provisions on employment and other economic indicators. The CEA's reports are the most comprehensive because they contain estimates of not only jobs supported by ARRA appropriations but also of jobs associated with other parts of P.L. 111-5 (e.g., unemployment and health insurance benefits, state fiscal relief, and tax provisions).

After the long economic expansion that characterized much of the current decade, the nation entered its 11th postwar recession in December 2007. It was not until November 2008, however, that the Business Cycle Dating Committee of the National Bureau of Economic Research announced that a substantial and widespread decline in economic activity had begun a year earlier. As part of its announcement, the committee noted that it "views the payroll employment measure, which is based on a large survey of employers, as the most reliable comprehensive estimate of employment. This series [the CES] reached a peak in December 2007."

The committee's announcement intensified congressional interest in passage of legislation aimed at encouraging creation of new jobs and warding off further loss of jobs. So, too, did comments equating the recession to the Great Depression. (See CRS Report R40655, *The Labor Market During the Great Depression and the Current Recession.*) This, in turn, sparked the interest of some policymakers in the job creation programs of the Depression period. (See CRS Report R4 1017, *Job Creation Programs of the Great Depression: the WPA and the CCC.*)

To mitigate all but one recession since the 1960s, Congress chose to increase federal expenditures on infrastructure (public works), thereby directly raising demand for goods and services to offset the reduced demand of consumers. (See CRS Report 92-93 9, *Countercyclical Job Creation Programs.*) But, there are a number of issues associated with using spending on public works to quickly create jobs during a recession. (See CRS Report R40107, *The Role of Public Works Infrastructure in Economic Stimulus.*)

When Congress considers spending on infrastructure to help stimulate a flagging economy, "how many jobs are created" is a commonly asked question. After first briefly examining trends in employment since the latest recession began, this chapter focuses on job creation estimates available in late 2008 associated with increased spending on traditional and so-called green infrastructure, placing a heavy emphasis on explaining the methodology often used to derive them and the difficulties associated with developing estimates for green economic activities in particular.

Once stimulus legislation is signed into law, the focus of Congress customarily turns to estimates of the number of jobs that result as federal funds are allocated to specific activities. In the case of the American Recovery and Reinvestment Act (ARRA, P.L. 111-5), which was enacted in early 2009, Congress included language requiring entities that receive ARRA appropriations from federal agencies to report the number of jobs created or maintained as a result and requiring the Council of Economic Advisers to report on the employment and other economic effects of ARRA provisions. The report closes with a review of what is known to date about the number of jobs associated with the stimulus act.

NET JOB LOSS

Total nonfarm employment declined steadily between December 2007 and October 2009, falling from 137,951,000 to 129,633,000. The great majority of this 8,318,000 job loss occurred after November 2008. Despite a small uptick in employment from October to November 2009, the number of jobs on employer payrolls fell the following month. Firms have been increasing their employment since then, however, with the number of jobs in April 2010 preliminarily rising to 130,161,000.

As is typical during economic downturns, employees in the goods-producing sector (mining, construction, manufacturing) have been the most adversely affected. Workers in the sector's construction industry began experiencing job losses even before the economy-wide downturn began.

Employment in the service-providing sector most recently peaked in December 2007, when the recession began. Some service-providing industries—utilities, education and health services— have continued to add workers. But, job losses elsewhere in the sector have far outweighed their gains. The financial activities industry began to lose jobs before the advent of the economy-wide downturn. This mirrors the above-mentioned trend in construction employment in part because real estate is a component of financial activities and it, like construction, has been hurt by the collapse of the housing market. Other components of financial activities, such as brokerage firms that packaged high-risk mortgages and the investors (e.g., banks) that purchased them, have been negatively affected by the housing market downturn as well.

Despite the widely expressed belief that the recession ended sometime in the third quarter of 2009, the pattern following the end of the prior 10 postwar recessions suggests that an uninterrupted rebound in jobs will not be immediate. According to a CRS analysis, in all but one of these recessions,

> the number of jobs on employer payrolls fluctuated for months.... Sustained job growth occurred within three to five months of the start of seven recoveries. In sharp contrast, steady job growth did not commence until March 1992—12 months after the July 1990–March 1991 recession ended—and not until September 2003—22 months after the March– November 2001 recession ended.[1]

INFRASTRUCTURE SPENDING AND JOB CREATION ESTIMATES

When in response to a recession Congress has acted to create jobs by raising demand for goods and services through increased federal spending, it often has chosen to direct the funds to infrastructure (public works) activities. Other means of direct countercyclical job creation— public service employment, fiscal relief to state governments, and employment tax credits—have been relied on much less often.[2]

Historically, public works has been synonymous with heavy and civil construction activities (e.g., road and bridge building, flood control structures and dam building). Today, it includes green economic activities or so-called green jobs. Although numerous studies on the emerging green economy have been released in the last several years, no consistent definition of green jobs exists at present. Green jobs seemingly are those in and related to industries that utilize renewable resources to produce their outputs (e.g., energy generated by wind, solar, and geothermal technologies) and jobs in and related to industries that produce energy-efficient goods (e.g., Energy Star appliances) and services (e.g., mass transit).[3] For this reason, the following discussion focuses on what is known about the job-generating impact of infrastructure spending broadly defined.

The section below begins with an in-depth examination of how job creation estimates usually are developed. The focus then narrows to look at two models that can be used to calculate the number of jobs nationwide dependent upon demand in the construction industry among others, and one model that can be used to calculate the number of jobs by state dependent on the construction industry among other industries. The section ends by reviewing the difficulties that researchers encounter in estimating the number of jobs supported by expenditures on green economic activities and the consequent caution that should be taken when utilizing these estimates in particular.

Job Creation Estimates: What Are They?

Interest in how many jobs are created by a particular type of economic activity has surfaced when the economy is in a downturn and policymakers seek to compare the relative advantages of different stimulus options. It also has arisen when policymakers want to know the impact of shifting expenditures from one federal budget category to another (e.g., away from defense and towards social services programs). Unless there is an *increase* in total spending, however, the number of jobs in the labor market would remain largely unchanged.[4]

Although there are other bases upon which to develop estimates of the number of jobs created by a given economic activity, an input-output (I-O) model of the economy often is utilized due to its cost-effectiveness.[5] An I-O model describes the interrelationships between industries in the production process, showing how the dollar value of a sale is distributed across industries at a particular point in time. It thus reflects how much of the purchased product comes from final and supplier industries. An I-O table might show, for example, the dollar value of roof trusses produced by the veneer, plywood, and engineered wood products manufacturing industry and the dollar value of bricks produced by the clay product and refractory manufacturing industry used by the construction industry to erect residential buildings.

The output requirements from each industry must then be converted to employment requirements. Employment requirements are derived from productivity estimates for each industry at a particular point in time. The total employment requirement associated with a given type of final demand (e.g., a water reuse program) is the employment in the industry producing the final product or service and in the supplier industries. In other words, it is an approximation of both the direct and indirect employment dependent upon/supported by the economic activity. It commonly is expressed as the number of jobs per billion dollars of expenditures valued in a particular year's dollars.

Like an I-O table, an employment requirements table is a matrix of hundreds of columns and rows. Each column displays the number of jobs supported in each of the industry rows by an expenditure of one billion dollars in the column industry. For example, one billion dollars spent in the construction industry supports (direct) employment in the various components of that industry (e.g., residential and commercial building, highway and bridge building) and (indirect) employment in the many industries that supply their goods and services to the construction industry (e.g., asphalt shingle manufacturing, fabricated metal bridge section manufacturing). An employment requirements table thus permits estimation of the varying impact of an expenditure on different industries and the varying impact of different kinds of expenditures.

Some Caveats

I-O models freeze technology and productivity at a particular point in time. Thus, the job-generating potential of an economic activity undertaken today could differ from that of an earlier period if there were technological and productivity improvements in the intervening years. Similarly, the estimates often are stated in terms of the number of jobs created for every billion dollars of expenditures, but a billion dollars spent in one year could buy less (or more) than a billion dollars spent in another year depending on changes in price levels over time.

There also could be differences in estimated versus actual job creation because I-O models assume that resources are unlimited. If, for example, the economy was performing at a fairly high level with plants operating near full capacity and with fairly few workers unemployed, the actual number of new jobs might fall short of the estimate due to capital and labor constraints. This is less likely to matter during a broad-based economic downturn.

Further, I-O tables do not necessarily differentiate between imported and domestically produced goods. As a consequence, the domestic employment impact of expenditures might be overstated to the extent that inputs are imported. Similarly, I-O tables typically do not express employment in terms of full-time equivalents (i.e., both full-time and part-time jobs are counted equally). Thus, programs which draw upon industries that rely relatively more on part-time workers (e.g., retail trade) might appear to create more jobs than programs that draw to a greater extent on industries employing relatively more full-time workers (e.g., manufacturing).

The Multiplier Effect

A more comprehensive estimate of the number of jobs created by a particular type of economic activity has three components:

- the number of jobs directly attributable to the activity,
- the number of jobs indirectly attributable to the activity, and
- the number of jobs induced throughout the economy as a result of the activity.

Induced jobs are those dependent upon the purchases of persons in direct and indirect jobs. For example, workers who are directly or indirectly employed as the result of a highway construction program might spend some portion of their wages in their communities at grocery stores, auto repair shops, and movie theaters.

Estimates of induced jobs or the multiplier are considered tenuous. To calculate the multiplier effect, one must estimate how much of the additional money earned by directly and indirectly employed workers will likely be spent versus saved. The actual number of jobs created by this added spending will further depend on economic conditions (e.g., the availability of labor, the inflation rate). As a result, there are widely varying estimates of the multiplier effect and those job creation studies that include induced employment utilize different multipliers.

Job Estimates and Construction Spending

The Federal Highway Administration

Perhaps the most widely known estimate of the employment impact of federal spending on our nation's roads comes from the Federal Highway Administration (FHWA). Although the FHWA twice updated its 1997 analysis, which estimated that $1 billion of federal-aid highway expenditures plus a $250 million state match supported 47,575 jobs, some proponents of stimulating job growth through increased federal spending on infrastructure continue to use this figure. The most recent update by the FHWA to 2007 indicates that a $1.25 billion expenditure on highway construction consisting of $1 billion from the federal government and $250 million from state government could support 34,779 jobs. If a state match is not required, "then $1 billion in Federal funds supports 27,800 jobs."[6] The jobs number has decreased over time in part because of increases in the price of inputs, such as asphalt and diesel fuel.

The FHWA breaks down the estimate of 27,822 jobs per billion dollars of federal spending on highways as follows:

- 9,536 construction-oriented jobs (i.e., jobs at construction companies working on the projects and at businesses that provide direct inputs to the projects such as asphalt, concrete, and guard rails);
- 4,324 jobs in supporting industries (i.e., employment at firms that provide inputs to the industries directly providing the materials and equipment utilized in highway construction such as producers of sheet metal who supply the manufacturers of guard rails); and
- 13,962 induced jobs (i.e., jobs throughout the economy dependent upon consumer expenditures from the wages of workers in "construction-oriented" and "industry-supporting" jobs).

Thus, induced jobs account for one-half of the total estimate.

The FHWA notes one caveat about I-O analysis in addition to those mentioned above; that is, the job estimate "utilizes the national average mix of construction materials and labor inputs. Specific projects and local utilization ratios will alter the estimated number of jobs supported."[7] For example, a different combination of materials and number of workers might be required for road resurfacing projects compared to bridge building or commuter rail projects.

The FHWA also states that

> [t]he employment figures have recently been used as a justification for including highway spending in an economic stimulus package. But with the exception of short-term resurfacing and preservation projects, highway funds spend out slowly, with only 27% of a project, on average, outlaying in the first year.[8]

BLS Employment Requirements Table

In recognition of the fact that "people want to assess the impact on employment of different policies or actions," the U.S. Bureau of Labor Statistics (BLS) makes available electronically free-of-charge to the public the employment requirements tables it develops as part of its employment projections program.[9] I-O and employment requirements tables developed and utilized by others often are proprietary and not made widely available.

The employment requirements tables are based on the official I-O tables for the nation that the U.S. Bureau of Economic Analysis (BEA) develops every five years. BLS takes the latest national I-O table available from BEA—in this case, 1997—and updates it to reflect more recent production and distribution technologies. It then utilizes the updated I-O table and recent labor productivity data to develop an employment requirements table. The employment requirements table referenced in this chapter reflects 2006 technologies of production and distribution as well as labor productivity. It is the table that was available in late 2008 when this chapter was first released.[10]

The BLS employment requirements table provides information for the construction industry as a whole. The construction industry, according to the North American Industry Classification System, is composed of three major subdivisions:

- construction of buildings (residential and nonresidential),
- heavy and civil engineering construction (highway, street, and bridge construction; utility system construction; construction of flood control structures, dams, and hydroelectric power generation facilities), and
- specialty trade contractors (foundation, structure, and building exterior contractors; building equipment contractors; building finishing contractors).

Some 11,768 jobs are directly and indirectly dependent upon $1 billion of spending on construction. A majority of the jobs are in the construction industry itself (i.e., 6,925 direct jobs).

The figure from the BLS employment requirements table for construction expenditures (11,768) is somewhat lower than the direct and indirect jobs figure for highway expenditures from the FHWA (13,860). Potential explanations for the disparity include differences in industry definition, data sources, method of updating the model, and time period.

The employment requirements available from BLS do not break out other types of construction that have been discussed as part of a federal job creation package (e.g., public school construction). BLS formerly conducted surveys to estimate full-time year-long employment associated with a variety of different construction activities, including new schools, hospitals, water and sewer facilities, roads, mass transit, and maintenance and repair construction. The survey information was last updated a few decades ago, however.

BEA's Regional Input-Output Modeling System (RIMS II)

From its Regional Input-Output Modeling System (RIMS II), the BEA produces estimates by geographic area of the employment, earnings, and output dependent on additional spending in hundreds of different industries.[11] For a fee to most parties, BEA utilizes either the 1997 benchmark I-O for the nation or the 2006 annual I-O for the nation adjusted by 2006 data from its regional economic accounts to provide these estimates at the subnational level.[12]

Table 1. Number of Direct and Indirect Jobs by State Dependent on an Expenditure of $1 Billion in the Construction Industry

State	Number of Jobs	State	Number of Jobs
Alabama	15,851	Montana	16,127
Alaska	11,009	Nebraska	13,946
Arizona	12,238	Nevada	11,459
Arkansas	15,306	New Hampshire	12,374
California	12,289	New Jersey	11,118
Colorado	12,575	New Mexico	14,279
Connecticut	10,709	New York	10,106
Delaware	9,518	North Carolina	15,555
District of Columbia	1,874	North Dakota	13,500
Florida	13,127	Ohio	14,391
Georgia	14,224	Oklahoma	16,232
Hawaii	11,614	Oregon	13,184
Idaho	15,860	Pennsylvania	12,390
Illinois	11,916	Rhode Island	10,767
Indiana	13,747	South Carolina	15,319
Iowa	14,330	South Dakota	15,316
Kansas	13,625	Tennessee	14,556
Kentucky	15,039	Texas	12,985
Louisiana	13,731	Utah	14,692
Maine	15,988	Vermont	14,883
Maryland	10,687	Virginia	12,085
Massachusetts	10,714	Washington	12,171
Michigan	13,354	West Virginia	13,834
Minnesota	12,998	Wisconsin	13,673
Mississippi	15,357	Wyoming	13,091
Missouri	13,241	United States	14,315

Source: Prepared by CRS from RIMS II estimates supplied by the BEA Regional Product Division in 2008.

As shown in **Table 1**, the number of jobs directly and indirectly supported by an expenditure of $1 billion in the construction industry in a given state ranges widely. The main reason for the disparity in job creation estimates is that each state has a different mix of industries within its borders. As a consequence, one state varies from the next in its capacity to supply all the intermediate goods needed to carry out construction projects. A secondary explanation is that earnings vary by state.

Job Estimates and Green Infrastructure Spending

Estimating the number of jobs dependent upon green infrastructure activities presents a greater challenge than estimates related to infrastructure projects as traditionally defined. The basis for most data collection by U.S. statistical agencies is the North American Industry Classification System (NAICS). It currently does not identify separately so-called green industries (e.g., those that utilize renewable resources to produce their outputs, those that manufacture goods which minimize energy use). For example, the NAICS disaggregates the electric utility industry into hydroelectric, fossil fuel, nuclear, and other power generation, transmission, and distribution. Such renewable sources of energy production as wind, solar, and biomass are not uniquely recognized; they are included in the "other" category. If harnessing the wind to produce electricity and plant material to produce biofuel requires a substantially different mix of inputs than relying on coal and gasoline, for example, the conventional I-O model does not seem well- suited as a basis for estimating the number of jobs supported by these green activities. Similarly, within NAICS, the construction industry does not have a unique category for retrofitting (e.g., installing additional insulation, fluorescent lighting, or energy-efficient heating and air- conditioning systems). Retrofitting likely requires a combination of inputs from supplier industries that differs from the mix for the top-to-bottom construction of buildings, once again making use of conventional I-O models problematic.

This recognized difficulty generally is either not mentioned, or how it is dealt with is not described, in the analyses of green job creation. One study, commissioned by the Center for American Progress and discussed in more detail below, does address the problem. The researchers explain that because "the U.S. government surveys and accounts that are used to construct the input-output tables do not specifically recognize wind, solar, biomass, building retrofitting, or new mass transit as industries in their own right," they created synthetic industries by combining parts of industries for which data are available. The researchers provided an example in the case of the biomass "industry:" they constructed it by combining farming, forestry, wood products, and refining industries; then they "assigned relative weights to each of these industries in terms of their contributions to producing biomass products."[13]

Further complicating the matter is the context and manner in which estimates of green jobs generally are presented. Studies often develop employment projections based on differing sets of assumptions and time horizons. For example, the number of direct and indirect jobs some 10 or more years in the future supported by an assumed increase in the demand for energy that is met by an assumed shift during the projection period from coal to wind and geothermal power generation. Some reports also include induced employment, but this is not always made clear. In addition, some analyses relate to a particular state. Their results may not be generalizeable to other areas because state economy's have different mixes of industries and may not be able to provide any or all of the inputs for a particular green output. Additionally, the assumptions and methodologies underlying the job creation estimates often are not clearly articulated, which makes thoughtful review of the results very difficult.

It should be noted that many of the studies by green economy proponents that were available when Congress was crafting stimulus legislation had not been conceived for the purpose of quickly stabilizing or increasing the number of jobs in the nation or in industries particularly hard hit by the recession. Job creation estimates from two organizations that proposed broad-based green economy strategies intended in part to stimulate the deteriorating labor market are briefly described below.

- The September 2008 report, *Green Recovery: A Program to Create Jobs and Start Building a Low-Carbon Economy*, was commissioned by the Center for American Progress (a research and educational institute). It represents an acceleration of a 10-year program included in a 2007 report (*Capturing the Energy Opportunity: Creating a Low-Carbon Economy*). The 2008 report's authors at the Department of Economics and Political Economy Research Institute (University of Massachusetts-Amherst), who relied on I-O analysis, estimate that almost 2 million jobs (935,200 direct jobs, 586,000 indirect jobs, and 496,000 induced jobs) could be created or preserved by a two-year $100 billion "green economic recovery program." Of the $100 billion total, $46 billion would be in the form of federal spending for such activities as public building retrofits, mass transit and freight rail expansion, and smart electrical grid development. Much of the remainder would be in the form of tax credits to encourage businesses and homeowners to retrofit commercial and residential buildings. The authors acknowledge that not all of the green activities

> can contribute equally to a short-term green economic recovery program. Some ... strategies are clearly capable of delivering within a year, while others will require as long as two years to be implemented.[14]

- In December 2008, the Apollo Alliance (a coalition of labor, environmental, business and community leaders) proposed *The Apollo Economic Recovery Act.*

> It is an initial step toward achievement of a 10-year $500 billion program to create 5 million green-collar jobs, which had been released in September 2008. The new initiative calls for federal spending of about $50 billion to create or maintain more than 650,000 direct jobs and 1.3 million indirect jobs. The derivation of these job creation figures is not always clear, appearing to rely much of the time on spending-to-jobs relationships estimated by other organizations. The proposed allocation of federal funds and associated job estimates include $10 billion to improve the efficiency and reliability of the electric transmission grid (131,000 direct and indirect jobs), $8 billion to repair roads and bridges (278,000 direct and indirect jobs), and $8 billion to encourage localities to replace aging buses and trains with U.S.-made clean-energy vehicles (37,600 direct jobs in vehicle manufacturing and 167,000 indirect jobs).

MEASURING JOBS SUPPORTED BY SPENDING PROVISIONS IN THE AMERICAN RECOVERY AND REINVESTMENT ACT

While crafting the American Recovery and Reinvestment Act (ARRA), Congress was concerned about timely tracking of the number of jobs whose creation or maintenance results from the legislation. The 111th Congress therefore addressed this matter in bill language much more than prior Congresses had in countercyclical job creation legislation.

Job Reporting by Recipients of ARRA Appropriations

At Title XV—Accountability and Transparency of Division A—Appropriations Provisions, P.L. 111-5 requires entities that receive ARRA appropriations from federal agencies (e.g., grant, loan, or contract recipients; states) to include in their quarterly reports to the agencies estimates of the number of direct jobs created and retained by infrastructure projects, for example.[15] Recipients of recovery funds were required to make their first submission of the required information in October 2009. Federal agencies are required to post the contents of these and subsequent reports on websites 30 days after the end of each calendar quarter. The Office of Management and Budget (OMB) was directed to provide guidance to help recipients prepare the reports, including the development of job estimates. The act further charged the Congressional Budget Office (CBO) and the Government Accountability Office (GAO) with commenting on the job estimates contained in the reports within 45 days after their submission to federal agencies.

Based on the self-reporting of recipients of ARRA appropriations, 640,329 jobs were saved or retained through September 30, 2009. Because the notion of a retained (saved) job caused consternation in some quarters, the OMB revised its guidance issued in June 2009. According to that guidance, upon which the aforementioned job figure was based, Congress' reference in ARRA to a job retained meant "an existing position that would not have been continued to be filled were it not for Recovery Act funding."[16] In response to feedback from the General Accountability Office, among others, the OMB revised its guidance on jobs saved so that recipients no longer will have "to make a subjective judgment on whether a given job would have existed were it not for the Recovery Act. The updated guidance [issued in December 2009] ... defines jobs created or retained as those funded ... by the Recovery Act."[17] Based on this definition, recipients reported that 608,317 jobs were funded by ARRA in the fourth quarter of 2009. Another 682,226 jobs were created or saved at ARRA recipients in the first quarter of 2010.

Job Estimation by the Council of Economic Advisers

Title XV of P.L. 111-5 additionally tasked the Council of Economic Advisers (CEA) with submitting quarterly reports to the Committees on Appropriations on the effect of ARRAprovisions on employment and other economic indicators. The CEA's mandate thus extends well beyond the above-described reporting requirements, which apply only to $271 billion in direct government investment spending out of a total of $787 billion.[18]

The first quarterly report of the CEA was issued in September 2009. Based on two different estimating procedures, it found that ARRA might have added some one million jobs to employer payrolls in August 2009 compared to what employment would have been in the absence of the legislation.[19]

As noted above, CBO was charged in ARRA with commenting on the number of jobs created or saved as a result of direct government purchases of goods and services, grants and loans to private entities, and grants to states and localities. Although it did so in *Estimated Impact of the American Recovery and Reinvestment Act on Employment and Economic Output as of September 2009*, CBO went further to provide a broader estimate than can be gleaned from the reports of primary and secondary recipients of more than $25,000 from appropriations in ARRA; it is an estimate more comparable to that of the CEA. Based upon information provided by macroeconomic models and historical relationships, CBO estimated that ARRA's tax cuts and outlay increases that occurred through September 2009 increased the number of people employed by between 600,000 and 1.6 million compared to the employment level without the law. The CEA's estimate of about 1 million additional jobs as of August 2009, discussed in the preceding paragraph, falls within the range estimated by CBO as of the third quarter of 2009.

In its second quarterly report, released in January 2010, the CEA estimated the effect of ARRA on employment through December 2009. It found that the stimulus law might have raised year-end employment by about 1.7–2.0 million jobs above what it otherwise would have been.[20] Similarly, CBO estimated in its report covering the fourth quarter of 2009 that ARRA's policies might have increased the number of people employed by 1.0–2.1 million.[21]

The CEA's third quarterly report, released in April 2010, showed ARRA's employment effect through March 2010. It estimated that the law might have raised employment by 2.2–2.8 million jobs above what it otherwise would have been as of the first quarter of 2010.[22] Similarly, CBO estimated in its report covering the first quarter of 2010 that ARRA's policies might have increased the number of people employed by 1.2–2.8 million.[23]

End Notes

[1] CRS Report R40798, *Unemployment and Employment Trends Before and After the End of Recessions*, by Linda Levine.

[2] CRS Report 92-939, *Countercyclical Job Creation Programs*, by Linda Levine.

[3] Related jobs include, for example, those in industries that manufacture wind turbines and install thermal-pane windows.

[4] Small differences in the total number of jobs could occur at the same spending levels if the economic activities to (from) which funds were being shifted were more (less) capital-intensive, for example.

[5] Another basis for estimating the impact of policy and other changes on the economy is conducting surveys. According to the U.S. Bureau of Economic Analysis (BEA), the advantage of the I-O approach to making impact estimates is the accessibility of the data sources required to develop the I-O model.

[6] U.S. Department of Transportation, Federal Highway Administration, *Employment Impacts of Highway Infrastructure Investment.* Available from author upon request.

[7] Ibid.

[8] Ibid.

[9] U.S. Bureau of Labor Statistics, *Layout and Description for 201-order Employment Requirements Tables*, Washington, DC, December 2007, p. 3, http://stats.bls.gov/emp/empind4.htm.

[10] BLS in late 2009 released an employment requirements table updated to reflect 2008 technologies of production and distribution as well as labor productivity. It is available at http://stats.bls.gov/emp/ep_data_emp_requirements.htm.

[11] For additional information on RIMS II see BEA, *Regional Multipliers: A User Handbook for the Regional Input-Output Modeling System,* http://www.bea.gov/scb/pdf/regional/perinc/meth/rims2.pdf.

[12] More specific detail by industry is available from the 1997 benchmark I-O than from the annual I-O. Therefore, Table 1 (Number of Direct and Indirect Jobs Per $1 Million of Output Produced by the Water, Sewage and Other Systems Industry) in CRS Report R40 107, *The Role of Public Works Infrastructure in Economic Stimulus*, was drawn from the 1997 benchmark I-O because the 2006 annual I-O provides data only for the utilities industry as a whole.

[13] Robert Pollin, Heidi Garrett-Peltier, and James Heintz, et al., *Green Recovery: A Program to Create Good Jobs and Start Building a Low-Carbon Economy,* Center for American Progress, Washington, DC, September 2008, p. 20, http://www.americanprogress.org.

[14] Robert Pollin, Heidi Garrett-Peltier, and James Heintz, et al., *Green Recovery: A Program to Create Good Jobs and Start Building a Low-Carbon Economy*, Center for American Progress, Washington, DC, September 2008, p. 5, http://www.americanprogress.org.

[15] Recipients of ARRA funds awarded to the Department of Transportation (DOT) are subject to Section 1512's job reporting requirement. Separately, at Section 1201, Congress required the DOT to estimate the direct, indirect, and total jobs created by transportation projects funded under ARRA. The DOT estimates thus are akin to the estimates for the entire bill that the CEA produces.

[16] OMB, *Implementing Guidance for the Reports on Use of Funds Pursuant to the American Recovery and Reinvestment Act,* M-09-21, June 22, 2009, available at http://www.whitehouse.gov/omb/assets m09-21.pdf.

[17] OMB, *Updated Guidance on the American Recovery and Reinvestment Act—Data Quality, Non-Reporting Recipients, and Reporting of Job Estimates,* M-10-08, December 18, 2009. See Part 2 of http://www.recovery.gov/ FAQ/recipient/Documents/m10-08%20Updated%20Guidance%20121 82009.pdf.

[18] The remaining ARRA funds fall into five categories: individual income tax cuts, a patch for the alternative minimum tax, investment incentives, aid to people directly hurt by the recession (e.g., unemployment insurance), and fiscal relief for state governments.

[19] Council of Economic Advisers, *The Economic Impact of the American Recovery and Reinvestment Act of 2009,* First Quarterly Report, September 10, 2009.

[20] Council of Economic Advisers, *The Economic Impact of the American Recovery and Reinvestment Act of 2009,* Second Quarterly Report, January 13, 2010.

[21] Congressional Budget Office, *Estimated Impact of the American Recovery and Reinvestment Act on Employment and Economic Output From October 2009 Through December 2009*, February 2010.

[22] Council of Economic Advisers, *The Economic Impact of the American Recovery and Reinvestment Act of 2009, Third Quarterly Report,* April 14, 2010.

[23] Congressional Budget Office, *Estimated Impact of the American Recovery and Reinvestment Act on Employment and Economic Output From January 2010 Through March 2010*, May 2010.

CHAPTER SOURCES

The following chapters have been previously published:

Chapter 1 – This is an edited, excerpted and augmented edition of a United States Congressional Research Service publication, Report Order Code R40244, dated April 5, 2010.

Chapter 2 – This is an edited, excerpted and augmented edition of a United States Congressional Research Service publication, Report Order Code R40173, dated April 9, 2010.

Chapter 3 – This is an edited, excerpted and augmented edition of a United States Congressional Research Service publication, Report Order Code R40620, dated March 12, 2010.

Chapter 4 – This is an edited, excerpted and augmented edition of a United States Congressional Research Service publication, Report Order Code RS22231, dated March 24, 2010.

Chapter 5 – This is an edited, excerpted and augmented edition of a United States Congressional Research Service publication, Report Order Code RL33657, dated March 10, 2010.

Chapter 6 – This is an edited, excerpted and augmented edition of a United States Congressional Research Service publication, Report Order Code RL34319, dated March 9,2010.

Chapter 7 – This is an edited, excerpted and augmented edition of a United States Congressional Research Service publication, Report Order Code RL30344, dated March 29, 2010.

Chapter 8 – This is an edited, excerpted and augmented edition of a United States Congressional Research Service publication, Report Order Code RL30354, dated March 31, 2010.

Chapter 9 – This is an edited, excerpted and augmented edition of a United States Congressional Research Service publication, Report Order Code R40438, dated March 18, 2010.

Chapter 10 – This is an edited, excerpted and augmented edition of a United States Congressional Research Service publication, Report Order Code RL33069, dated April 21, 2010.

Chapter 11 - This is an edited, excerpted and augmented edition of a United States Congressional Research Service publication, Report Order Code RL30520, dated March 12, 2010.

Chapter 12 - This is an edited, excerpted and augmented edition of a United States Congressional Research Service publication, Report Order Code RS22354, dated April 15, 2010.

Chapter 13 - This is an edited, excerpted and augmented edition of a United States Congressional Research Service publication, Report Order Code RL33186, dated April 2, 2010.

Chapter 14 - This is an edited, excerpted and augmented edition of a United States Congressional Research Service publication, Report Order Code RS22204, dated May 13, 2010.

Chapter 15 - This is an edited, excerpted and augmented edition of a United States Congressional Research Service publication, Report Order Code RL34424, dated April 12, 2010.

Chapter 16 - This is an edited, excerpted and augmented edition of a United States Congressional Research Service publication, Report Order Code RS21883, dated April 15, 2010.

Chapter 17 - This is an edited, excerpted and augmented edition of a United States Congressional Research Service publication, Report Order Code R40080, dated May 26, 2010.

INDEX

C

D

E

F

G

H

I

R

S